Forces of Order

Forces of Order

Policing Modern Japan

David H. Bayley

UNIVERSITY OF CALIFORNIA PRESS

Berkeley / Los Angeles / Oxford

University of California Press
Berkeley and Los Angeles, California

University of California Press, Ltd.
Oxford, England

Originally published in 1976 by the University of California Press under
the title *Forces of Order: Police Behavior in Japan and the United States*.
The original edition was extensively revised for the preparation of this
new edition.

Library of Congress Cataloging-in-Publication Data

Bayley, David H.
    Forces of order : policing modern Japan / David H. Bayley—2nd
ed.
        p. cm.
    Includes index.
    ISBN 0-520-07261-8 (alk. paper).—ISBN 0-520-07262-6 (pbk.: alk. paper)
    1. Police—Japan.   2. Police—United States.   I. Title.
HV8257.A2B383   1991
363.2'0952—dc20   90-41028
                                                                          CIP

Printed in the United States of America
9 8 7 6 5 4 3 2 1

The paper used in this publication meets the minimum requirements of
American National Standard for Information Sciences—Permanence of Paper
for Printed Library Materials, ANSI Z39.48–1984. ∞

To
W. W. LOCKWOOD—
teacher, friend, and exemplar

Contents

Preface

Americans are often urged to study foreign countries and cultures, the usual reason given being the need to overcome parochialism and to broaden intellectual horizons. These are valuable purposes, to be sure, but they obscure another one, which is equally important and often overlooked. Foreign travel is a means of learning about oneself and one's society. What is distinctive in one's own world, too familiar usually to be recognized, becomes obvious by comparison with the lives of others. It is important to discover what differences there are among the peoples of the world; it is no less important to discover what makes these differences alien.

This book is an attempt to learn about the police problems of the United States by studying Japanese police institutions. Japan is a particularly apt comparison with the United States. It is modern and affluent, congested and urbanized. It belongs to the world's "developed" nations. Comparisons between the United States and Japan are not vitiated by disparities in technical capacity, educational levels, wealth, or dominant modes of production. What stands out between the two is culture, not modernity. The thrust of the analysis will be to note differences in institutional practices between the nations' police, then to explain why the practices diverge in characteristic ways. In this way, it should be possible to highlight what in American history, culture, and character shape police performance today.

A study of the police also provides a new vantage point for viewing contemporary Japanese society. Police penetrate society more completely than any other governmental agency, and police officers see things that most private citizens do not. Their perspective, though not representative, is no less authentic than any other. And it may have the advantage of being more extensive. The police are also a part of society. Because society works in them one can learn something about the society by observing them. Borrowing from the anthropologists, the police may be regarded as a village—not the only one but a real one nonetheless.

The book does not provide a complete description of Japanese police institutions; Japanese experience is drawn on selectively in order to illuminate contemporary American police affairs. The topics discussed reflect my own troubled preoccupations—preoccupations I am sure are shared by many others. Moreover, the book focuses on patrol work. This reflects my strong belief that the success or failure of any police force is determined by procedures affecting behavior in encounters, especially face-to-face, between police and citizens. Matters of formal organization, forensic technique, and equipment, which preoccupy so much of the professional literature on the police, will be ignored unless they affect contact-behavior directly. The neglect of patrol work by so many observers, let alone writers of fictional works about the police, is curious in several respects. Patrol activity accounts for the bulk of police manpower; criminal investigation, considered by so many the essence of policing, is a relatively small specialty. Patrol officers provide almost all emergency help; they are the only police officers most people will ever meet. Furthermore, patrol activity is much more open to public gaze than criminal investigation. Because the rights of suspects as well as victims must be protected and because surprise is essential in detection, criminal investigation is largely invisible to outsiders. Paradoxically, then, the public knows least about the police work it is most interested in and cares least about what it can know best. And its interest bears no relation to what most police officers do most of the time.

This revised edition represents *Forces of Order* as it would be written in the early 1990s instead of the middle 1970s. The objective of both editions is the same, namely, to discover what is distinctive in the Japanese approach to policing. But because a great deal has changed in both Japan and the United States in the past fifteen years, a fresh new look is certainly required.

In the new edition all factual material has been brought up to date. New or expanded discussions have been added about police corruption, "substitute prisons," and allegations of involuntary confessions, organized crime, juvenile delinquency, narcotics trafficking, and foreign workers. A chapter from the first edition dealing with riots and their control has been omitted because of a sharp decline in such activity, although discussion of the orientation of the Japanese police toward security threats has been expanded. The original edition unaccountably failed to explain why Japan has such remarkably low crime rates in comparison with other industrial democracies, though the book did contain several hints. The new edition concludes with a discussion of this topic. Finally, because American policing has not stood still either, some differences originally found between Japan and the United States are no longer true. Such comparisons have been revised to reflect the changed American scene.

Police officers in Japan are legally and ostensibly like police officers in the United States. No problems of comparability arise. There is a question, however, whether generalizations can properly be made about police based on national units. Can a characteristic of police operations be fairly called Japanese or American? Are police practices sufficiently homogeneous in each country so that such generalizations are intelligent? In Japan they are. Japan has only one police force; its system is not a patchwork of overlapping forces and jurisdictions as in the United States. Though command of operations is decentralized among the country's forty-seven prefectures, policies are so standardized that it is proper to refer to the *Japanese* police. In the United States problems of generalization are undoubtedly more acute. I believe it is fair to speak of *American* practices for the following reason: differences along any dimension of comparison are greater between any American force and the Japanese police than between any two American forces. American police forces are more similar to each other than to the Japanese force. This conclusion is subject to testing, and I invite readers to determine from their own knowledge whether features of police activity discussed in the book are more similar within each nation than between them.

The study is based on about two years of intensive field research in Japan distributed over twenty years and many visits. The research in Japan involved observation of police operations and interviews with hundreds of officers. Because operations are organized for the most part in terms of police stations, I made a selection of police stations located in a variety of socioeconomic areas—urban, rural, heavy industrial, upper-class residential, university, commercial, entertainment, and so forth. The sample was drawn from five prefectures—Tokyo, Aomori, Osaka, Kochi, and Fukuoka. Generally about five days were spent studying each station. Observation of police operations was carried out mostly at night—the busiest hours for the police. I would accompany officers working in patrol cars or in Japan's unique police boxes (*koban*). Formal interviews were held with the chief of each police station (or his deputy) and with the heads of each major section—patrol, criminal investigation, crime prevention, and administration. Because I was particularly interested in contact-behavior, interviews were held with at least one officer at every rank level within the patrol section of each station. Interviews were also conducted with all ranks of detectives but not necessarily in each station. The police are organized into prefectural commands, so it was important to talk to senior officers at prefectural headquarters. This meant the chief of the prefecture and the heads of each functional section. Some specialized operations are organized on a prefectural, as opposed to a station, basis, and they required additional study—riot control, traffic regulation, vice surveillance, and some criminal investigation.

Choices about sites to visit and persons to interview were made entirely by me. No attempt was ever made to deny me access to a location, an officer, or an operation (subject to the legal requirements of confidentiality). Indeed, I often discovered that I was more hesitant to ask to see a particular operation, out of fear of being considered presumptuous, than police officers were to show it to me. I soon sensed that Japanese officers, being experienced professionals, would have thought less well of me if I had not asked to see sensitive situations and talk to critically placed personnel. Altogether, the police were as accessible as I could ask, certainly as accessible as the canons of scholarship require. I am deeply grateful to the Japanese police for the trust in me which this openness represented.

Traveling and working with the police provides an extraordinarily varied and intimate view of any society. In Japan I have accompanied the police at all hours into bars, jails, dance halls, fish markets, striptease shows, security posts, schools, movie theaters, private homes, pedestrian malls, Mah-Jong parlors, apartments, restaurants, pawnshops, public baths, shops, entertainment arcades, temples, and gangster offices. This book is about the human events that occurred in those settings and the way in which the police related to them. As varied as the settings, the events had one quality in common—they were real. They were not staged or contrived or acted out for the tourist. Some events were dramatic—a lost child or the hospitalization of an alcoholic husband. Some incidents were hilarious, as when an elderly woman asked my patrol companions to have me—referred to as the *gaijin* (foreigner)—eat her four-year-old grandson because he was misbehaving. Many events were acutely embarrassing to the people involved—teenagers who had been caught breaking into a high school, a businessman helplessly drunk, homosexuals arrested in a public place. And some were poignant. I remember particularly a distinguished chief of police who, retiring after thirty-three years of service, acknowledged my presence among the audience—some of whom were in tears—when he gave his farewell address to his men. For an outsider to be allowed to be part of such human events is a great privilege. Time and again I asked myself what right I had to intrude into the lives of so many people. Scholarly observation often seemed like an act of trespass. Yet the Japanese people—police and private persons alike—not only permitted me to enter their lives as they lived them, they consistently pretended that I was inconspicuous. For such generosity and consideration, any expressions of gratitude are inadequate.

Though access to police operations and personnel was faultless, there are still important questions to be raised about the veracity of my findings. To what extent can a scholar, and a foreigner to boot, expect to be told the truth by police officers about police matters? It would be naive to think that Japanese officers were not apprehensive that I would portray them in an unfavorable light. They were concerned about the reputation of their organization and their reactions to me were instinctively cautious. This is true of police officers everywhere, whether in Bombay, New York, Stockholm, or Tokyo. At the same time, police institutions are not impenetrable to scholarship. Police officers in most countries want their point of view to be presented. If they find a researcher sympathetic and willing to listen, they seize the opportunity to present life as they see it and live it. This is precisely what the researcher wants, for it allows dialogue to begin that can lead to the building of trust. In the Japanese case, my being a foreign professor aided this process. Japanese police officers think that their own scholars insufficiently appreciate the job of the police and habitually approach the police with strong ideological biases. My interest, therefore, was subtly flattering, according them the serious academic attention they thought they deserved. Moreover, they were impressed by the fact that I wanted to find out about daily operating procedures, rather than simply about certain highly publicized events or aspects of police work. Being an American helped as well. Japanese police officers are proud of their accomplishments and want foreigners to know about them. To show these to an American, whose police system they believe to be in serious trouble, was especially attractive. This is not to suggest that they were completely forthcoming about their own defects. Of course they tried to show themselves to best advantage. For a researcher, however, unwillingness to communicate is a far more serious obstacle than desire to impress. Handling bias and building rapport are what interviewing is all about; without ready communication the researcher cannot begin to employ the skills of his craft. Japanese police officers were anxious to talk, and because they felt they had little to hide—a point that will be discussed in chapter 1—they were far less defensive than many American officers I have interviewed.

One method of building rapport is to demonstrate shared expertise. People in most occupations like nothing better than to talk about their work to interested and informed outsiders. I have studied police operations in several countries—Australia, Britain, India, the United States—for over twenty years. The police institution is not new to me. By referring to police practices elsewhere with appropriate detail, I could convince Japanese officers that I was a serious student of their work. As my knowledge of Japanese procedures grew, I could compel more frank exchanges by citing specific observations and facts. On several occasions when a pointed question of mine had been met with vague generalities, I responded by noting gently but frankly that I actually had seen the contrary. Rather than being affronted, my informants consistently paused, laughed, and complimented me on the unusual penetration of my research. They would then go on to supply additional information. Their readiness to reply to contradictory fact with forthright candor is an admirable trait.

Finally, the process of building rapport is something the Japanese understand explicitly. One of the words Japanese use to discuss interpersonal relations is *ninjo*. The other is *giri*, and both will be discussed in detail later. *Ninjo* refers to sympathy, warmth, empathic identification between two persons. Whereas only social scientists talk much about rapport in the United States, every Japanese can recognize and discuss the amount of *ninjo* in a relationship. *Ninjo* enhances rapport; in some ways it is rapport. Police officers were willing, therefore, to shape their response to me according to whatever subtle links of warmth and sympathy our meeting generated. They were not locked into a posture of reaction by my formal attributes; they were open to the creation of personal bonds that transcended official roles. This did not happen in every case, but it was a possibility that increased the likelihood of obtaining candid responses.

In summary, Japanese police officers were as quick as American officers to perceive the thrust of my questions, to determine potential embarrassment. Because, however, they were proud of what they were doing, admired expertise, and were open to the interplay of personality, frank exchanges with Japanese police officers were not usually difficult to obtain.

The most serious handicap from which this study suffers is my inability to speak Japanese. I was forced to work entirely through an interpreter. How much I missed as a result I cannot begin to estimate. The costs were greater in conducting field observations than in formal interviews. Indeed, there are advantages to using an interpreter in an interview. Translation, though it prolongs interviews, provides moments of respite during which the researcher can make notes and organize thoughts before plunging into another question. Control is easier to maintain, though nuances are undoubtedly missed that should affect the course of the conversation. In field observation there are no advantages at all, apart from having an extra pair of eyes. There is so much that might be important, yet winnowing decisions have to be made. At a street altercation, for example, what should the researcher tell his interpreter to tell him: what is each person saying, what are the identities of each speaker, how much respect is being shown, what is the issue, who is trying to mediate, what seems to be the emotion behind the words of each speaker, and so forth? A great deal can be learned by simply watching, listening for tones of voice, and observing gestures and facial expressions. But inferences based exclusively on observation are apt to be misleading; the researcher can be wholly wrong and never know it. The longer a researcher and his interpreter work together, the more sensitive they become to each other's needs. The interpreter understands more fully what the researcher is interested in; the researcher learns when he must be quiet and allow the interpreter to listen uninhibitedly. Enormous patience is required on both sides.

To the extent that it was possible to minimize the disadvantages of working in a language I did not understand, I was able to do so through the ability, sensitivity, and intelligence of Nozomu Nakagawa, who has served throughout my work in Japan as my interpreter. "Naka-san," as he allows me to call him, began by being my interpreter, became a colleague, and ended as a friend. Not only was he a faithful voice and keen ear, he contributed original insights to the research and often prompted me about matters that I would have neglected to explore. Having lived for several years in the United States, he understood which aspects of Japanese culture an American would misperceive or overlook. With infinite care he explained the subtleties of many situations until he was sure I understood. Because he has been with me throughout the project, he has come to understand the purposes of the research and to anticipate my needs for information.

It often seemed to me that our relationship was the reenactment of a famous comradeship from literature: that of Don Quixote and Sancho Panza. Like Don Quixote, I was the taller, thinner, older of the two. I possessed a set of objectives intelligible fully only to myself. Like Sancho Panza, Naka-san had to mediate between my driving vision and the reality of life in Japan. Often I stood mutely amid a host of attentive Japanese, like an abstracted statue, as Naka-san tried to fit my desires to the possibilities of the social setting. He had to watch as I strove with false impressions, waiting for the appropriate moment to teach me that what I perceived were really windmills. And he felt Sancho Panza's anxiety that his Don might suddenly say or do something totally out of keeping with propriety.

I am very grateful for the encouragement and intellectual support provided by many American experts on Japan. As a group, they proved to be most unclannish, not at all resentful of a comparativist poaching in their preserve. They introduced me to friends, gave invaluable advice about tactics, and shared their knowledge and insights. Most important of all, they reassured me that the study was both useful and feasible. I hope that after reading this book they still believe so. I am particularly indebted to Lawrence W. Beer, Joyce C. Lebra, Chalmers Johnson, W. W. Lockwood, Marius B. Jansen, John Haley, Hirose Wagatsuma, and Rodney W. Armstrong. Mikio Kato and the staff of the International House of Japan, Tokyo, provided crucial technical assistance, wise counsel, and a friendly home away from home. The initial study was made possible by grant No. G5-33052 from the National Science Foundation. The most recent fieldwork was sponsored by the Japan Foundation, with generous supplemental support from the All Japan Crime Prevention Association.

My greatest debt is owed to countless police officers throughout Japan who generously gave their time, experience, and hospitality. Many of them have become personal friends. I hope that what I have written justifies in some measure the faith they have had in me. The Japanese have done their best to help me understand their country and its police system. If I have failed to do so, the fault is mine.

1

Heaven for a Cop

Japan is a long way from the United States. With respect to law enforcement it is a different world.

Ask a senior police officer anywhere in Japan—a station chief, riot-troop commander, or head of a detective section—what kind of misconduct by subordinate officers causes him the greatest concern and he will invariably cite off-duty traffic accidents, drunkenness, and indiscretions with women. Almost as an aside he may mention that police officers are sometimes careless with their pistols, discharging them accidentally or having them stolen. One listens in vain for concern about the disciplinary problems that trouble commanders in the United States—brutality, rudeness, corruption. Even off the record, when rapport has been built through hours of technical talk, shared patrol experiences, and innumerable cups of green tea, Japanese officers steadily maintain that the major discipline problems involve off-duty behavior, especially driving, drinking, and womanizing.

To an American this kind of testimony is incredible. American officers, though hardly forthcoming on this topic, would not be nearly as bland and disingenuous. So the suspicion grows that Japanese officers are not being candid. They may be reluctant to tell an outsider, especially a foreigner, the true state of affairs. Or, alternatively, perhaps they themselves do not know what is really going on. Rather than dissembling, they are simply ill-informed.

1

If they are not being candid, the fault is systematic. What they report privately is exactly what they tell their public, and both are supported by official statistics. In 1988, for instance, there were approximately 220,000 police officers in Japan.[1] Only 15 of them were discharged for misbehavior. Departmental punishments—meaning temporary suspension, reduction in pay, and formal reprimands—were given to another 97 officers.[2] Compared with the incidence of police misconduct in the United States, this is a drop in the bucket. The New York City police department, which has 26,000 officers, dismissed 55 in 1988, more than three times the total for all Japan. Even a moderate-sized force like the one in Portland, Oregon, with 766 officers, in 1988, either fired or pressed into resigning 3 officers, almost one-fifth the Japanese total. Lesser punishments were awarded to 97 other officers.[3] The reasons for punishing officers in Japan were mostly trivial. Only 5 were dismissed for criminal actions such as corruption, fraud, or theft. The most common reason for punishing a police officer, including firing, was the failure of supervision by superior officers, mainly related to undue force in handling suspects, or the loss of an officer's police identification card. There were 35 of these in 1988.

In a representative year less than five officers are punished in connection with corruption.[4] Theft and extortion, too, are rare. This record is not as reassuring to the public as it might have been before the 1980s. Several cases have come to light of police officers receiving money for tipping off gambling parlors about impending raids. The former chief of the Osaka police, then serving as director of the National Police Academy, committed suicide in 1982 when newspapers broke the story of these events during his tenure. Nonetheless, disenchantment is by no means general. Newspaper reporters and the public tend to dismiss corruption as a phenomenon confined to the Osaka and Kobe areas. Moreover, they think it is minor—not involving narcotics or organized crime—and that it rarely runs through entire stations or units.

Brutality—unnecessary physical force—occurs sometimes in the handling of disorderly drunks, as the police themselves admit, and occasionally in the course of criminal investigations. Prompted by several

1. National Police Agency, *White Paper On Police, 1988* (Tokyo: The National Police Agency, 1988), p. 118. These figures are for authorized strength; actual strength is somewhat less.
2. Data provided by the National Police Agency. These figures include officers found guilty by courts.
3. Data provided by the police departments of New York City and Portland, Oregon.
4. Data supplied by the National Police Agency.

cases of convictions, sometimes of capital offenses, being overturned by
the Supreme Court on the grounds of involuntary confession, defense
lawyers have campaigned for changes in the law regulating the detention of suspects under investigation. To the great embarrassment of the
Japanese government, they have taken their case to the United Nations
Commission on Human Rights. Neither the public nor the media seem
greatly concerned, believing, as most experts do, that such excesses are
confined to a few of the very small number of suspects detained in
Japan.

Another piece of evidence that discipline in the police may be as
good as the official records show is that there is no m vement among
the public for the creation of new mechanisms of supervision and investigation of misconduct. There is already a form of civilian review outside the police. This is the Human Rights Bureau of the Ministry of
Justice, established in 1948. There are human rights offices in every
major city, plus 1,200 volunteer counselors throughout the country.
They receive complaints about violations of rights at the hands of government servants as well as private citizens. Amazing as it may seem, the
number of complaints against the police brought to the Human Rights
Bureau has been falling every year. In 1987 only 50 complaints were
received in all of Japan.[5]

The skeptic may argue that a low number of complaints indicates
that people are simply not sensitive to police misconduct, not that behavior is uniformly good. Although this is plausible and will be explored later, the media appear to be attentive. Police misdeeds are big
news in Japan. The police are continually irritated because the press
singles out the crimes and misdemeanors of off-duty and even retired
police officers. Police reporting is one of the largest areas of specializa-
tion in print journalism. The major dailies assign as many as ten reporters to the headquarters of the Tokyo Metropolitan Police Department,
with additional staff at the eight district police offices. Reporters assidu-
ously cultivate personal contacts within the force so they will not be
dependent on official versions of events. This may, of course, be a two-
way street, with implicit understandings struck about the limits of re-
portability. Recognizing this possibility, one can at least say that the
media are in a position to know, that notable exposés have occurred,
and that the police believe that the media are eager to pounce.

The fact is that a transformation did occur in police behavior in
Japan in a relatively short period of time immediately after World War

5. Information provided by the Ministry of Justice, Tokyo.

II. It is associated with democratization and is one of the most prized developments of the postwar period. Japan's contemporary record of excellence with respect to police behavior is striking, then, not only in relation to the United States but in relation to its own past.

In sum, if generality of agreement among people in a country is the mark of truth, then Japanese police behavior is astonishingly good. The incidence of misconduct is slight and the faults trivial by American standards. Though a cynical American may always wonder if enough is known about the conduct of individual officers—whether by himself or by insiders—he must begin to consider the disturbing possibility that police conduct need not inevitably, recurrently, require substantial improvement.

Japanese police operations are not conducted in an atmosphere of crisis and declining public confidence. There has been no spate of special investigations or national commissions. Surveys show that the public believes that police performance is very good. Their respect for the police is high. There are some pockets of hostility, mostly among ideologues of the left. University students tended to be very hostile to the police during the late 1960s and early 1970s, when large political demonstrations were organized. These are now rare, and violent confrontations between police and protestors occur almost exclusively in connection with the development, and now the expansion, of Narita Airport.

The Japanese police display a pride in themselves that is quite remarkable. They are supremely self-confident, not doubting the worth of the police role in society or the public's support of it. The annual *White Paper on Police* betrays no deep-seated anxiety about the position of the police in modern Japan. Police officers are neither defensive nor alienated. Though they have a strong sense of belonging to a distinct occupational community, solidarity has been self-imposed. They have not been driven in upon themselves by a critical public, isolated among their own kind. There has been no "blue power" movement in Japan, no organized effort among police officers to fend off threats to police autonomy. Officers do not feel victimized in pay or benefits, though they can cite improvements they would like in working conditions. Strikes by police officers are unheard of and the regulations banning formation of police unions are unquestioned. Recruitment of new officers is relatively easy, the number of applicants running at twelve times the number of vacancies.[6]

6. Information provided by the National Police Agency.

American police officers view other agencies in the criminal justice system as uncertain allies in the fight against crime. Resentment is particularly bitter against the courts, which they claim have unduly restricted the activities of the police or are being too lenient with arrested offenders. Japanese detectives, by contrast, are more outspoken about their own shortcomings than those of others. Getting them to evaluate the effect of judicial decisions on police performance or criminality is like pulling teeth. Although they sometimes complain about lenient sentences, they do not appear to feel that their investigatory powers have been unduly limited. They do not talk about being "handcuffed."

The primary purpose of any police force is to protect people from crime. The crime rate in Japan is so low in comparison with that of the United States that Japanese police officers seem hardly to be challenged at all. This accounts, to some extent, for their self-confidence. The rate of serious crimes per capita is over three times greater in the United States than in Japan. In 1987, for example, the crime rate for homicide, rape, robbery, assault, and larceny all together was 1,131.2 per 100,000 people in Japan; it was 3,681.9 in the United States.[7] There were six-and-a-half times as many murders per person in the United States in 1987 as in Japan—8.3 compared with 1.3 per 100,000 people.[8] New York City alone, with a population of just under 8 million, had 1,672 murders in 1987—almost exactly as many as Japan, which had a population of 122 million.[9] Tokyo, with a population just over 8 million, very similar to New York's, had only 133 murders.[10] The incidence of rape is twenty-five times higher in the United States than in Japan (37.4 per 100,000 persons versus 1.5 per 100,000 in 1987). In the New York metropolitan area, a woman is fourteen times more likely to be raped than in Tokyo. The most mind-boggling statistic has to do with robbery—taking property with force or threat of force. The rate is over one

7. Computed from the *White Paper on Crime, 1988,* p. 5, and *Sourcebook of Criminal Justice Statistics, 1988,* p. 427.

8. U.S. Department of Justice, Bureau of Justice Statistics. *Sourcebook of Criminal Justice Statistics, 1988* (Washington, D.C.: U.S. Government Printing Office, 1989), and Japan, Ministry of Justice, Summary of the *White Paper on Crime, 1988.* All figures that follow dealing with crime are from the same sources except where noted otherwise.

9. In 1987, 1,584 homicides were known to the police in Japan.

10. It might be objected that using crime figures from New York City biases the sample of American criminality. That is not so. Although it is true that cities have higher crime rates than rural areas, New York City ranked only ninth among U.S. cities in 1988 with respect to the incidence of homicide. Moreover, its homicide rate of 25.8 per 100,000 was less than half the rate of the number one ranked city, namely, Washington, D.C., which had a rate of 57.9. FBI statistics, *New York Times,* 13 October 1989.

hundred thirty-nine times higher in the United States than in Japan. In 1987, for example, there were 1,874 robberies in Japan and 517,000 in the United States, with 412 in Tokyo and 78,890 in New York City.[11] The reason for this enormous discrepancy has to do with the prevalence of guns in the United States. A drawn gun is a palpable threat. Japan, however, is a totally disarmed society; criminals hardly ever carry firearms. Theft is less dangerous to its victims in Japan than in the United States, therefore less likely to become a robbery, because thieves are less able, perhaps less willing, to injure people.

The Federal Bureau of Investigation in the United States analyzes trends in crime according to an index composed of the seven most serious crimes: murder, forcible rape, robbery, aggravated assault, burglary, larceny theft, and motor vehicle theft. To underscore just how different Japan is from the United States with respect to crime, consider this fact: there are four times as many serious crimes committed per person in the United States as there are crimes of all sorts, even the most petty, in Japan.[12] In 1987, for example, there were 13,508,700 serious crimes in the United States; in Japan, there were 1,577,929 crimes of all sorts.[13]

Yearly increases in the crime rate—the incidence of crime per person—in the United States are as inevitable as death and taxes; they have ceased to be news. It is hard to believe, therefore, that crime rates in Japan fell from 1948 to 1976 by 45 percent. Since then crime rates have risen very slightly each year. The 1987 rate is 17 percent higher than in 1976. The crime rate in 1987 was just about the same as it was in 1966. In the United States, by contrast, the rate for serious crime has doubled since 1966.

Narcotics addiction and drug abuse, which baffle and frighten the American public, are a relatively small problem in Japan, one that seems to be contained. In 1987, 22,337 persons were arrested for drug

11. The legal definition of robbery is the same in both countries, as are the criteria for classifying robberies, according to police officials responsible for collecting crime data in both countries. One possible source of confusion comes in distinguishing robbery from extortion. In Japan, a person deprived of property because he could not resist is a victim of robbery; a person deprived of property because of fear of assault is a victim of extortion. In 1987, there were 11,855 cases of extortion in Japan. If all these were classified as robberies, the total for robbery would still be substantially lower than in the United States.

12. Referring in Japan to crimes under the Penal Code, but excluding negligence cases.

13. The rates respectively are 5,550 per 100,000 for serious crime in the United States and 1,288 per 100,000 for Penal Code offenses, excluding negligence, in Japan.

offenses in Japan. Most of these—20,643—were in connection with stimulant drugs (methamphetamines). Of the remainder, 1,464 persons were arrested for marijuana use or sale and only 304 in connection with what Americans would regard as hard drugs.[14] There were no arrests connected with "crack"—smokable cocaine. By contrast, 937,400 people were arrested for drug offenses in the United States in 1987. Drug arrests in Japan are 1.8 per 100,000; in the United States, 38.4.

Nonetheless, the Japanese are concerned because the trend is rising. Although hard-drug problems have remained vanishingly small, stimulant offenses rose dramatically after 1970, from less than 1,000 persons arrested to 24,022 in 1984. Since then there has been a slight decline. The Japanese refer to this as the "second methamphetamine epidemic," the first being in 1954 when 55,000 persons were arrested.[15] It should be noted that Japan faced and defeated a stimulant-drug epidemic before. Its people, including the police, believe that it can do so again. Drugs are not regarded as a crisis out of control.

Japan's crime rates are remarkable not only by American standards but by those of the developed democracies generally. For example, its homicide rate was 1.3 per 100,000 persons in 1987, compared with 8.3 in the United States, 4.1 in France, 4.3 in West Germany, and 5.5. in Britain. For robbery, Japan has a rate of 1.5, whereas West Germany has 46.0, Britain 65.4, and France 46.0.[16] The point is that Japan's crime rates are remarkably small by international standards but America's are remarkably high.

Can these figures on the incidence of crime in Japan be accepted at face value? Are there any reasons for believing that they may be less reliable than American figures? I do not think so. Both countries have studied nonreporting by victims to the police. They show that the rate of nonreporting is higher in the United States than in Japan. The National Policy Agency in Japan compared survey results from both countries for similar kinds of crime in 1970 and found that the true incidence of theft was 82 percent higher than reported figures in Japan, and 122 percent higher in the United States. On the basis of this evidence, differences in crime rates between the United States and Japan cannot be discounted because of differences in the willingness of people to report crime to the police. Unfortunately, although the United States has

14. *White Paper on Police, 1988,* chap. 5.
15. M. Tamura, "Japan: Stimulant Epidemics Past and Present," *Bulletin on Narcotics* 41, nos. 1 and 2 (1989): 83–93.
16. *White Paper on Police, 1988,* p. 19.

conducted national surveys of victimization yearly since 1974, Japan has never again done so. While there is no reason to suspect that reporting of crime to the police has sharply declined since then, one would like to be reassured.

Official figures on crime in Japan should be accepted as evidence of a profound difference in the incidence of criminality between Japan and the United States. This conclusion need not be based exclusively on statistics; it is supported by quite obvious differences in the quality of life. The streets of Japan are safe. Americans who live for a while in Japan soon begin to experience a liberating sense of freedom; they forget to be afraid. They learn to walk through city streets by night as well as day and not fear the sound of a following step, the sight of a lounging group of teenagers, or the query of a stranger for directions. Vandalism is rare; even graffiti is unobtrusive, at most penciled mustaches on subway billboards. Public telephones show no signs of tampering and bus drivers make change. Every foreign visitor has a story of surprising acts of individual honesty—money left untouched in hotel rooms, lost purses returned, currency found again in the pocket of a suit brought back from the cleaners. In commuting to police operations I have walked at all hours through neighborhoods of every conceivable social condition and I have never experienced the slightest apprehension. Only twice did the police warn me about areas that should be avoided at night—the Sanya section of Tokyo and the Airin area of Nishinari ward in Osaka. These are Japan's "Skid Rows."

While the safety of Japanese cities cannot be overemphasized, representing as it does a qualitative difference in civility, Japan is not quite paradise. It has criminal problems—violence, gangsters, extortion, political corruption, and rape. It has the pathologies of any society. Reducing crime is an important part of Japanese police work, one that the public appreciates. Subjective concern with crime is not directly proportional to objective incidence.

The Japanese record should convince thoughtful Americans to reassess two popular explanations about rising crime rates. First, crime is often attributed to urbanization, the clustering of people more densely into compact areas. Japan's population is about half that of the United States, yet it is crowded into a land area no bigger than California. There are 800 people per square mile in Japan and 62.5 per square mile in the United States.[17] Almost two-thirds of Japan's 121 million people

17. Foreign Press Center, Tokyo, *Facts and Figures of Japan* (1987 edition), p. 10, gives the density of the Japanese population as 320 per square kilometer and of the United States as 25.

live concentrated around three metropolitan areas—Tokyo, Nagoya, and Osaka. Population density in Tokyo is 38,000 per square mile compared with 24,089 per square mile in New York City.[18] Almost one-fourth of all Japanese live within thirty miles of downtown Tokyo—30 million people.[19] What would Americans do to one another, one wonders, if half of them lived in a space no larger than California? Would crime rates fall, as they are doing in Japan?

Second, Americans often explain criminality in terms of their history, especially the frontier tradition of individual self-assertion, violence, rough-hewn justice, and handguns. Americans accept the aphorism that violence is as American as apple pie; they believe that their unique tradition underlies contemporary lawlessness. Yet Japan's history has also been marked by blood, creating a legacy that touches contemporary culture. Political assassinations, for instance, have been much more common there than in the United States. Martial arts have always played a large role in popular culture. Japanese glorify the sword-wielding samurai every bit as much as Americans do the straight-shooting cowboy. Violent samurai dramas saturate Japanese television as monotonously as westerns do American television. Japan made a virtue at one time of unquestioning loyalty to the Emperor and, by extension, to military discipline. It has openly fought to create an overseas empire and has committed acts of brutal oppression. If Japanese social relations are tranquil today, it is not because their national experience is a tale for children.

These two theories may be so beguiling to Americans because they not only seem to explain, they also excuse. Urbanization is a fact of life; it has occurred and there is little that can be done about it. The past, similarly, is beyond the reach of social engineering. Therefore, crime is inevitable. Nothing can be done. The appropriate response is not collective action and self-appraisal but individual acts of self-protection—stronger locks, guns in the bedside table, migration to suburbs, large dogs, and avoidance of streets at night. These theories allow the face in the mirror to escape responsibility.

Police work in Japan is not only less demanding than in the United States, it is also vastly less dangerous. Guns play a very small part in crime. In 1987, for instance, only 265 crimes involved the use of handguns. Out of 7,778 violent crimes committed in Tokyo in 1987, only 14 involved the use of handguns.[20] The unexpected in police work is

18. *Facts and Figures,* p. 11, and *U.S. Statistical Abstract, 1989,* p. 34.
19. *The Economist,* "Tokyo in Torment," 8 April 1988, p. 21.
20. Information supplied by the Tokyo Metropolitan Police Department.

much less threatening than in the United States. Police officers are not haunted by fear of the sharpshooting assassin, the armed motorist, or the panicky criminal. The most dangerous weapon a police officer encounters is a knife or, occasionally, a sword. Since police officers carry nightsticks and .38-caliber revolvers, and are rigorously trained in hand-to-hand combat, the odds are solidly in their favor. They do not go in armed convoys, as has happened in American cities, and it would be considered outlandish for an officer to carry an auxiliary small-caliber pistol concealed in a pocket, as some American police officers do. Less than twenty police officers are killed each year in Japan as a result of felonious acts, and less than one by firearms.[21] In 1987 alone, 65 American police officers were killed by firearms. During the same year, 2,789 were assaulted with firearms, 605 sustaining injuries.[22]

From an American point of view, contemporary Japanese society is an anomaly. It is affluent, mobile, congested, technologically innovative, and penetrated by mass communications. In outward appearance, it is so like the West as to lack intrinsic interest; it is neither exotic nor traditional, as less developed countries are. Yet this country, with all the attributes Americans consider modern, has a crime rate that is low and declining. Streets are safe and narcotics addiction is infinitesimal. Law enforcement is conducted virtually without stress. Police officers are proud rather than defensive. They perceive the public as supportive, the political environment as benign. The ordinary citizen expects exemplary behavior from police officers and has been given few reasons for believing this unrealistic. How has this remarkable combination of modernity and tranquility been achieved? How can it have happened that a country so similar to the United States can be heaven for a cop?

21. Information provided by the National Police Agency.
22. *Sourcebook of Criminal Justice Statistics, 1988*, pp. 462–67.

2

Koban

Police operations in Japan are based on a unique system of fixed police posts. There are two kinds: *koban* in cities and *chuzaisho* in rural areas. Personnel of koban change each shift; they report for duty at a police station and fan out to the koban. A chuzaisho is a residential post, manned around the clock by a single officer—occasionally two—who lives with his family in attached quarters. The number of personnel in a koban varies considerably depending on the area, from as few as two to as many as ten or twelve in a single shift. In physical appearance hardly any two koban are the same. A koban may be a narrow two-story structure stuck like a chip in a crevice between two tall office buildings. Or it may be a detached circular one-story building located beside a busy intersection. A koban may be a small house on the bank of a canal or one among a row of glass-fronted shops in the arcade of a railway station. Some share structures with other enterprises. One, for example, has a restaurant above it and a bar in the basement below. Koban are stuck on traffic islands, in converted cafes, and under railway overpasses. They fit wherever they can, making do with space available. The only features common to all are a round red light globe hung over the front door, which glows at night, posters of wanted men pasted to a bulletin board on the front wall, and walls painted a dull gray. Chuzaisho look like ordinary but nontraditional homes. Some in northern

Japan have recently been built to resemble alpine cottages with sharply peaked roofs. Because farm homes are not dispersed in single units over the countryside but cluster in communities, chuzaisho are usually located in moderate-sized villages, each on its own small plot of land.

There are about 6,600 koban in Japan and just over 9,000 chuzaisho. Though chuzaisho outnumber koban, koban are the more important posts because almost four-fifths of the population live in urban areas. Koban serve small, very densely populated areas. In metropolitan Tokyo, for instance, where there are approximately 1,000 koban, the average area covered is about 0.22 square miles containing a population of 8,500. Chuzaisho cover about 3,000 people on average and areas up to 18 square miles.[1]

Unlike the United States, police operations in Japan have not been organized in terms of the patrol car. Fixed posts outnumber patrol cars—"*patr'o* cars," as the Japanese say, rather than "*p'trol* cars"—almost five times.[2] Osaka, Japan's second largest city, is representative of the urban distribution of personnel between cars and koban: one-fifth of all patrol officers work in cars, four-fifths work in koban.[3] During the 1960s the relative importance of patrol cars to koban was a matter of lively debate in police circles. During that time the number of koban and chuzaisho declined by 20 percent while the number of patrol cars increased by 57 percent. The reduction was largely accounted for by chuzaisho rather than koban: 25 percent in chuzaisho, 7 percent in koban. There has been no further decline of fixed posts in favor of patrol cars since then because the Japanese police recognize the disadvantages of shifting to more mobile deployment, despite possible economies from covering larger areas with fewer personnel. They know, for one thing, that the public is adamantly opposed to the abolition of koban.[4] Moreover, mobility is not as important a consideration for Japanese police as for American. A smaller proportion of land is devoted to streets in Japan than in the United States: only 15 percent of

1. National Police Agency, March 1989.
2. In 1989 there were 3,034 police cars in Japan: one-third assigned to traffic and two-thirds to patrol. There were 1,241 police stations, 6,569 koban, and 9,059 chuzaisho. National Police Agency.
3. National Police Agency, 1988.
4. Demonstrated originally in a public opinion survey, National Police Agency, Committee on Comprehensive Countermeasures, *Interim Report* (Tokyo: National Police Agency, 1970), chap. 3. Available only in Japanese. This is now an article of faith among police managers, supported by the larger number of requests for establishment of koban, which the police are unable to grant.

the land area of Tokyo, for example, is composed of streets, compared with 27 percent in New York and 43 percent in Washington, D.C.[5]

Patrol car operations are integrated closely with koban activity. A patrol car's chief function is to increase the number of men on the street actively patrolling, since koban personnel patrol intermittently. Because cities are highly congested and a koban's area of jurisdiction is small, patrol cars do not possess an advantage in response time. Koban personnel, on foot or bicycles, frequently arrive first in response to calls for assistance. Patrol cars also provide transportation between koban and the police station, carrying prisoners to the station for processing and detention and police officers for consultations. To encourage close cooperation between cars and koban, patrol cars must pass each post at regular intervals, and driver and partner are required to take short rest periods at koban.

Several small changes are occurring in the koban system. The number of koban is growing slowly to cover newly built-up areas around cities. Correspondingly, the number of rural chuzaisho is declining as farmland is reduced. For example, the number of koban grew from 6,229 in 1975 to 6,641 in 1987, while the number of chuzaisho declined from 9,938 to 9,045.[6] At the same time, the number of police stations is rising slightly, owing to the subdivision of large suburban jurisdictions to cope with rising "bed-town" populations.

Koban development is hindered, however, by two factors, land prices and personnel. Because of the astronomical rise in urban land prices in the past decade, owners are less willing to donate land free of charge to the police, and the police find it difficult to pay commercial rents.[7] Nor are there enough personnel to cover existing koban around the clock. The Tokyo Metropolitan Police Department considers the minimum complement for a koban to be twelve officers—three officers, including a supervising sergeant, on a four-shift rotation. When police officers are unavailable for duty because of sickness, calls for service, or duties elsewhere in the city, koban may be left unattended. Although they are generally left open so that the public can use the phone to sum-

5. Tokyo Metropolitan Police Department, Traffic Division, March 1989; Department of City Planning, New York City, January 1990.

6. National Police Agency, 1988.

7. According to the *Economist,* land in Tokyo and Kanegawa prefectures, which include Tokyo city and Yokohama, was worth as much as all land in the entire United States in 1987. At 1987 exchange rates, a piece of land in central Tokyo the size of a piece of typewriter paper was worth $12,000. "Tokyo in Torment," p. 22.

mon aid, the public complains sharply. In Tokyo the police have attempted to cover some areas with mobile vans, known as mobile koban. This is not popular, since they are not a reliable presence. Tokyo has also created 150 satellite koban, some of which are posts staffed for only eight hours during a day as needed, whereas others are no more than resting posts for foot patrols where an emergency phone is available for public use.[8]

The most crucial function of koban is to provide information to people about locations and addresses. Japanese neighborhoods are a maze of narrow lanes and one-way streets; houses are built on every inch of land, sometimes seeming to be inside one another, reachable only by narrow paths. To make matters worse, most streets—apart from major avenues—are unnamed, and houses are numbered in the order in which they were constructed, rather than according to location. If several houses are built simultaneously, they all have the same block number. Places are located by specifying areas within larger areas—like saying New York, Manhattan, mid-town, East Side, and then giving a number. It has been suggested that this system fits a culture in which houses have social value only within immediate families and neighborhoods. Japanese rarely entertain at home, apart from close relatives; business friends and acquaintances are entertained in public facilities.[9] There is no need, then, for an impersonal numbering system. For people who must find a Japanese home and do not already know its location, the host either arranges a rendezvous at a known place nearby or provides a small map.

Koban officers say that it takes at least two years before they know an area thoroughly. Newcomers cannot even respond to emergency calls successfully without the assistance of more-experienced officers. When a patrol car receives an emergency call over its radio, a curious sequence frequently takes place: the car brakes to a stop, the dome-light is switched on, and the officers consult detailed maps. If they cannot pinpoint the location, they go to a koban in the area and look at maps there. Since koban officers are the experts on each neighborhood, patrol cars are often guided to the spot by watching for koban patrol officers on bicycles and following them. Even koban staff sometimes charge out into the night, only to discover they do not know exactly where to go. They mill around, asking passersby for help, until the person who telephoned can find *them*. An illustrative case of the difficulty of finding

8. Patrol Division, Tokyo Metropolitan Police Department, March 1989.

9. Chie Nakane, *Japanese Society* (Berkeley and Los Angeles: University of California Press, 1970), chap. 4.

places in Japanese cities occurred one muggy summer night when a patrol car was directed to investigate a report that a woman had been molested on her way home from work. The car roared up and down streets searching vainly for the right number. At one point the officers abandoned the patrol car and spent half an hour in a light drizzle running through meandering lanes. They finally broke off their fruitless search to spend seven minutes consulting with officers in a koban. After fifty minutes had elapsed, they succeeded in finding the unhappy woman's apartment. It turned out that the distraught woman, who claimed her breast had been touched on the stairway of a subway station, had incorrectly given her block number to the dispatcher. Since she had not thought to leave her phone number, the police could not call her back to receive proper directions. Though the police were very late in this case, they performed a minor miracle in getting there at all. The officer in charge, sweat-streaked and damp, grumbled as he got back into the patrol car that it was a good thing she wasn't being murdered.

The neighborhoods surrounding koban are generally more heterogeneous in terms of class and activity than is the case in the United States. Within two hundred yards of a koban it is not unusual to find a cluster of bars and restaurants, lower- or middle-income homes tightly packed together, a street or two of small shops, a small foundry or machine-tool factory (scarcely more than garage enterprises), a movie theater with garish advertisements, and a clutch of expensive houses with high walls and enclosed gardens. A "residential area" in Japan is any place where people live, even if they may live in tiny apartments over stores or on narrow streets behind commercial districts. Neighborhoods are not easy to type economically. For one thing, they do not seem to have the life cycle of obsolescence so common in the United States. Though zoning is almost haphazard, economic decay is less pronounced. The explanation for this paradox may have to do with the intrinsic value of space in Japan. Space is not a throwaway item to be discarded by one class of owners when its newness wears off. Space, especially in cities, is too valuable to be left to rats, dust, and darkness. Neighborhoods renew themselves through piecemeal development.

Over a third of the people who need police help seek it from a koban.[10] Almost 60 percent use the telephone, either an emergency number or an administrative one, and about 12 percent go in person to

10. Survey by the National Police Research Institute in Tokyo, Osaka, and several rural police stations (private communication, February 1989); 28.3 percent sought help directly at the koban, 2.9 percent contacted officers on foot patrol, and 5.4 percent asked for help during the regular visit by koban personnel to residences.

a police station. Altogether, just under half of all requests for police assistance (48.3%) are made in person. This represents only a small decline from twenty years ago, when 56 percent of requests were conveyed in person, despite the fact that the proportion of telephones per capita has risen sharply since then.[11] Most of the requests that come to koban are not urgent. Of the 62 percent of the public that came to a koban in 1988, only 14 percent reported being the victims of crime.[12] The most common reason was to report a lost item or turn one in (31.5%). Nineteen percent asked for directions; 6.3 percent needed information about driver's licenses or other motor-vehicle matters; 8.3 percent reported traffic accidents; 2.4 percent sought counseling; and 2.1 percent reported violations of traffic regulations, mostly illegal parking.

Koban are adaptive institutions, their character shaped by the setting in which they are located. They are more than sources of emergency aid; they are community service facilities. Some koban have been equipped with area-wide loudspeaker systems for making announcements of general interest. At least one koban plays a musical chime early in the morning to serve as a time-check for a neighborhood composed largely of apartment houses. The most dramatic example of sensitive adaptation is in the Sanya section of Tokyo. This is an area inhabited by derelicts, misfits, and unskilled laborers hired each morning as casual labor. They live in flophouses and find their only pleasure in scores of small stand-bars. Because many of the people are too improvident to own watches, the koban has mounted a large illuminated clock on the front wall, which helps the men report to work on time. Many people in Sanya like to keep small fish—a Japanese passion—which they catch in small commercial pools. Because they are too poor to afford tanks and equipment, the koban has built a concrete fishpond outside its front door. Fish are deposited there and the owners come back every week or so to see their fish and leave a few hundred yen to pay for food. Transients may also use the koban as their postal address. At a similar koban in Osaka the police were instrumental in obtaining a color television set from the municipal government, which was mounted on a pedestal in a park and turned on for several hours every summer evening. It provides the only nonalcoholic entertainment many of the residents can enjoy.

11. Survey by the Prime Minister's Office, reported in the Japanese journal *Public Opinion*, December 1972.

12. National sample survey by the National Police Agency. Information supplied by the NPA, March 1989.

Koban officers are the first line of police response. They are the first on the scene of any emergency. They have the best chance to capture criminal suspects and the greatest responsibility for forestalling violence. Their decisions determine how most situations will be handled. Though they experience the excitement of jumping into the unknown, they work in anonymity and their responsibility is short-lived. The more serious a situation or the more difficult to settle, the quicker they are supplanted by specialists dispatched from the police station or prefectural headquarters. Rarely do they have the satisfaction of following a case through to a conclusion. They labor under the burden of being regarded as the foot soldiers of police work—jacks-of-all-trades but masters of none. One rainy night the phone rang clamorously in a koban; the officers on duty characteristically jumped to answer it as if letting it ring twice would be an unforgivable sin. Informed that a traffic accident had occurred nearby, they set out pell-mell on white police bicycles. They found a sports car slewed around at the end of a long underpass, its front end shattered against the median divider. The driver had been thrown out and lay huddled on his side a few feet from the open door. Illuminated by the yellow light of sodium lamps, blood from a deep cut above the driver's ear streamed along the rain-streaked concrete, mingling with the fluids from the broken car. The patrol officers diverted traffic around the scene, kept spectators back, and administered first aid while waiting for the ambulance to arrive. It could be heard in the distance hurrying toward the accident, its siren pulsating in the night, "wah-oo, wah-oo, wah-oo." In a few minutes experts in traffic investigation arrived from the police station. They went to work with tape measure, chalk, and camera, and the patrol officers returned unnoticed through the drizzle to their koban.

Investigation of all but the most trivial crimes is conducted by detectives. The koban patrol officer merely preserves the scene of the crime and rounds up witnesses. Detectives also do most of the criminal surveillance, like watching for pickpockets and sex offenders. Detectives, who always work in plainclothes, use koban as bases, coming in to use the phone, to interrogate a suspect, or to have a cigarette and a cup of tea. Outsiders are sometimes startled when a disreputable looking individual marches boldly into a koban and without a word of recognition from uniformed personnel takes over a desk and a phone. Koban play a surprisingly small role in processing suspects. Decisions to arrest are made for the most part at the police station. Suspects are questioned briefly in koban, but if further inquiry is needed, they are transported by patrol car to the station. Unless an officer is assigned to a koban where the incidence of crime is especially high, he may serve for years without filling out an arrest paper.

Generally the activities of patrol officers and specialists mesh easily. Friction occasionally develops when differences in vantage points create differing operational imperatives. For example, twice in one evening patrol officers were summoned to take care of a drunken man who was pestering a bar owner. The second time they were called they took the man into custody and had him transported to the station for holding overnight. The detectives in charge decided the incident was trivial and released the man. Like a bad penny, he turned up within minutes at the bar, his anger doubled because he had been reported to the police. So for a third time koban patrol officers were called out to deal with the same situation. When they returned to the koban, they spoke contemptuously about deskbound detectives who could not appreciate the difficulties of street work. The officer in charge of the koban—a sergeant—felt compelled to talk to the detectives by phone, explaining the koban's point of view. He then suggested to his own officers that the matter had been discussed firmly enough and he didn't want to hear any more about it. Koban patrol officers also become irritated from time to time if they are asked to devote a lot of attention to matters within the purview of specialists which koban personnel do not consider very important. They often complain about the extra work involved when special campaigns are organized against illegal parking or traffic accidents. They begin to feel harried and are conscious of having to slight work which they think is more important to the safety of their immediate area.

Koban come under the command of police stations. The station is where officers report for duty, keep equipment, train, send suspects, obtain information, and sometimes eat and sleep; it is where supervisory authority over them is concentrated. Station staffs range in size from as few as 16 to as many as 500 in Tokyo.[13] Stations are organized into sections according to the nature of the work performed: patrol, traffic, crime prevention, criminal investigation, security, and administration.[14] About 40 percent of total police manpower is in patrol, 15 percent in criminal investigation, 13 percent in traffic, 11 percent in security, 6 percent in crime prevention, 5 percent in riot police, and 2.4 percent in administration.[15]

13. The smallest station is in Aomori prefecture; it serves a remote area of fishing villages and farm communities.
14. The Security Division deals with subversive activities and counterintelligence.
15. Data provided by the National Police Agency for 1989.

Police stations in turn come under the supervision of prefectural headquarters. The prefecture is the highest level at which day-to-day command over operations is exercised. Although there are national as well as regional police commands, they provide only administrative services. Only in extreme emergencies would they direct operations. Japan has forty-seven prefectures; they are very much like states in the United States, only much smaller, on the order of a large American county. In nine prefectures where a large city dominates the prefecture—Osaka and Tokyo, for example—prefectural and city police headquarters are coincidental. In other prefectures, police operations in cities are managed by police stations reporting to prefectural headquarters.

A koban patrol officer, to function successfully, must cultivate the ability to listen patiently. Police officers spend endless hours allowing people to demonstrate that they are alive, have problems, feelings, values, and a uniqueness that is significant. Listening is often an end in itself; it makes no contribution to further action on the part of the police officer or the private individual. For example, one evening at 10:30 a working-class woman about fifty years old came into a koban. She had a nervous, tense face and was followed almost immediately by a small unshaven man of the same age. They sat side by side on a wooden bench and began to talk separately across a desk to two young officers. The woman glanced secretively at the man as she talked, her face betraying distaste and fear. Several times, when they heard their stories diverging, they broke off to shout at each other, calling the other a liar. It turned out that the woman's son and the man's niece had been caught by the police that afternoon sniffing glue. The man, believing his niece to be in bad company, came to the woman's house that evening, rudely pushed his way inside, and threatened the boy if he came near his niece again. When the stories were told, the senior officer of the koban, also about fifty years old, rebuked the man sternly, his voice rising in anger, for attempting to "act like a policeman." The man had no right to enter another's house, to threaten, or to punish. Two other officers joined in the lecture and after about ten minutes the man, thoroughly chastened, went home. Clinging to what remained of his dignity, he muttered that he was satisfied that the matter was now in the right hands and he did not intend to pursue it further. The woman, however, still agitated, settled more deeply onto the bench and had a heart-to-heart talk with the senior officer about the difficulties of bringing up an independent-minded teenage boy without a husband in the house. The officer listened sympathetically for almost an hour, gently giving advice.

On another occasion three men came into a koban—a taxi driver of middle age, informally dressed, and two rather mean-looking young men, one with a misshapen ear and a face deformed into a lopsided triangle. The taxi driver had refused to chase the car of a friend of the two young men. They had tried to goad him into it by disparaging his driving ability. He had then angrily ordered them out. But they had refused to get out, arguing that it was raining hard and they were not where they wanted to go. So the driver brought them all to the koban, where they sat in a line in front of the sergeant's desk, telling the incident from their respective points of view. None of the three raised their voices or used harsh words; they sat almost companionably, exchanging cigarettes and smiling, though more out of embarrassment than warmth. Only the taxi driver occasionally showed irritation, for he still rankled from their insult to his professional ability. None of the men wanted anything from the others, and the police never considered filing charges against them. The sergeant listened attentively, once in a while injecting a word or two. The rain fell, the men talked, the police listened. After half an hour they went away; they could be seen sitting together for a few minutes more in the taxi outside. The sergeant concluded simply that they had wanted to "clear up their hearts."

Koban also attract hangers-on who ingratiate themselves with the police and with whom the officers feel involved. The police refer to them as "police maniacs." One of these has the habit of bringing gifts, such as a box of candy, to the koban when he has money in his pocket after working for several days. Another habitually tries to sleep in a koban. When the officers rush out on a call and leave the koban unattended, he sneaks in and goes to sleep on a bench. If a patrol car comes by, the man explains in detail where the officers have gone, promises not to go back inside, and gives deep bows of farewell as the car pulls away. "Maniacs" are mainly a lower-class phenomenon, derelicts or casual laborers, befuddled with alcohol or retarded. They are harmless and pathetic, desperately wanting a little companionship. Some retired men from higher classes are also drawn to the police, coming to koban regularly to give advice or to assist in giving directions. Regardless of class, the motivation is the same—to provide a semblance of belonging in otherwise empty lives.

Sympathetic listening is not easy. It becomes especially difficult the more tired an officer becomes, and Japanese officers, who work incredibly long hours, have ample reason for feeling exhausted most of the time. Most patrol officers are on duty fifty-six hours a week. They work what is called a three-shift system, which involves working one day from 8:30 A.M. to 5:15 P.M., then the next day from 8:30 A.M. to the following morning at 8:30 A.M., then a day of rest, and reporting the fourth day to begin the cycle anew. Though the time served on duty each week is fifty-six hours, official working time is forty-four hours. In each twenty-four-hour tour of duty, officers are allowed to take eight hours' rest, but they may only do so if circumstances allow. It is not unusual for officers to work the full twenty-four hours, catnapping and grabbing bites to eat on the fly. In order to ensure that officers are on duty an average of fifty-six hours per week, a complicated scheme for distributing extra days off through the month has been devised. Tokyo prefecture is unique in the country in having a four-shift system, with duty hours being fifty-five hours per week and working hours forty-four.[16]

The hours that police officers work are irregular as well as long. They never work the same hours two days in a row—except on the novel four-shift system. The Japanese are familiar with the American system where officers keep to one period of duty for a substantial period of time, commonly a month. This system was tried briefly in Japan just after the war but it was not found congenial. Japanese homes are small and sleeping in the daytime is difficult. If officers are to get adequate rest, they are better off sleeping in facilities provided by the police than going home. Furthermore, because many officers do not own cars, they are dependent on public transportation. Public transportation, however, shuts down from approximately 11:00 P.M. to 5:00 or 6:00 A.M. Police officers could not get home during those hours even if they were let off work. The irregularity of working hours plays havoc with the family life of police officers. Getting home after twenty-four hours on duty, an officer is exhausted, yet it is mid-morning and his family has not seen him for a whole day. He is faced with an awkward choice. He can try to stay awake and drag through the day or go to sleep immediately and find himself wide awake in the evening and faced with a new shift the following morning.[17]

16. Police officers are the hardest-working segment of a hard-working people. The average workweek in Japanese industry in 1987 was approximately 43.2 hours; it was 38.5 hours in the U.S. Keizai Koho Center, *Japan 1989: An International Comparison*, p. 68. Police officers are given twenty paid holidays a year, but few officers take all of them. It is part of the police mystique that a dedicated police officer never takes all the vacation allowed.

17. The disjointed sleeping schedule of Japanese police officers may fit deep cultural patterns with respect to sleep. Americans frequently notice that Japanese people seem to be able to take short naps anytime and anyplace. Japanese children are raised so they can

The arduousness of the Japanese system cannot be justified on the ground of putting more officers on the street during peak hours of crime. The police are busiest between 8:00 P.M. and 2:00 A.M.—a pattern found in most industrial nations. The three- and four-shift systems put two shifts on duty during the day, from 8:30 A.M. to 5:15 P.M. Actually, one shift staffs koban and patrol cars while the second does special assignments like traffic enforcement or makes mandatory visits to residences. One argument in favor of Tokyo's four-shift system has been that it allows officers to begin their longest tour—twenty hours at a time—at two o'clock in the afternoon, so that they are fresher and more alert when evening comes. The four-shift system provides qualitatively, not quantitatively, better coverage.

Only patrol and traffic personnel work irregular day-night schedules. Detectives and administrators work a six-day week, composed of approximately eight hours of duty each weekday and four hours on Saturday.[18] Of course, when an investigation requires night work, detectives disregard the clock. Special precautions are taken with personnel who do exacting work where a lapse due to tiredness might have serious consequences. Patrol-car drivers, for instance, are not allowed to drive longer than three hours at a time without an hour's rest, and every two hours they are required to take a ten-minute break.

Tiredness, for patrol officers especially, becomes a way of life. When one has been on duty for a long period, fatigue becomes a throbbing physical burden, like a feverish pressure weighing down one's shoulders. Patrol officers spend much of their time on their feet, standing in front of koban answering questions, patrolling, and responding to summonses. By nighttime the impulse to sit is overwhelming; an officer's feet seem to grow hot and expand in size. But it is precisely at night, when fatigue is greatest, that police officers are busiest. They particularly dread getting a call at 2:30 A.M. just before most of them are due to get their first sleep in eighteen hours of duty.

To remain alert, let alone civil, in such circumstances is a major ac-

---

sleep anywhere. A common sight in Japan is infants sleeping upright strapped to their mothers' backs. Unlike American children, Japanese children do not need to lie down to fall asleep. Sleep rituals—such as being prone, having darkness, quiet, and uninterrupted periods of time—may be less important to the Japanese. If this is true, then the irregularity of duty hours does not exact the psychic cost in Japan that it would in the United States. Japanese officers are not adapting to a peculiar shift-system. Rather, the shift-system fits established sleep patterns.

18. Rank has its privileges. Above the rank of inspector, officers usually serve only during the day unless there is an emergency.

complishment. Patience is particularly needed with the happy drunks who find the police convenient objects for teasing. A party of young men, for instance, pretended to ride away on the bicycles belonging to a koban. A tall, well-dressed man, sodden with drink, stood truculently in front of a koban berating the police for being lazy, unable to display authority, and wasting time. Patrol officers tried gently to move him on, but he kept returning, as soon as they would turn him loose, like a yoyo on a string. Some teasers have a genuine comic gift. A short wiry man about fifty years old, four front teeth missing, and wearing a bedraggled cloth hat, spent an hour and a half one evening in front of a koban re-enacting drills from his days in the Imperial Army. His stock response to suggestions from the patrol officers that he go home was to draw himself to stiff attention and give a crisp salute. The officers always returned it, even though they knew it encouraged him. People like this mean no harm; they simply want human interaction. What few people understand is that by late evening even smiling is an effort for a police officer. And drunks are unpredictable. An officer cannot be sure when one will begin to talk loudly, drawing a crowd, and then pugnaciously criticize the officer for the mistakes of the entire organization.

A koban is not simply a place of work; it is a home where officers eat, sleep, and relax. It is an "offstage" area denied American patrol officers deployed in automobiles. Housekeeping is an important part of koban life—sweeping floors, brewing tea over a gas ring, or washing cups. These chores are usually performed by the most junior officers. Every koban has an extra room, located behind or above the main office with a raised tatami floor where officers eat their meals and rest or sleep. Some have television sets and well-used boards and counters for playing Go. Meals are brought from home, then warmed up on the gas ring, or sent in from nearby restaurants. Officers are prohibited from eating in public in uniform. Green tea is always available. In summer officers drink soft drinks, cold barley tea, and a sweet drink of fermented milk known as Calpis. During the evening and night, patrol officers announce their intention to go off duty and retire to the sleeping room where they unroll mattresses and bedding provided and get three or four hours sleep. Later they emerge rumpled and heavy-eyed, as their turn comes to relieve tired officers. In a few lucky koban a woman comes regularly to prepare tea or to arrange a small vase of flowers. In one case these services were performed every evening by a cabaret hostess on her way home from work. Services are voluntary, and they bring a welcome feminine touch to a drab male world.

Koban are not particularly cheerful places. Like police facilities the world over, they are serviceable but dilapidated. Desks and chairs are generally worn and scarred, like a collection from a used-furniture store. Visitors sit on metal folding chairs, which throughout Japan are bent, so that the sitter must continually make an effort to sit back or else slip onto the floor. Floors are grimy and the walls, painted gray or dull pastels, are spotted and peeling. The only ornamentation is provided by large maps or chalk-boards, and sometimes vases of arranged flowers. There are always a few bulky cabinets against the walls for storing confidential records, pistols, items of equipment, and the innumerable forms that plague police work.

Different generations are represented among the personnel of a koban, just as they would be in a private home. The supervising officer is usually a sergeant. Sergeants tend to be a generation older than most of the patrol officers in the koban. They have the air of wise and experienced old bears surrounded by energetic cubs. Their style is to lead their charges by example and a quiet word rather than by active command. They tend to stay close to the koban unless a particularly difficult situation arises, letting the young officers do the running. Sharp-eyed and observant, they stand in the background, allowing the patrol officers considerable freedom. When it is necessary, they come forward unobtrusively to handle a belligerent older drunk, to calm a distraught woman, or to deliver a lecture on duty to erring teenagers.

Senior officers make sure that the routines of the koban are discharged. If they leave the koban, they pass over to another officer a braided blue lanyard containing all the keys to the koban kingdom. Patrol officers must make their personal marks—their "chops"—in the logbook when going off or coming on duty. Dishes must be washed and floors swept. During the slack daytime hours, patrol officers visit the homes of the people who have recently bought cars, in order to certify that private parking spaces are available. So great is the pressure on space in larger urban areas that this has become a requirement for automobile ownership. There is a lively trade in phony certificates among car salesmen. Each officer is responsible for visiting each residence and business twice a year in a designated subarea of the koban's territory.[19] This is the "residential survey" and requires considerable investment of time. From these visits are produced the files that allow koban personnel to provide directions in an instant to almost every person or business in their area.

19. This will be discussed in detail in chapter 5.

The procedures of koban and the demeanor of personnel vary only slightly among different parts of the country. In Tokyo an officer is required to stand out front to be accessible for easy questioning twenty-four hours a day, even in the depths of winter. The Tokyo Metropolitan Police Department also insists that the front doors to koban be left fully open at all times. This makes them cold and uncomfortable except near the ever-present, movable kerosene heaters. Other regions are more lax, partly because they are not the "front-face" of Japan and partly because patrol officers elsewhere generally serve twenty-four-hour tours of duty beginning at 8:30 A.M. and are exhausted by evening. Patrol officers are not supposed to take their hats off in public, and this includes the office of the koban. But they do, especially during slow hours and in less prepossessing parts of the cities.

There is more punctilio among Japanese police than American. Many of them put on white gloves when they leave a koban for patrol or when they drive a patrol car. When they enter or leave a koban, patrol officers salute senior officers present. They also bark a muffled, unintelligible word that sounds like "oess." Its meaning is unclear. Some officers thought it was a contraction of "gokuro san desu," meaning "thank you for your trouble," others that it derived from "ohiyo gozaimasu," meaning "good day." And still others thought it had no literal meaning but was a traditional greeting in judo clubs and among high school students.

The requests that flow into a koban are wonderfully varied. Most are ordinary, of course, such as directions, explanations of a law, or mediation. But many are surprising. If people have lost their money or overspent in a night on the town, they can come to a koban and be loaned enough money to get home. Koban in busy entertainment areas, especially those adjacent to railway or subway stations, keep a box of small change for transactions of this kind; the procedure, which involves nothing more complicated than signing a ledger, takes only a minute. Officers say the return rate is very high, as much as 80 percent. People unfamiliar with an area come to koban late at night to obtain recommendations for suitable hotel accommodations. Officers make suggestions and sometimes telephone to make sure a room is available. A koban is an all-purpose source of help. One day, for example, two teen-age boys carrying a small plastic bag containing goldfish wondered if a koban had any distilled water so that the health of the fish would not be impaired in transit. An embarrassed middle-aged man asked if officers had a tool that might repair the zipper on his fly, which would not close. A pair of needle-nosed pliers was found, and the function was restored.

Children emerge most poignantly out of the human parade that passes through koban. A mother shopping on a hot, humid Saturday came to a koban to ask for water for her baby's bottle. While the officers warmed the bottle over a gas ring, she sat, tired and distracted, soothing her fretful baby. Children near public parks, especially in residential neighborhoods, drop in to say hello and in the hope that they will be given a piece of candy. The anguish of lost children is particularly moving. Some simply cry, others are frightened into vacant immobility, and some somberly talk with officers about their lives and pleasures. One six-year-old girl in a bright red dress sat bravely for fifteen minutes till her father found her. As he took her onto his lap, absentmindedly answering the officer's questions, her face slowly crumpled and two enormous tears silently slid down her golden cheek. A young boy, not quite five, became separated from his mother during a crowded outdoor festival and was brought to a koban. After almost half an hour the mother had sense enough to come to the koban for help. Seeing her son sitting safely on a straight chair, she flew across the room and slapped him in the face, saying "Why did you walk away?" Before the startled officers could more than gasp in protest, she sank to her knees and put her head in the crying boy's lap, sobbing her own relief.

Children learn early lessons about citizenship in koban. Around parks they often find coins that have dropped out of pockets of people who have sat on the benches. If the children turn them in, as well as other lost items, many koban reward them with a small printed card filled in with the child's name, the date, and the particular deed performed. The cards ask parents to praise the child for his action. Officers often make a show of receiving lost coins and putting them in a lost-and-found box. Then they give the child a reward of equal amount, which in fact comes from their own pockets. The lesson is that lost money belongs to the loser but virtue has a tangible reward. Valuable losses—wallets, glasses, packages—involve more red tape. A form must be filled out giving the finder's name and address. After a specified period, the finder may claim the lost item. One child found a wallet during a summer festival. His father urged the officer not to go to the trouble of filling in the form; he wanted to take his son back to the excitement of crowds and booths. The officer insisted, however, pointing out that this was an important occasion to teach duty to the child. The poor father, caught between responsibility and pleasure, fidgeted helplessly for twenty minutes while all the proprieties were observed for his five-year-old son.

The sheer numbers of people that pass through the koban present peculiar problems. Throughout Japan a worn sign appears on the door of koban toilets saying "Broken. Do not use." Koban plumbing is as good as any other but assistance has practical limits.

There is a rhythm to daily life in a koban. It is marked by changes in pace of work, nature of requests, kinds of people who need help, the level of noise, and the stresses of fatigue. Each hour has a unique ambiance, so that an experienced officer knows intuitively what time it is without having to consult a clock. Take, for example, a warm summer night in a koban located in the middle of an entertainment section of a Japanese city. During the day there will be hardly any calls for assistance. A few people will ask directions, usually to shops and department stores. Women predominate on the streets. Officers get caught up on paperwork, patrol sporadically against vehicles parked illegally, and go out on the house-to-house visitations. As the sun sets, the tempo picks up, until by eight o'clock movies, restaurants, bowling alleys, and sweetshops are pulsating with life. Streets, thronged with people of all ages and sexes, are as light as day, shop windows agleam with merchandise of all sorts. A few young married couples stroll slowly in matching kimonos, often with a freshly scrubbed child in tow. Footwear is as diverse as the people—shoes, high heels, sandals, zoris, and tennis shoes with the heels folded down so they can be put on and off without undoing the laces. The clop-clop of clogs echoes in the streets, worn alike by middle-class men in kimonos and lower-class workers. About ten o'clock a change occurs. Stores begin to close, their corrugated steel shutters clanging down with a roar. Display lights are extinguished, robbing the streets of their brilliance; shadows begin to form. Two women in their early twenties come into the koban, asking for directions to a bar where a friend works. They have just arrived by train from another city and have no place to stay. Attractive, dressed in bright colors, they laugh and chatter for fifteen minutes while one officer locates the bar on a map and another makes a hotel reservation for them. As the crowds in the street begin to dwindle, the proportion of men increases. Young men with bowling bags surge suddenly out of bowling alleys as if still caught up in the excitement of sport. Small knots of men with their arms around one another's shoulders, laughing and unsteady, stroll leisurely toward transportation terminals. Patrol officers are called to tend a drunken man who has passed out on the sidewalk near a pool of his own vomit. A friend comes with a taxi, and the police return to the koban.

About 10:00 P.M. a teenage couple about eighteen years old come to report that the girl has lost a purse containing all her money, credit cards, and the sundry documents essential to modern life. Neatly dressed, she sits in front of the desk, weeping quietly, head down, as the police fill out the standard form with her name, address, contents of the purse, and the circumstances of its loss. Her companion, dressed in a long, white, old-fashioned car coat, stands beside her holding her hand. As she signs the form a police officer turns from the phone to tell her that the police station reports that her purse has already been found and can be picked up at a nearby koban. The girl's head rises incredulously, then, as everyone nods confirmation, her face breaks into a radiant smile and she clutches the boy in a joyous hug. As they leave the koban to reclaim the purse she bows several times at the door to the assembled officers, her expressive, tear-stained eyes crinkling to slits as she smiles. A half hour later, she and the boy return to the koban, their arms full of cans of hot coffee purchased at the ubiquitous sidewalk vending machines. Bowing to everyone, she distributes them throughout the koban, even to the observing foreigner.

At 11:30 P.M. the working day ends for legions of hostesses from bars and cabarets. They are the night's last surge of humanity in darkened and rapidly emptying streets. Carrying small bags or traveling cases like a badge of office, some are dressed in traditional kimonos, their heads piled high with shining black hair; others wear Western clothes, mostly slacks, a few shorts, and high heels. A few prance proudly like mettlesome racehorses, but most shuffle tiredly. Glamor and make-believe behind them, they are like any group of working women, glad to be done with another day.

The evening deposits people in the koban like flotsam on the shore. A tall man with glasses, dressed casually in used clothes, is brought to the koban after being found riding a bicycle from which all identifying marks have been removed. He will not give his name and has no written identification. His speech is halting, almost a stammer, and never consists of more than a word or two. He seems to be struggling inside himself, as if he cannot connect his mind and tongue. The officers try to coax him into a coherent response; they plead, cajole, and finally get angry. The longer they work with him the more paralyzed he becomes, collapsing into the dark world inside himself like a spent balloon. At first he was a puzzle to the police, now he is a problem. He cannot take care of himself and the police do not know where he lives. After a host of phone calls have produced no clues to his identity, he is taken by patrol car to the police station for holding overnight. Another man is brought in who is dressed only in undershorts and has bright orange patches of mercurochrome on his elbows and knees. He is about fifty years old, gap-toothed, with a stubbly beard, and is totally bald except for a horseshoe of black hair over his ears and around the back of his head. He sits cross-legged on the concrete floor and drunkenly though coherently makes speeches to the watching officers. His wife, a drab figure in the background, with an intelligent face marked by cares she cannot handle, wants him committed to a mental hospital. The man has not worked for two years because of an automobile accident that injured his shoulder. He suffers bouts of depression during which he hurts himself and frightens his wife. After a few minutes the man is carried away, shouting in protest, to a night-cell. His wife stands with simple, enduring dignity among the strange police officers and, as the night deepens and grows chill, tells them softly about her husband's tragedy. The officers listen, shuffle, and grow quiet. A little later an elderly woman, probably sixty-five, wants to spend the night in the koban. Dressed in a shapeless dress and a black stocking-like hat, she moves as if benumbed, clearly unaware of where she is. She is taken to the police station where she settles down for the night on a wooden bench.

So many of the people the police see regularly, and to whom only they attend, are defeated, bedraggled, and helpless. Some have been abused by their own vices, some by circumstances they could not control. All are pitiful and lost, the hope gone out of their lives.

The night runs down; midnight comes and goes. On the faces of the officers beards become noticeable. Not having shaved since early morning, they begin to look haggard and slightly disreputable, their faces etched by fatigue. Under the fluorescent lighting uniforms appear dull, colorless. Officers light cigarettes with the languid, studied deliberation of working men enjoying a symbol of respite. Police officers are not allowed to smoke in public. So they do so in the koban in interludes between activity. Patrol-car officers similarly either come to the koban for a smoke or find a secluded back street or dark corner of a park. Police officers do not smoke nervously, combining a cigarette with work, but take their time, lingering over every puff, as if participating in a life-giving ritual.

The night's last task, apart from waiting for emergencies, is to discipline the cruising taxis. Because all public transportation closes down shortly after midnight, unwary revelers are at the mercy of the taxis. Exploiting their advantage, taxi drivers refuse to pick people up at the taxi-ranks where people stand in line and the driver has no choice about whom he must serve. Instead, the taxis park nearby, waiting for desperate people to agree to pay twice the going rate and holding out for long-distance trips. Lines at the taxi-ranks grow a block long and people complain bitterly to the police. The officers make a halfhearted attempt to stir up the parked taxis, but they snap on their lights and flee like starlings as the officers come close.

Toward two o'clock as the lines of waiting people diminish, quiet and coolness comes to streets that shortly before were fevered with activity. Shadows now are deep; a few sodden men sleep on benches. Whiffs of steam rise from wheeled stalls around which a few people sit in the light of kerosene lanterns eating noodles and boiled fish. Most of the patrol officers look forward to rolling themselves in the koban's bedding. Finally the koban is left to two bleary-eyed officers who are charged with keeping a flickering watch over the now still night.

3

Street Behavior

Japanese police officers are addressed by the public as "Omawari-san"—Mr. Walkabout. This is an accurate reflection of what the public sees the police doing most of the time. Foot-patrolling is done out of koban usually for periods of an hour. Patrols are more common at night, when officers work in pairs. Patrolling by foot is more tiring than it looks. Patrol officers amble at a ruminative pace that allows thorough observation. It is like browsing or window-shopping with none of the satisfaction of actually getting somewhere. Patrolling by automobile, which is much less common than foot-patrolling, can be frustrating too. Because of the narrow congested streets of Japanese cities—for example, only 13 percent of Tokyo's twelve thousand miles of streets are wide enough for two-way traffic—patrol cars are forced to move at a snail's pace.[1] There are often no sidewalks, and utility poles are built in the street several feet from the edge. Pedestrians, including small children, eddy along the streets, in and out around parked cars, delivery vans, stacked crates, and utility poles. Intersections are so tight that a patrol car cannot turn from one street to another in a single motion but must jockey back and forth.

Patrolling is by no means a matter of high adventure. For the most

1. Information furnished by the Traffic Division, Tokyo Metropolitan Police Department.

part it consists of watching and occasionally answering questions. Patrol officers rarely discover genuine emergencies; the chances of coincidence between the officers and sudden need are simply too remote. Patrolling does not reduce reaction time or particularly enhance availability. What patrolling does is to demonstrate the existence of authority, monitor persons who might be or have been involved in disreputable activity, correct minor inconveniences—such as illegally parked cars—and generate trust through the establishment of familiar personal relations with a neighborhood's inhabitants. On patrol, the police are alert for different kinds of problems in different places. In a residential area they watch for people who appear out of place or furtive. In public parks they give special attention to loitering males. Around major railway stations they look for runaway adolescents, lured by the glamor of a big city, who could be victimized by criminal elements. They also watch for "teyhaishi"—labor contractors—who pick up and sell unskilled laborers to construction companies. In a neighborhood of bars and cabarets police officers stare suspiciously at stylishly dressed women standing unescorted on street corners. They determine whether wheeled carts piled with food or cheap souvenirs are blocking pedestrian thoroughfares. Throughout every city they pay particular attention to illegally parked cars and cars that have been left with their doors unlocked.

According to any objective measure, patrol duty is of unquestioned importance. Officers assigned to koban and patrol cars account for the largest proportion of contacts between police and citizens. More officers are assigned to patrol work than to any other police endeavor— about 40 percent. Nonetheless, patrol work does not enjoy an honored place in police service. Indeed, it has the lowest prestige of any specialty. A telling indication of this is the seating arrangement of senior officers of a police station or prefecture when they meet together. Hierarchy in Japanese organizations is openly acknowledged and instantly recognized. In a police station, the chief[2] sits at the head of a rectangular seating arrangement. Immediately to his right sits the deputy chief, who is responsible for administration. Below the chief and the deputy come the heads of the criminal investigation section and the security section. Lowest of all, farthest from the chief, is the head of the patrol section. He is invariably the youngest in seniority among the section chiefs. At prefectural headquarters, division status[3] has been given to

2. *Keisatsu-sho-cho.*
3. *Bu.*

criminal investigation, security, crime prevention, traffic, and administration. Patrol has attained division status only in eleven prefectures. In
the remaining thirty-six, it is a section within the crime-prevention division.[4] Japan's elite police officers, who are recruited directly into the National Police Agency, view patrol work as the least attractive stepping-
stone to a successful career; they much prefer to be assigned to criminal
investigation or security.[5] At prefectural headquarters, the chiefs of
many divisions are elite officers sent from the National Police Agency.
Patrol sections are directed by officers promoted from the lower ranks.
The practice is rationalized by referring to the necessity of having patrol
chiefs with extensive experience as patrol officers. There is merit in this
reasoning, though it is hard to see why this should be more true of patrol work than of criminal investigation or traffic regulation or security
surveillance. If the police establishment were really committed to raising the status of patrol, it would insist that elite officers be given more
extensive on-street experience precisely so they could be assigned to senior patrol positions.

It is interesting to note that the greatest amount of prestige after the
chief in any Japanese police organization goes to the head of administration. In the United States, administration is considered a necessary
evil, a fit place for persons without the ability to hold active commands.
The relative status of administration within the police organizations of
the two countries indicates a profound difference in the evolution of
each system. The Japanese police were created from the top down by
explicit acts of central government initiative during the Meiji period,
1868 to 1889 especially. Function followed organization. In the United
States, police forces grew haphazardly out of patrol and watch activities in thousands of autonomous communities. Organization followed
function.

Though American police organizations evolved out of street responsibilities, the prestige of patrol is no higher than in Japan, except in relation to administration. Most American patrol officers covet detective
status. They want to get "out of the bag," as they call their uniform, and
to be less bound by routine. The difficulty of raising the prestige of patrol is the same in Japan and the United States: how can routine work
performed by a majority of police personnel be made to seem exalted?
Because new recruits are always assigned first to patrol duties, patrol

4. Tokyo was the first prefecture to promote patrol to division status. This occurred
in 1967. Before that, it had been part of the Guard Division.
5. See chapter 4.

work is associated with beginners. Not only beginners but leftovers, for it is out of patrol that men are recruited to criminal investigation or any other specialty. There is a tendency for the ablest men to transfer out of patrol work as soon as possible.

The uniform of Japanese police officers is rather formal in appearance, except in the summer. It consists of a four-button single-breasted coat worn over white shirt and tie. In the winter the coat and trousers are black; in spring and autumn steel blue, the material being lighter weight than in winter. A Sam Browne belt is worn over the jacket—that is, a belt with a strap diagonally over the chest to the opposite shoulder and across the back again to the belt. In summer police officers resemble American police, shedding coat, strap, and necktie, and wearing an open-necked steel-blue shirt with matching trousers. Short-sleeved shirts are popular. The police cap is peaked in front with a short black visor. On the front above the visor is the gold emblem of the police—a five-pointed star enclosed by cherry branches. Rank insignia are worn on coat lapels or breast pocket. There are no identifying numbers or name tags. Shoes are black and vary in style. Officers assigned to motorcycles and patrol cars often affect ankle-length boots. Only socks have escaped standardization, and when policemen cross their legs a wide assortment of lengths and colors are displayed.

Over the uniform, patrol officers wear the distinctive tools of their trade. Patrolling officers carry two-way radios so that they can contact headquarters for information or assistance. In several cities officers carry a small radio receiver, located in the breast pocket, connected by a thin cord to a button-speaker worn in the ear. Patrol officers learn to live with murmuring voices in their ears and sometimes have the distracted look of people living in two worlds. The receivers allow police headquarters to send patrol officers instantaneously from one place to another, like radio-dispatched patrol cars. Police batons—"nightsticks"—are straight pieces of turned wood exactly sixty centimeters long (twenty-four inches) with a leather thong that can be wrapped around the wrist. When not being carried in the hand, they are attached to the belt through a metal loop. A .38-caliber revolver is carried in a holster and attached to the shoulder by a braided lanyard. Handcuffs are kept in a pouch on the belt. All equipment is standard issue and worn according to an identical format all over Japan: pistol on the right, handcuffs left-rear, nightstick down the left leg. There are no individual touches such as one sees on the uniforms of American police—no pearl-handled pistols or reverse-draws. Perhaps the most distinctive item of equipment is not visible—fifteen feet of light rope, strong enough to hold a man's weight, kept in a trouser pocket. Following the ancient art of rope-tying known as Hojo, officers are taught a variety of knots and ties by which they can fashion restraining lines, tourniquets, rescue hoists, and additional handcuffs.

When a Japanese police officer is out on patrol he makes a special point of talking to people about themselves, their purposes, and their behavior. These conversations may be innocent or investigatory. The law provides that police officers may stop and question people only if there is reasonable ground for suspecting they have committed or are about to commit a crime or have information about a crime.[6] Nevertheless, standard procedure on patrol is to stop and question anyone whenever the police officer thinks it may be useful. The tactic has proven very effective. Seventy-five percent of all arrests for Penal Code offenses are made by koban and chuzaisho officers.[7] Most of these are made through these "field interrogations." In Osaka, for example, 73 percent of the arrests in criminal cases made by patrol officers in 1988 were made from on-street discovery and questioning.[8] In Tokyo, 34 percent of the people arrested for Penal Code crimes in 1986 were arrested as a result of street interrogations,[9] whereas 44 percent were the result of interrogations by detectives of already arrested persons. Moreover, the importance of patrol questioning as an enforcement tactic has been increasing. In Tokyo the proportion of arrests resulting from patrol questioning rose from 6 percent to 33 percent between 1972 and 1978; in Osaka the proportion of criminal cases cleared by this method rose from 7 percent in 1972 to 18 percent in 1988.[10]

Not only do officers learn to question people adroitly on the street, they become adept at getting people to agree to come to the koban so that more extended, less public inquiries can be made. People are under no obligation to do so, any more than they are to stop and answer questions.[11] The key to success with these tactics is to be compelling without

6. The Police Duties Execution Law, Article 2.

7. *White Paper on Police, 1988,* p. 37.

8. Information supplied by the Osaka Prefectural Police.

9. Murayama, "Patrol Police Activities in Changing Urban Conditions—The Case of the Tokyo Police" (Paper prepared for the International Sociological Association, 1988), p. 19.

10. Murayama and Osaka Prefectural Police.

11. Police Duties Execution Law, Article 2.

being coercive. This in turn depends on two factors: a thorough knowledge of minor laws, and the manner of the police officer. The first provides pretexts for opening conversations justifiably. People who park illegally, ride bicycles without a light, or fail to wear helmets when riding a motorcycle are inviting officers to stop them and ask probing questions. Officers then proceed in a manner that is politely presumptive, asking for information on the often explicit argument that respectable people would not possibly object. Or patrol officers may bluff them into cooperating by saying that they are suspected of being a missing person, and if they cannot prove their identity, they will have to come to the police station for further investigation. This is similar to an American tactic of threatening people who give false names with arrest because the name belongs to a suspect in a very serious crime.

In Japan, unlike the United States, bicycles present a never-ending opportunity for police officers to stop people because the bikes are defective, are being ridden without a license, or do not have proper registration. Major cities are awash in bicycles, ridden for the most part among pedestrians, since it would be foolhardy to ride them in the streets and in many areas there are no sidewalks.[12] Predominantly white, but with a sprinkling of blues, reds, greens, and yellows, these small three-speed clunkers are used by people of all ages for shopping, visiting, or traveling to bus and train stations. A constant sound in the residential parts of Japanese cities is the screech of rusty brakes on cycles moving at a walking pace, alerting people that a cyclist would like to get by. Since the bikes are rarely locked, commuters frequently appropriate ones not belonging to them, from the thousands available, when they cannot find their own, morally secure in the sense that they will return them the next day and that no sane person would ever steal one for profit. Patrolling officers frequently encounter these innocent criminals in their street interrogations.

The importance with which the police view on-street interrogations is indicated by the pride that patrol commanders take in the skill of particular koban or officers as shown by the number of resulting arrests. In addition, prefectural and national contests are held each year to recognize officers who are best at it. One officer assumes the role of suspect and another is given eighteen minutes to discover essential facts about him. Judges evaluate the subtlety of technique. Senior officers continually impress upon new recruits the importance of learning to ask

12. The law was amended in 1986 to allow bicycles to be ridden on sidewalks.

questions in inoffensive ways so that innocent people are not affronted and unpleasant scenes can be avoided.

A tall man in soiled clothes, carrying a shopping bag, was stopped along a dark street lined with warehouses. He talked amiably with one officer, readily giving his name and address. The other patrol officer moved several yards up the street and quietly spoke into his two-way radio in order to determine whether the man was on the list of wanted persons. Each prefecture, or major city, maintains an "A-B-C Index" listing wanted persons, stolen objects, and criminal records. Searching these lists takes at most ten minutes, allowing officers to hold people in conversation while information is uncovered that will determine the officer's course of action. Use of two-way radios is often done so casually that interrogated persons are unaware they are being investigated. When headquarters reported that the soiled man was not wanted, the officer rejoined his colleague and the police terminated the conversation with some hearty advice about not drinking too much.

On another night a young man with shoulder-length hair, light-blue jeans, white shirt, and desert boots was asked to accompany two officers to a koban. He was questioned about his identity, occupation, and residence and requested to show the contents of his pockets. He wanted to refuse, but his nerve failed and he meekly complied. Finding that the young man was not on the wanted list, the police bowed him out the koban door with profuse thanks—"doomo arigato gozaimashita." In a small park two patrol officers found a man in dark glasses, no tie, and with a heavily bandaged arm; he was resting on his haunches near a low iron railing. The man was drunk but docile and happy. One officer squatted down with the man and talked to him while his partner determined by radio that the man was not wanted. After providing and lighting a cigarette for the suspect, the officers walked on, leaving the man still hunkered down by the fence. Late at night a man in a white shirt and good-quality trousers was found in a small public garden near the rest house of a famous temple. He was reading a newspaper under a lamppost. Suspecting that he might be a peeping tom, the police persuaded him to come to a koban. They checked whether he was wanted, whether he had a criminal record, and even whether the transistor radio he was carrying had been stolen. Absolved on all counts, the man was dismissed with smiles and thanks.

It is often helpful in an interrogation for the police to examine personal possessions. This is a very delicate matter. Unless placed under arrest, individuals are not obligated to reveal the contents of their pockets, purses, or parcels.[13] For their own protection, police officers frequently pat the outside of a suspect's clothing—a frisk—to determine whether he is carrying a weapon. And they often get people voluntarily to show what they are carrying, usually because to object would seem suspicious. For instance, a young man was stopped a little after midnight because his motorcycle was making too much noise. His license was examined and the identifying number on his motorcycle was checked to determine whether it had been stolen. When the police asked pleasantly whether they could see inside the satchel suspended from the handlebars, the young man readily agreed. An officer unpacked the bag item by item, asking questions about many of them. Finding only personal effects, he repacked the bag, and the motorcyclist continued on his way after being warned to get his muffler fixed. A groggy bum asleep near the men's room in a park had the contents of two shopping bags searched. They contained several pounds of cigarette ends.

Cues that the police use in choosing people to interrogate are hard to pin down. Sometimes the procedure is routine, accompanying a minor infraction. Other times the police are genuinely suspicious. As in the United States, police officers are trained to recognize the incongruous: well-dressed people in low-class neighborhoods, poorly dressed people in rich ones, heavy bulky clothing on a hot summer night, a business suit worn with crepe-soled shoes, disheveled clothing. Attention is attracted by unnaturalness of manner, such as ducking into an alley when the police are seen or conversely, being overly casual with the police. Then again police officers may simply be curious. They select targets of opportunity as they are presented: leather-jacketed owners of motorcycles, adolescents hanging around a railway station, unescorted young women, a group of youths walking a street at 1:00 A.M., a lone cyclist on a dark street, a car parked on a scenic overlook, two surly-looking men standing beside a sports car near a bar. Street "stops" and interrogations undoubtedly fall most heavily on young males. There is good reason for this: they are the most numerous part of any nighttime crowd and crime rates among them are higher than for other portions of the population.

Patrol officers make other kinds of discriminating judgments as well. They decide which laws to enforce among many and whether circum-

13. Police Duties Execution Law, Article 2(4).

stances require the application of a particular law. Patrol officers daily overlook a host of minor infractions, like spitting on the street, talking roughly in public, or carrying potential weapons, such as iron bars or glass-cutters. They decide when a situation is sufficiently dangerous or disturbing to warrant action. A man urinating in the Ginza at noon will be bundled off without a moment's hesitation; late at night in a back street in Shinjuku he will be ignored.[14] In lower-class neighborhoods drunks are allowed to sprawl asleep in the entrances to movie theaters shut for the night; if they sleep on the floor of a railway station, they are awakened and taken outside. A middle-aged woman, about ten o'clock at night, was displaying stuffed animals on the walkway of a shopping arcade. Two patrol officers genially said hello to her, totally ignoring a clearly lettered sign directly over her head that said sidewalk vending was prohibited by order of the police department. Several blocks farther on, the same officers demanded that a mobile food stall in a less crowded place be moved down the block. The difference in their responses was due to the character of the people involved: the woman was pleasant, orderly, and law-abiding and had used the spot for a long time; the man pushing the food stall was sneaky, nonchalant in a studied way, and known to be affiliated with a local gangster group. At a busy railway station on a Sunday afternoon a Communist student in a red helmet harangued the passing crowd for about forty-five minutes through an electric bullhorn. Other students passed out leaflets. Even though the activity was conducted no more than ten yards from a koban and the police knew that the students did not have the required permit, nothing was done. At the entrance to a large subway station, left-wing students obtained permission from the chief of police to deliver speeches from the top of a private bus. They were allowed five minutes. After thirty minutes had elapsed two patrol officers sauntered across the street from a koban and told them their time was up. The students continued unabashedly for another hour without further notice from the police.

Traffic enforcement too raises delicate issues because most offenders do not consider themselves morally at fault. They are apt to be resentful of any regulation directed at them personally. The police are forced to calculate the value of preventing accidents against losses in public re-

14. The Ginza is the downtown commercial section of Tokyo; Shinjuku is a more moderately priced area with a more youthful clientele. It is also one of the largest urban transportation hubs in the world and a popular shopping area.

spect for law and the police. Traffic police officers openly acknowledge applying a rule of thumb to speeders—they allow between six and fifteen miles per hour over the speed limit. And they may be even more generous depending on circumstances. A man driving at 50 m.p.h. in a 30 m.p.h. zone was stopped by police officers but only given a lecture about the irresponsibility of endangering the lives of his friends. Leniency may become institutionalized. In Tokyo the traffic division publicized a policy of giving "friendly warnings" rather than citations in all but the most flagrant cases. Patrol officers learn to ignore illegally overloaded trucks, especially dump trucks hauling dirt around construction sites, because they know that to stop them would hamper completion of the work and lead to longer periods of traffic congestion. Drivers of defective vehicles are subject to fines but generally are advised instead to make repairs as soon as possible. Professional drivers tend to be treated more severely than owners of private vehicles because they are presumed to be better informed about traffic rules.

Principles governing the use of discretion are not codified or set down in writing; they have the character of custom among police officers. Several factors seem to be involved in determining when illegal behavior will be tolerated. First, enforcement is modified according to place. Officers judge what the public in a particular area has become accustomed to. Second, police forces have their own traditions; over time notions about tolerable limits for different kinds of behavior become accepted within the police community. The policy of allowing a margin over the speed limit is an example, as is toleration of sidewalk vending in prohibited areas. Third, police officers try to judge the effect of their actions upon future behavior of the individuals involved. A warning is often as effective a deterrent as an arrest, and a good deal less costly and time-consuming. Conversely, legal penalties may be an insufficient deterrent for some offenses, so rueful toleration becomes the only practical policy. Police officers appreciate an investment of time that is commensurate with results. Drunks sleeping in public places, for instance, may be more trouble to arrest than the arrests are worth in terms of changed behavior. Fourth, police officers have their own preoccupations. They may decide, for example, that it is more important to continue to patrol against sex offenders than to check upon gambling in a Mah-Jong parlor. Fifth, police officers are sometimes motivated by sympathy for offenders. On one occasion when a minor accident occurred between a taxi and a private car, officers repressed evidence that the taxi driver had been drinking. If results of the "breathometer" test had been recorded, the taxi driver would have had his license suspended. The officers decided that the punishment would be too severe, since no one had been hurt in the accident, both drivers were adequately covered by insurance, and the taxi driver had a blameless record. The taxi driver was ordered to sleep for two hours in his taxi beside the koban before going home. Undoubtedly, he will be more cautious about drinking and driving another time, and the police will have gained a staunch friend.

Who are the people who become police officers in Japan and are required to make these discriminating judgments? Are they unusual in some respect—for example, in experience, intelligence, or probity? The typical Japanese police officer is thirty-five years old, male, married, and high-school educated. He comes from a marginal middle-class family and has been raised outside the larger metropolitan areas.

In terms of sex, police officers are not at all representative of the population. Only 1.9 percent are women, as opposed to 7.6 percent in the United States.[15] Women are currently employed in twenty-five prefectures, concentrated especially in large cities, such as Tokyo, Osaka, and Nagoya. Official policy is to promote the hiring of more women. Women were recruited first in Tokyo, beginning in 1946, though only a handful were employed before 1970. Half of the approximately 4,100 female police officers are assigned to traffic regulation, where they ticket and impound illegally parked vehicles, and 20 percent to the counseling of juveniles.[16] Other cities have female traffic wardens, who wear a distinctive uniform but are not sworn officers. Policewomen do some plainclothes work, mostly against pickpockets and shoplifters. A few have been assigned during daylight hours to busy koban to assist in giving directions. No attempt has been made to integrate them into patrol work on an equal footing with men. Policewomen do not carry guns. One reason given, in fact, for the failure of smaller prefectures to recruit women is that they did not have enough speciality assignments where women could be used.

The educational level of police officers is higher than that of the general population, and efforts are being made to raise it even higher. All

15. National Police Agency for 1988 and the *Sourcebook of Criminal Justice Statistics, 1988,* p. 88, for 31 October 1987. In the larger work force, women constitute 39.8 percent in Japan and 43.8 percent in the U.S. *Japan Times,* 24 February 1989.

16. *White Paper on Police, 1988,* p. 118.

police recruits must have graduated from high school; in the general population the figure is about 92.7 percent.[17] In recent years, about 40 percent of recruits to the police have graduated from a four-year university; 33 percent in the population as a whole. In the United States police are slightly better educated than the population as a whole. The average educational level among American police is 13.6 years completed; among the general population twenty-five years of age and older, it is 12.2. Thirty-five percent of police have no college education, compared with 63 percent of the general public.[18]

Police officers are upwardly mobile in terms of social class. The fathers of police officers are most likely to have been blue-collar workers or small entrepreneurs rather than white-collar workers in large organizations, on the one hand, or manual laborers, on the other. This is true of American police officers as well. Police officers prize advanced education highly and are determined their children will go to college. Though police officers show great pride in their vocation, few of them want their children to follow in their footsteps. Disruptive work schedules are cited as the primary detraction. A contributing factor may be uneasiness about the occupational status of the police. Though survey data are lacking, the fact that Japanese officers consider a career in the police—apart from elite service in the National Police Agency—transitional in the history of their families indicates that they share with American police a sense of status inferiority.

By and large, police officers grew up in the prefectures in which they serve. Interestingly, the proportion of local officers seems to decline the more urbanized the prefecture is. In Aomori prefecture in the north and in Kochi prefecture in the south, almost all the force is local. In Osaka, about half the force is local. In Tokyo, only about 19.7 percent of all police officers were born in the city.[19]

In Japan's large cities, therefore, citizens deal commonly with police

17. Foreign Press Center, Tokyo, *Facts and Figures of Japan* (1987 edition), p. 98. This is higher than in the United States, where it is estimated that about 76 percent of the population over age eighteen has finished high school. *The World Almanac and Book of Facts, 1989*, p. 219, from the U.S. Bureau of the Census, 1987.

18. David L. Carter et al., *The State of Police Education* (Washington, D.C.: Police Executive Research Forum, 1989), pp. xii and 38; and *Statistical Abstract of the United States*, 1989, p. 131.

19. Information supplied by each prefectural force. In the Tokyo police force, more men are recruited from the Tokyo prefecture than any other prefecture. In order, the next major contributing prefectures are Kagoshima, Hokkaido, Saitama, and Chiba. Information furnished by the Tokyo Metropolitan Police Department, March 1989.

officers who are migrants to those communities, officers who have been recruited from less urbanized prefectures. It is not clear, however, whether these officers are rural or city people. It is possible that these recruits actually came from other cities. The data available show only prefecture of origin and not the size of the community where recruits lived. It is possible that even in less urbanized prefectures most police officers grew up in the city parts of those prefectures. Observers of employment patterns generally have suggested that many employers, especially in manufacturing enterprises, prefer workers from rural areas because they are believed to be more tractable, disciplined, and hardworking.[20] Though many police officers agree with this view, there is no evidence that police recruiters in the large cities deliberately discriminate against persons from the local area or in favor of noncity people from anywhere. They say that if they could fill their quotas locally, they would do so. The failure to recruit young people from the larger cities seems to be attributable to different evaluations of the attractiveness of the career between rural and urban young men. There could be various reasons for this: lack of jobs outside the large cities, appeal of a large city to people in the hinterlands, varying perceptions of the congeniality of police work.

When Japanese officers are out on patrol, their demeanor is self-effacing, low-key, and undramatic. Unlike American patrol officers, they do not play a visible role in public unless specifically activated to do so. In the language of the theater, they do not fill space positively unless a specific situation requires it. They do not move habitually as if laden with authority that must be defended. They do not swagger or posture. They see but they rarely take notice. Loitering teenagers or hoodlums do not draw challenging stares so typical among American police officers. In public places the police are as inconspicuous as postal workers. The public rarely gives them more than a passing glance.[21]

The lack of authoritative posturing by police officers is a reflection of

20. For example, James C. Abegglen, *The Japanese Factory* (Glencoe, Ill.: Free Press, 1958), p. 137. Rural workers are supposed to have "stable natures."

21. The inconspicuousness of patrolling officers extended to me as well. Despite my height and light brown hair, people took great pains to avoid noticing me. Only by turning suddenly could I surprise people glancing covertly at me. During about nine months of working with the police on the street over a period of fifteen years, only a few drunks and two bad characters openly inquired about my presence. One evening, for example, as I was standing in front of a koban in a lower-class neighborhood, a drunk said truculently to a senior patrol officer standing next to me, "I don't like to see Yanks." Gesturing down the street, the officer said calmly, "Then don't see him."

general social mores: the Japanese seek to preserve privacy in public places. People move as inviolable units; they go to great lengths to avoid eye contact with one another. This particular custom shows up in an extreme form among members of criminal gangs: they consider a direct stare to be a challenge and have been known to strike a person who does it.[22] So Japanese police are conforming to social custom when they avoid intruding visually without specific cause into other people's lives.[23]

There is an important difference between what privacy in public means in Japan and in the United States. The privacy the Japanese prize is a matter of sight, not of sound. The reverse is the case in the United States, if police behavior is an accurate indication. Relative to one another, Japanese police officers are sound intrusive, Americans sight intrusive. American patrol cars carry powerful spotlights mounted on the side, sometimes more than one; Japanese patrol cars do not. Patrol cars in Japan are invariably equipped with loudspeakers; patrol cars in the United States have only recently become so. Japanese police officers hardly ever shine flashlights onto people without cause. In parks they discreetly turn their lights aside from young lovers embracing on benches. American police make a game of seeing lovers jump when the spotlight hits them. And to catch a couple in a car *in flagrante delicto* is a great coup. American police shine their lights everywhere—onto the porches of private homes, at windows of stores, into yards, between buildings, and into residential areas from low-flying helicopters. In Japan koban and patrol-car police officers make constant use of built-in loudspeakers. The nondriving member of a patrol-car team typically sits with the microphone in hand, volume on ready for instant use. They even tap the microphone in place of using their horns to move people aside. Verbal admonitions are constant. "Don't double-park along this street"; "Your door is not firmly closed," spoken to a car moving ahead in traffic; "Will the owner of the car with license number such-and-such come and move it, it is illegally parked"; "You are crossing against the light, please go back"; "Stop first, then make a right turn." So natural is the commentary that whimsy as well as sarcasm creeps in. To a pedes-

22. All Japanese I have spoken to about this accept it as being true. And with reason. I have twice heard young tough street characters excuse hitting someone because the victim had looked them in the face.
23. The only Japanese who, while not staring, would notice me while I was patrolling with the police, by briefly looking me in the eyes, were bar hostesses and entertainment women going to work.

trian hurrying across a street at mid-block, "You're looking proud"; from a koban to pedestrians, "You are now at an intersection and as the light is changing you should be thinking about keeping your eye on the light"; as the light changes, "Time is money, better hurry across the street"; and to pedestrians defying a red light, "Red means *stop,* not *run.*" Americans would be intensely irritated by such directives. One can imagine their stony faces, mutterings of "Drop dead," and occasional rude gestures.

On patrol Japanese officers are less suspicious than their American counterparts. They seem less alert, their heads turn less frequently to see what is going on all around them. They walk through a crowd as if going for a bite to eat, not like self-conscious wardens of public order. Perhaps this is because there is objectively less to be suspicious about. But the lack of inquisitive alertness may relate as well to the norm about visual intrusions: Japanese officers may be less comfortable than American officers in prying with their eyes.

There is very little cynical posturing among Japanese patrol officers. They exchange fewer knowing smiles than American police officers when confronted with the devious, tawdry, commonplace persons of the police world. It does not seem to be essential to their image that they cannot be surprised by the foibles of mankind. They need not demonstrate publicly that they are a knowing in-group.

Japanese police officers patrol only in public places like stations, streets, and parks. They do not enter bars, restaurants, or shops unless required to do so. Even in lower-class areas where police officers are more free in their intrusiveness, they avoid public accommodations privately owned. There are a few exceptions to this. Patrol officers do enter dance halls to check for people who are under eighteen years old. They also go into movie theaters, with the permission of the owners, looking for sleeping derelicts or for underage youths if the motion picture being shown has a restricted rating. Because the officers do not want to disturb or alarm the audience, they usually make their observations from the rear of the seats, which, as they admit, is not a very effective way to determine who is underage. They enter bars, cabarets, and nightclubs late at night after the customers are supposed to have gone in order to detect violations of the closing laws.

Examining Japanese and American patrol behavior together, several instructive contrasts stand out. Japanese patrolling is more pervasive, due to the proximity of koban and the prevalence of foot patrols, yet much less authoritative than American. They become an assertive audible part of any public scene whenever they choose. They visit private homes twice a year and conduct discreet interrogations of people who arouse their interest. But their visible presence is informal; it does not involve acting out an official role. American police, by contrast, are more fitful in their presence, because they depend so much on the automobile, and more formal. Physical presence is more official than the Japanese; it is never self-effacing. American officers, however, are generally silent though always watchfully alert. In short, the Japanese police force is pervasive, unofficial, and low-key, while the American is occasional, official, and self-conscious. Police authority is conveyed more informally in Japanese than in American society. American police seem to make up in threatening visual presence what they lack in pervasiveness.

The language police use is a crucial variable in police behavior. As in the United States, language among Japanese police officers varies with the locality and the person contacted. To taxis and trucks clear-cut orders are given by patrol-car police because their drivers are frequent violators and are hardened in their relations with the police. To a double-parked taxi an officer says "Move!" rather than "Please move your car, it is double-parked," as he might to a private car in a residential neighborhood. To squabbling laborers outside a bar police say "Stop fighting!" rather than "Please stop fighting," as they would to drunken businessmen in the Ginza. In addition to varying between requests and commands, modes of address change to indicate degrees of politeness and respect. These are difficult to understand through translation but are readily recognizable to Japanese, who make fine distinctions in the choice of words and grammatical forms depending on the status of the other person. Indeed, recruits do video-monitored role-playing during training to learn to fit language to situations and persons. Without changing tone a police officer can switch from a polite form of address in talking to his partner to a rude form in speaking to a prostitute standing on a street corner. The language officers use with street riffraff would be deeply insulting to a respectable Japanese. They also tend to be less respectful to laborers, drunks, and young males with long hair, especially if their manner is sullen or unresponsive. Less polite language does not always indicate disrespect. Since language forms vary with class, the use of high-tone expressions with working-class people would be considered insulting because it would dramatize through its incongruity their lower status. This is true in English as well, where exaggerated politeness is used occasionally to demonstrate place. For example, an American police officer may respond to the criticism of a lower-class black by saying, "Yes *Sir, Mr.* Jones."

Patrol officers are constantly reminded by senior officers to be restrained verbally. Nevertheless, anger occasionally breaks through and they become tough and threatening. When hoodlums are questioned in the back rooms of koban, the doors are sometimes banged shut and shouting can be heard. On one occasion three middle-aged women caught for soliciting for a strip show abused the police in loud shrill voices all the way through a crowded arcade. The officers made a point of turning down a narrow well-lighted lane off the main thoroughfare, where one young officer suddenly turned on the women and shouted "Shut up!"

Talking back to the police is not common but it does occur. The three women just mentioned—known as "catch" women—argued that they did not like being carted off "like cats" and kept saying loudly for the benefit of the crowd, "Don't push me," "Don't hit me," though the police were doing neither. A drunken man who had punched a friend in a bar insisted that the police use the polite form of "You" in talking to him and refused to get into the patrol car until the officers said "please." The rudest behavior toward the police that I saw in nine months of field observation came from a man selling strawberries from the back of a flatbed van in the early evening. Angered at being ordered to pack up because he was obstructing the street, he said truculently, "If I go, why don't you," and later, "I'll go, but I'll be back many times." One other time I surprised two young men in motorcycle jackets, who thought we had passed, surreptitiously giving "the finger" to the patrolling officers. I thought I was home.

Patrol officers often adopt a humorous approach to the people they deal with. Driving around a corner near a street of bars, an officer growled out the window like a tiger at four men urinating against a building. A patrol car came alongside a young man in sports clothes walking in a dark park. He was known to the officers as a sneak thief who robbed preoccupied lovers. "What are you doing?" said an officer. "Swimming," said the man, though the night was chilly. Rather than being affronted, the officer replied, "Pool is closed. You better go home." Three officers were called to a home where an estranged brother had come to pester his working-class family for drinking money. The officers led the man, boisterously drunk, up the street. Patting him on the shoulder, they gave him a mock lecture: "Are you a Japanese man? You don't act very manly. You should act manly or maybe we should cut off your penis. Maybe we should throw you in the river. How about that?" The man smiled groggily, wanting to play up to the humor, and finally managed to stagger to the koban.

Sometimes the humor misfires. A young hippie-type with dark glasses and red knitted cap pulled down over his head was given permission to use a koban toilet. Three of the patrol officers, the same age as the young man, kidded him about his hat. He replied that he had bad brains and the hat was to protect them. When kidded about his dark glasses, however, he produced a document showing that he was half-blind. The officers were abashed and immediately apologized. Attempting to divert conversation, they asked where he was going. Sensing his advantage, the young man wondered pointedly whether the question was official or private. If private, he said, he did not intend to say. And with that he sauntered off, leaving the officers thoroughly discomfited.

Swearing and crude language is not common among Japanese police officers. For one thing, it is difficult for a Buddhist to be blasphemous, which removes a whole genre of expressive language as Americans understand it. There are, to be sure, coarse expressions in Japan, but many of them are not understood across class lines. Earthy language is not much used among officers themselves, let alone with members of the public. It is not a badge of membership in the police community, as it is in the United States. If a Japanese police officer wants to be disrespectful, he does so by manipulating the forms of speech, especially by changing in subtle ways the indicators of status, familiarity, and respect.

The one constant element in the working life of koban patrol officers is people in endless need. In many instances there is very little the police can do to help; assistance consists largely in providing an opportunity for a grievance to be registered. For example, late one evening in July two patrol officers were called to a small bar. It was a single room scarcely twenty feet on a side, capable of serving at most twelve people sitting at several diminutive tables. Small metal Christmas trees hung from a ceiling that was barely head-high. The bar was deserted except for the three heavily made-up women who ran it. They told about a man wearing sunglasses who had drunk quickly by himself, gone to the toilet, and ducked out the back door leaving a bill of forty-five dollars. There was no hope the man would be found and the women seemed to know it. They talked slowly, dispiritedly, the smoke from their cigarettes drifting to the ceiling. Sometimes police assistance is rejected. Responding to a 110 call, officers found a bedraggled young woman in a shapeless dress sobbing in a back alley, her right cheek bruised, her nose bloody. A tough-looking stocky man about thirty-three years old standing nearby was questioned by the police. The injured woman, leaning against a dirty brick wall and uttering dry hysterical sobs, refused to give her name or the man's and would not even say whether he had hurt her. Two other women dabbed at the injured woman with handkerchiefs and confided to the officers that the man and woman were living together. But they too refused to give names. The police knew that the woman was a prostitute, so they concluded the man was her pimp. Since the officers had not seen the assault and the woman refused to press charges, there was nothing they could do. With disdainful nonchalance the stocky man took the sobbing woman firmly by the wrist and led her away. It was clear that the compulsions of this woman's life could not be loosed by police intervention.

Sometimes the help that the police give is acknowledged, and for a moment officers feel a sense of accomplishment. A woman had an attack of severe stomach cramps. She was brought to a koban; the police tried to reassure her and make her comfortable on a wooden bench while an ambulance was summoned. Three hours later her teenage son came back to report that she was fine and to offer the family's thanks to the men of the koban. Another time a blowzy woman in a yellow scoop-necked T-shirt and dowdy black skirt ran across a busy street and threw her arms around the waist of a patrol officer. Her face twisted with fright, the woman used the officer as a shield against a crew-cut man pursuing her who had a heavily bandaged right hand. The two were living together, she said, though they were not married. He was becoming more and more violent, and the woman wanted him arrested and committed to a hospital. The man was held for the night and the woman, after calming down, was sent home.

On rare occasions there may be a dramatic emergency, the kind that police work is supposed to be all about but hardly ever is. Teenagers had a fight in a remote coal-mining village and a young woman was stabbed in the stomach. She was taken by ambulance to a hospital. The police wrapped up the bloody knife and brought her assailant to a koban. He stood benumbed in the center of a throng of officers and reporters, saying over and over again, "I'm sorry, I'm sorry, I'm sorry." [24] A detective became separated from his partners when he chased two gangsters, supposedly dealing in drugs, through a maze of alleys and twisting lanes.

24. *Gomen nasai, gomen nasai.*

The police radio broadcast an announcement that a police officer was in danger, which brought patrol cars speeding from all over the city. On foot and in cars, a small army of officers ran up and down streets, looking desperately for their lost colleague. Ten minutes later he turned up on his own, winded but unhurt, and the patrol cars were ordered back to routine patrol. In another incident, two patrol cars responded to a report that a fight had occurred near a Buddhist temple. They found two dirty, ragged men who had injured each other with broken beer bottles. Blood-streaked and grimy, the men sat on the steps of the temple while their heads were wrapped in incongruously clean white bandages by ambulance attendants. The police dispersed a small crowd of curious bystanders who were fascinated by pools of blood, almost purple in color under the light of fluorescent street lamps, that had fallen on the pitted stone steps.

The needs of most people are not dramatic and the help the police give produces indeterminate results. Many people do not even know they need help and the police grope to find an appropriate response. A typical example was a middle-aged man found about midnight sleeping on a bench in a river-front park. Near him was parked an expensive, gaudily outfitted bicycle. The man had evidently been employed at some time as a construction laborer because he wore the soft, two-toed boots that look like a dinosaur's footprint and a foot-wide woolen cumberbund. Such belly-wraps are common among manual laborers; they are supposed to prevent stomach problems by keeping the midriff warm. Sleepily rubbing his eyes in the light of police flashlights, he ruefully remarked that this was the most terrible night of his life. He had been robbed, so he could not prove his identity, and now he was picked up by the police on suspicion of stealing a bicycle. Because the handlebars of the bike had been knocked awry and the chain had come off, he could not even ride home. The police treated him with good humor and he soon began to laugh at his fate. The police took him and his outlandish bicycle to a koban where, in the course of a few hours, they would make repairs to the bicycle, find out whether it had been stolen, and try to determine whether the man's identity was genuine.

The most striking aspect of the variety of situations confronted by police officers is their compelling, unforced naturalness. The police see masses of utterly ordinary people who have become enmeshed in situations that are tediously complex and meaningful only to the persons immediately involved. The outcomes are of no interest to the community at large; the newspapers will not notice if matters are sorted out or not;

superior officers have no way of recording the effort patrol officers expend in trying to be helpful; and the people themselves are incapable, by and large, of permanently escaping their predicaments. Police officers are responsible for tending these individuals, for showing that they appreciate—even when they are tired, hurried, bored, and preoccupied—the minute ways in which each person is unique. It is, perhaps, the greatest service they render.

4

Discipline and Responsibility

In 1987 an Osaka woman accused the police of embezzling a large sum of money she had found in a supermarket. In addition, the police shamefacedly admitted that they had initially dismissed her story out of hand and had falsely accused the wife of the owner of the supermarket of failing to bring the money to a koban, as the finder had been assured she would do. The upshot was that the officer was fired, his station chief was transferred, and the senior officers of the prefecture, including the chief, were required to pay monetary damages of two million yen (about $16,000) to the family of the defamed woman. Not long afterward it was revealed that officers in a police station in Hyogo prefecture had received several million yen over four years from the government's legal betting corporation for providing protection against gangster intimidation—a clear case of the cure being as bad as the disease. Finally, several defendants have recently been released from prison, often after long periods, because retrial had shown that the evidence for conviction had been fabricated or their confessions had been coerced.

In the United States stories of police misconduct are sad but not especially remarkable. They are the stuff of innumerable films and TV dramas and of cynical shrugs by a resigned public. In Japan, however, revelations like these were almost unthinkable until the last decade. Although corruption scandals had marked the immediate postwar period, they had then been almost unknown until the late 1970s. Since then misbehavior seems to have increased to the extent that the police are edgy and concerned and the public, according to a leading national newspaper, "has an accumulated sense . . . of distrust toward the police."[1]

How much misconduct exists in Japan? It is, of course, impossible to know. Misconduct is undoubtedly a greater problem than is suggested by the mere handful of officers dismissed each year for brutality or corruption. At the same time, it is probably considerably less than in the United States, unless the Japanese are being hoodwinked in a wholesale conspiracy by the police, journalists, prosecutors, and defense attorneys. Many of the scandals dramatically reported involve police officers committing criminal acts when off duty for reasons of passion or financial distress. The press finds major scandals sufficiently rare that it still gives full play to accounts of officers being arrested, and then automatically dismissed, for driving while intoxicated in their own private cars. Corruption appears to occur almost entirely on the margins of vice, especially in connection with tip-offs about raids on gambling parlors. It does not seem to involve narcotics trafficking or prostitution. Moreover, organized corruption involving groups of officers in a single station or unit has so far been confined to the Kansei region around Osaka and Kobe. The rest of Japan has been immune. Physical brutality seems to occur as isolated events of overreaction by individual officers.[2] The charges of ill-treatment of suspects under investigation who are held in police jails are more disturbing because they appear to involve behavior that may be institutionalized and condoned. Although deplorable, such events stem not from a lack of discipline but, rather, from a different discipline. This subject will be explored in chapter 7.

Although Japan has not yet seen the need to set up special prosecutors or high-level government commissions to investigate the sporadic cases of misconduct, and there are no calls for more meaningful civilian oversight, the police themselves have shown concern. The National Police Agency recently ordered that internal investigation units in all prefectures be expanded and more senior officers put in charge. Each

1. The *Asahi Shimbun* quoted in the *New York Times,* 5 November 1984, p. 2, in an article by Clyde Haberman entitled "Police in Japan: Badges Have Lost Their Sparkle."
2. For example, while making an arrest a detective kicked a young thinner addict in the stomach. The man subsequently died. The detective was fired, the chief of the prefecture received a reprimand, and his salary was reduced for a month by one-tenth.

prefectural force has also created and publicized a special telephone number that citizens may call with complaints about police performance. Plans are afoot to create a single national number for this purpose.

Setting aside the unresolvable question of the amount of improper conduct that exists in Japan, what have the Japanese done to ensure that such actions remain rare, if not eliminated altogether? In discussions in the United States about ways of producing responsible police behavior, several factors are thought to be especially important: training, pay and benefits, supervision, and accountability. Let us see what the Japanese have done with respect to each.

The training given recruits in Japan is much more extensive, thorough, and practical than in the United States. Formal training in a police school in Japan lasts for eighteen months for high school graduates and twelve months for college graduates; it lasts not more than six months in the United States.[3] Both the duration of training and the curriculum are standard throughout Japan. Mandatory training standards in most, but not all, states in the United States have occurred only in the last fifteen years.[4] Formal training is also a more serious hurdle to appointment in Japan. Five percent of the candidates sent to the Tokyo police academy, for example, fail to complete the course. Comparable data for the United States are, as usual, lacking because of extreme decentralization. Appointment as a probationary officer has often been criticized, however, as being tantamount to final confirmation because training programs fail to weed out the incompetent.

Formal training is longer in Japan despite the fact that the educational level of recruits is higher than in the United States. About one-third of all police officers have four-year college degrees, while almost half of current recruits in the larger cities have them. In the United States the average educational level is 13.6 years of formal education, meaning not quite two years of college credit.[5] Considerable time is given in Japanese police schools to "moral education and general cul-

3. National Police Agency and the International Association of Chiefs of Police, 1989. Actually the Los Angeles police department requires seven months of academy training, the longest in the U.S. In other large cities, academy training varies from 400 to 1,000 hours, or approximately 2.5 to 6.25 months.

4. The minimum training standard is usually 400 hours (2.5 months). Training Division, International Association of Chiefs of Police, November 1989.

5. David L. Carter, Allen D. Sapp, and Darrel W. Stephens, *The State of Police Education: Policy Direction for the 21st Century* (Washington, D.C.: Police Executive Research Forum, 1989), p. xii. Based on a survey of 699 state, county, and municipal police forces, including all departments serving populations of 50,000 and more.

ture." For example, the Tokyo academy devotes 10 percent of the curriculum for high school graduates and 8 percent for college graduates to Confucian precepts, the history of *bushido* (way of the warrior), samurai traditions, and the values and attributes of humaneness.[6]

The Japanese also recognize that more learning can be accomplished in a few months on the street than in a host of school lectures and demonstrations. Accordingly, they have integrated school with training on the job. After completing a year of police school, high school recruits are sent into the field for three months. College graduates go for the same length of time after eight months. High school graduates then return to school for six months and college graduates for four months.

There is also much more in-service training in Japan. Upon promotion to noncommissioned officer ranks, sergeants spend three months at one of the eight regional training schools and assistant inspectors spend two months. An officer promoted to inspector is sent for six months to the national police college in Tokyo. Every year approximately ten thousand police officers undergo training upon promotion, and forty-two thousand do technical courses lasting from three weeks to a year. Finally, serving junior officers are often given monthly homework assignments designed to keep particular skills fresh. For example, they may be required to fill out appropriate arrest papers for a particular situation.

The material rewards for being a police officer are roughly comparable between Japan and the United States. The total yearly salary of a Japanese patrol officer is about $27,000; in the United States it is $29,000.[7] A Tokyo patrol officer earns about $29,000, whereas a New York City patrol officer earns about $39,000.[8] Salary figures for Japanese include base salary plus allowances and the fixed yearly bonus. Al-

6. Tokyo Metropolitan Police Department, March 1989.

7. National Police Agency, 1989, and *Sourcebook of Criminal Justice Statistics, 1988,* p. 80. The figure for the United States is for officers in cities of over 100,000 in 1987. This comparison is more appropriate because most police forces in the United States are very small. Seventy-nine percent have less than 24 officers, with the average being about 12. Ibid., p. 78. Japanese police forces are organized in terms of prefectures, and the smallest force contains 1,100 officers (Tottori) and the largest 40,000 (Tokyo). "Patrol officer" (*junsa*) in this context designates a rank, not a function. It is the lowest and most numerous rank in both countries. Figures represent estimated averages, since pay within ranks varies according to seniority. Dollar equivalents were calculated at 125 yen per dollar, the prevailing rate during 1989.

8. New York City Police Department, 1989, and Tokyo Metropolitan Police Department, 1989. The New York City figure represents total base salary for "police officers" with three years seniority in 1989.

lowances are extensive, amounting to 34.6 percent of base pay. They include supplements for dependents, housing, commuting, assignment to supervisory positions, overtime, and working nights and holidays. The largest item is the bonus, amounting to 40 percent of base wage and paid in three installments during the year.

If yearly income (base pay, allowances, bonus) were the total benefits earned by Japanese police officers, they would be less well off economically relative to their American counterparts, since the cost of living in Japan is higher than in the United States.[9] However, Japanese police receive extensive fringe benefits in the form of services that American police supply out of their salaries. Approximately 47 percent of all police officers live in housing furnished by the police, for which they pay little or nothing.[10] In Tokyo, for instance, where the cost of housing is astronomical, accommodations for police families are offered at a tenth of the market price. Free medical care and hospitalization are provided to all police officers; their families may use the same facilities at concessional rates. Restaurants, laundries, and barber shops are available to officers at a fraction of the market price. Police officers may also join two cooperative associations that provide health, disability, and retirement benefits supplementary to those awarded by the government. The associations make low-cost loans and sell consumer goods at discount prices. The halls of police facilities are often crowded with racks and tables displaying clothing and household appliances. One of the associations has built hotels in famous cities and vacation resorts, where policemen, their families, and even their friends (if space is available) may obtain excellent rooms and inexpensive food.[11]

Japanese police must retire at the age of sixty, except for senior commissioned officers, who may be asked to retire earlier to make way for the promotion of more able junior officers. This is called the "pat on the shoulder," a nudge from behind, indicating that the person is standing in the way. No one tries to resist this pressure, and most are found alternative employment in private or community-service companies. Pensions are equivalent to about 55 percent of base salary.

The value of fringe benefits would easily bring Japanese compensa-

9. Keizai Koho Center, *Japan 1989: An International Comparison*, p. 75.
10. In this case, of course, they would not be given a housing allowance. National Police Agency, 1989.
11. Figures are not available for fringe benefits in the United States. In New York City, however, which has strong unions, fringe benefits for patrol officers with three years seniority are about 15 percent of base pay.

tion up to American salary levels. But American police too have fringe benefits. If my impression is correct that fringe benefits in the United States are not usually as generous, especially since housing is normally not included, then monetary rewards are about the same, with perhaps a slight edge to the Japanese.

More meaningful than comparing police salaries in the two countries is a comparison of the returns to police officers relative to other occupations. How competitive are police wages and benefits in relation to other forms of employment? The average salary of Japanese patrol officers—base pay plus bonus and allowances—is 10 percent above the average for all private-sector workers.[12] In the United States, patrol officers earn on the average slightly below what workers do in private industry.[13] Only workers in the construction trades earn more than police. Japanese and American police officers are therefore situated similarly with respect to the overall wage structure in each country.

To recapitulate, being a police officer is equally attractive in material terms in Japan and the United States, relative to other occupations. In absolute terms, Japanese police are slightly better-off, though a precise comparison of fringe benefits might change this conclusion. There is one additional condition that American officers would consider a major disadvantage: Japanese police are prohibited from supplementing their income through private employment. In American language, they cannot "moonlight."[14]

The amount of base salary earned by police in Japan depends on three factors—seniority, rank, and education. All police officers receive automatic increments in salary each year, which become smaller the higher the rank. Patrol officers get just under 4 percent a year, thus doubling their salary in about twenty-five years. The annual rate of increase declines the longer the service. It is greatest during the first twenty years, declining after age forty. Police service has been made more attractive for university graduates by giving them four years' seniority at the outset. This differential between college and high school graduates is lost upon promotion in rank. Salary also increases with advancement in rank. Passage of a written examination is required for promotion

12. Y3,375,000 versus Y3,047,000. *Japan 1989*, p. 69.

13. $20,690 per year for patrol officers in the United States (*Sourcebook of Criminal Justice Statistics, 1989*, for 1987); $22,800 for all private enterprise, including agriculture, 1987; $23,894 excluding agriculture (*Statistical Abstract of the United States, 1989*, p. 403).

14. Some minor exceptions are allowed: with permission of a senior officer, they may help run a family store, manage an apartment, or teach English.

from patrol officer to sergeant, sergeant to assistant inspector, and assistant inspector to inspector.[15] Beyond inspector, promotions are made on recommendation of superior officers. From patrol officer through inspector a rise in rank wins a raise in pay less than 1 percent higher than what an officer had already achieved through seniority. Thus a patrol officer with ten years' service earns as much as a sergeant with seven years' service. A patrol officer with thirty years' experience could earn as much in base salary as his station chief if the chief had the rank of superintendent—which is common—and only fourteen years' seniority. Faithful service is rewarded as much as substantial promotions in rank.

Internal supervision is considerably more strict in Japan than in the United States. American supervisors stress the development of individual initiative; Japanese supervisors, errorless performance. Koban patrol officers work under the watchful eye of a sergeant; assistant inspectors tour groups of koban once or twice every shift. Only during foot patrols, which rarely last longer than an hour, are patrol officers in any sense on their own. For all but the most routine events, a sergeant or senior patrol officer will come to the scene minutes after initial response. The chief of a station's patrol section monitors radio communications, especially at night, by means of a portable receiver. Even among themselves, patrol officers continually advise and caution one another. When a patrol car, for example, prepares to start across an intersection, the officer who is not driving mutters "O rai" (all right) to the driver to indicate no car is approaching from his side. Police officers in the United States would resent this kind of routine "front-seat" driving. American patrol officers climb into their police cars at the beginning of a shift and are on their own for eight hours, unless they become involved in an unusually serious incident. American officers even eat alone, in contrast to Japanese patrol officers, who are not allowed to eat in uniform in public places and so return to the koban or police station at mealtime. Senior officers in the United States continually talk about the importance of not blighting the enthusiasm of young officers. The mores of the American police community militate against active on-street supervision. Challenged by public opinion to demonstrate that internal discipline is strict, American officers therefore regulate the only

15. Under a policy begun in 1973, officers with good records are now being promoted without examinations to sergeant after 14 years, to assistant inspectors after 10 years as sergeant and at age forty, and to inspector after 10 years as assistant inspector and at age forty-five. This is being done to reward meritorious service as well as to allow retirement of almost everyone at the rank of sergeant.

part of an individual officer's conduct that they can get at, namely, the officer's relations with the organization. This makes discipline a matter of nagging formalism, covering dress codes, accounting for expenditures, reporting daily events, and indenting for equipment. Supervision in American police forces is a smokescreen for substantial freedom of action on the street. Individual performance is monitored only by peers.

Variations in supervision between Japan and the United States mesh with respective deployment mechanisms. Koban facilitate close supervision; patrol cars undermine it. In Japan most decisions about arrests are made at the patrol station, not on the street. Except in emergencies, patrol officers ask suspects to accompany them to the police station, where senior officers can dispose of the case. Police officers keep in close touch with senior staff and specialists by koban telephone. Because telephones are more private that two-way radios, koban officers can obtain informal advice from headquarters in a way that American police cannot. Where American officers have perfunctory exchanges with headquarters dispatchers, Japanese officers have long conversations in which they examine situations in great detail. Japanese officers are aware that mobility diminishes the effectiveness of supervision. They give special attention to the selection of personnel assigned to patrol cars and motorcycles, especially since increased independence is one of the recognized attractions of the work.

Supervision can also be more extensive in Japan because the ratio of supervisory officers to junior grades is higher than in the United States. Patrol officers (*junsa*) make up 44 percent of the force in Japan and approximately 75 percent in the United States.[16] In Japan the ratio is 1 sergeant to every 1.3 patrol officers, in the United States, 1 to every 6.4. Officers above the rank of sergeant make up 21.6 percent of personnel in Japan compared with 13.3 percent in the United States. Thus, the ratio of what are sometimes called management/command personnel, as opposed to frontline supervisors, is 1 for ever 2.1 patrol officers in Japan and 1 for every 5.6 in the United States.[17]

Strict supervision entails special obligations for senior officers. They are held accountable for the behavior of subordinates more strictly than

16. National Police Agency, 1989; and *The State of Police Education: Policy Direction for the 21st Century* (Police Executive Research Forum, Washington, D.C.), p. xi.

17. The proportion of patrol officers in Japan has declined sharply relative to higher ranks, especially sergeants, during the last twenty years. In 1972 patrol officers made up about 75 percent of the force, exactly the proportion existing in the United States today.

is the case in the United States. Twenty-nine percent of officers who were disciplined departmentally in 1988 were punished for failures of supervision. The most common punishment in such cases was a written reprimand that appears on an officer's record. A few were suspended or had their pay decreased.[18] In a typical case, the chief of a detective section had his pay reduced by 10 percent for several months when a detective in his charge allowed a suspect to take poison and die. The chief of a police station was demoted in rank because an off-duty police officer had his pistol stolen in a Mah-Jong parlor. Officers are required to leave their weapons in the stations, and this officer's failure to do so was attributed to inefficient supervision on the part of the chief. Another station chief was demoted when a patrol officer was arrested for raping several adolescent girls. Station chiefs are admonished when subordinates are arrested for drunken driving off duty. As one would expect, punishments to superiors are more severe when the subordinate's misconduct was on duty rather than off, and when there is a clear link between the activities of the superior and the mistake of the subordinate. In Japan, superior and junior officers share liability for mistakes. This creates a bond between them, which is symmetrical and not based exclusively on fear. A superior officer is viewed as more than a punishing judge; he is a partner in responsibility who may be punished for an error on the subordinate's part.

The responsibility of superior officers for the behavior of subordinates is not unique to the police; it is a general cultural pattern in Japan. When a submarine, for example, struck a fishing boat in Tokyo bay, killing thirty-one, the director-general of the Defense Agency resigned. When the father of one of the radical youths captured after a hostage-taking and siege in 1972 saw his son arrested on television, he went into the backyard and hanged himself in shame for his failure as a parent. And the director of food services on Japan Air Lines committed suicide after an episode of food poisoning was traced to an infected finger of one of his employees.

The system of supervision in the police cannot be understood properly without reference to the ubiquitousness of hierarchy in Japanese social relations. Police officers are aware not only of rank gradations but of seniority within ranks. They mold their speech and behavior according to whether the officer they are dealing with is above or below them in status. Even partners in a patrol car address each other differently

18. Information provided by the National Police Agency.

DISCIPLINE AND RESPONSIBILITY   61

depending on their relative roles. The senior partner will be addressed as "shacho" by the junior, while the junior partner will be called by his surname. (Americans are sometimes puzzled by the Japanese practice of exchanging name cards upon first introduction. These cards contain important clues to status and allow each person to adopt the manner appropriate to the other's social position. Japanese travelers in the United States recount their anxiety at having to meet people socially without knowing something about their station in the world, and they find a cocktail party very unsettling.) But strenuous attempts are made to smooth the hard edges of the hierarchical system. A senior officer who could not mix on easy terms with his subordinates would not be well regarded. Supervisory personnel frequently put on fatigue clothes and perform menial work alongside their men. They also join lower ranks in playing sports or at social occasions. At a dinner or lunch for a visitor four or five ranks will be present. Conversation is general and subordinates participate without embarrassment. Though a superior can dominate if he wants to, lower ranks often inject observations and point out forgotten facts. Senior officers are pragmatic and they appreciate the value of experience. They have no trouble deferring to it over rank. In koban, for instance, sergeants and assistant inspectors frequently step aside and allow a situation to be handled by a young patrol officer who may know the area better than they.

The arrangement of furniture in police offices provides important clues to the nature of relations among ranks. In the office of a chief of a station, the chief's desk will stand on one side of the room with a chair behind it but none in front. On the other side of the room will be several sofas and armchairs grouped around a coffee table. When the chief is at his desk, he deals quickly with subordinates he summons—to give an order or elicit a point of information. The subordinate does not sit down and talk with the chief across his desk. When the chief wants to have a discussion, he goes and sits in an armchair at the head of the coffee table. Chiefs spend much of their time sitting in overstuffed armchairs listening and talking to their staff in what an American thinks of as an informal situation. The same is true in headquarters' offices as well. The senior officer's individual work is done at his desk. When he deals with subordinates, other than in a clear command situation, he deemphasizes social distance by making himself physically accessible. In American society, where hierarchy is less clearly felt, a superior commonly remains seated behind his desk, inviting visitors to sit opposite him. Even staff conferences are conducted from behind the sheltering desk. Paradoxically, then, in the less rank-conscious society—where subordinates often address superiors by their first names—leaders physically demonstrate authority differentials, while in the society where hierarchy is explicit, leaders insist on collegial physical groupings. It is as if each society had developed customs for offsetting fundamental characteristics of social structure. The reason for these compromises may be pragmatic. Hierarchy and collegiality—the one to facilitate command, the other to facilitate egalitarian communication—are both necessary for the efficient operation of complex organizations. Though Japan and the United States appear at first glance to have emphasized different qualities, devices have been generated which ensure that the opposing quality is not lost.[19]

The final factor to consider in trying to explain how Japan tries to limit misconduct is accountability. That is, what mechanisms have been established to enforce responsible conduct upon the police from outside? The network of external constraint upon the Japanese police bears a striking resemblance to the system in the United States. This is not surprising, since the contemporary constitution, criminal codes, and statutes relating to police powers were laid down between 1945 and 1952 during the Occupation.[20]

Every police force is accountable to a civilian Public Safety Commission.[21] There is one in each prefecture and another at the national level that supervises the National Police Agency. Public safety commissions are similar to regulatory agencies in the United States in that their members, who serve for fixed terms, are nominated by executive authority and confirmed by appropriate legislative bodies.[22] Great pains are taken to ensure that the commissions are nonpolitical. Members cannot be appointed from legislative assemblies, hold executive office in a political party, or engage in political action. A majority of a commission cannot be from the same political party. Public safety commissioners are charged with supervising all police operations. They appoint

19. This is an excellent example of a general point that social structures arrayed at opposing ends of an abstract linear continuum tend in practice to decay toward a common center. I am indebted to Marion J. Levy for first bringing this point to my attention.

20. This is not strictly true. The Police Law was passed in 1954. Its provisions concerning public accountability and individual duties and responsibilities changed very little from the Occupation period. What changed most was the pattern of national organization, particularly the size of police jurisdictions and coordination between local and national levels. This will be discussed in chapter 8.

21. The Police Law, Article 38.

22. See chapter 8 for further discussion.

and dismiss prefectural chiefs of police; they must approve promotions and transfers; and they make recommendations concerning punishment for disciplinary violations.

The prefectural legislatures, along with the national Diet, hold the purse strings. Chiefs of police, as well as other senior officers, are frequently summoned before these bodies to answer questions about police performance, crime, and public order.

Japanese police are subject to the criminal law. If a police officer is accused of a crime, the public prosecutor's office—part of the Ministry of Justice—is required to conduct the investigation as well as the prosecution. The police force is not put in a position where it might be tempted to protect its own personnel. Police officers can also be sued for civil damages. If damages are assessed as a result of actions occurring in the course of duty, they are paid by the government. Officers are not liable personally, as is often the case in the United States.

Civilian oversight is enhanced by the Human Rights Bureau of the Ministry of Justice, established in 1948, which solicits complaints about infringement of civil rights by private and public agencies. In addition to an official staff in every major city, the bureau uses twelve thousand civilian counselors scattered throughout the country to discover violations of rights. Though the bureau does not have compulsory powers of investigation, it can ask for an accounting from the police and make recommendations concerning punishment. The number of complaints brought to the bureau about the police has been declining steadily over the past forty years. In 1987 there were only fifty, but they tended to involve more serious infractions than were taken directly to the police, such as physical violence, illegal confessions, and unlawful arrest, investigation, and seizure.[23]

The mass media in Japan is a very important but diffuse mechanism of accountability. It is free and vigorous and not reluctant to publicize police misdeeds. It is fair to say that stories about the police, especially their imperfections, are among the most popular features. For example, when bystanders alleged that police officers had failed to jump into a lake to rescue people from a capsized boat, a headline the next day read, "Are You Like the Navy?" referring to sailors from a Japanese submarine who rammed but did not assist victims from a sports-fishing boat. When the police disregarded the claim of a drunken street-person that he had killed someone, a local newspaper published the story. The

23. Information provided by the Ministry of Justice.

police then investigated and found a body. The chief of the prefectural police committed suicide.

Though all these mechanisms are familiar to Americans, it is difficult to assess whether they exert as much active supervision as in the United States. There are certainly fewer civil suits and criminal prosecutions against police officers, proportionately, in Japan than in the United States. The number of civil rights complaints lodged with the Ministry of Justice are negligible. The press, though avid, only occasionally reports matters that are very serious. Is this because the amount of misconduct is genuinely small or because misconduct is hushed up? Reciprocal back-scratching between reporters and police officers has certainly been alleged, as has collusion between prosecutors and the police to conceal violations of the criminal law. It is also often said that the Japanese public is not "rights conscious," that it acquiesces too easily to overbearing official action. Moreover, public safety commissions do not play an active role in disciplinary investigations; they leave matters in the hands of uniformed personnel unless there is a major scandal. All that one can say, then, is that the mechanisms of accountability appear to be vital: their existence is valued, their use has been legitimated, and they are in fact regularly used. If they are not used as often as might be the case in the United States, it could be because police conduct is better.

At the same time, there is one very serious impediment to external oversight in Japan that does not exist in the United States. Action against individual officers is more difficult to initiate because police do not wear badges or numbers that make them identifiable individually. The introduction of such marks has been considered periodically by the police, and was again a hot topic in the late 1980s, but has always been rejected. Opponents have argued that identification would allow criminals, especially gangsters and political radicals, to pick out and victimize individual officers. Others have objected that the great majority of unerring police would feel as if they were being branded because of the misdeeds of a few. All of this seems strained to Americans—or to Europeans, for that matter. It is also ironic that police recruits wear numbers throughout their academy training, precisely so that instructors may assign responsibility and correct defects in performance.

In relation to what Americans think are important factors in producing high standards of individual police performance, Japan is doing at least as well and often better than the United States, the sole exception being its reluctance to make police officers individually responsible in the public eye. There may, therefore, be objective reasons for what seems to be Japan's superior record. But analysis cannot stop here. The factors that Americans think are important for reducing police misbehavior do not exhaust the possibilities. Police behavior in Japan is molded self-consciously in ways that would rarely be thought of in the United States. What are these unique constraints? And are they applicable in the United States?

Responsible behavior is secured in Japan by developing the allegiance of the individual to the work group in such a way as to legitimate its disciplinary claims on him and to intensify his feeling of obligation not to offend against it. The work group in Japan dominates personal life. It has the emotional overtones of a family—a word police officers use frequently to describe the kind of emotional fulfillment they want to achieve in the group.[24] In such a setting discipline is generated by the chemistry of membership rather than the arrangement of formal structure. Duty is personal; it is part of belonging. Failure to act properly is an act of disloyalty against one's brothers rather than an offense against codified rules. American police officers would find supervision according to the Japanese model frustrating and repressive. Not so the Japanese. To them it is protective and liberating because it tells them how to ensure respected membership in the most important community of their adult lives. Discipline, then, is not simply a condition of service; it is a guarantor of continued emotional fulfillment.

Police officers in the United States continually ask that disciplinary rules be set forth in writing so they may know the limits of their independence. They want a clear demarcation between areas of initiative and subservience. In Japan the group's oversight is constant and nearly without limit. Until 1954 police officers were not supposed to marry without the permission of their superiors. Even today they are advised to end a match when it is considered unsuitable. Senior officers frequently act as marriage brokers, arranging for young men to meet respectable young women and persuading parents that a marriage should be endorsed. Young unmarried officers are admonished to be discreet in meeting their sexual needs, to avoid unsavory female friendships, and to visit prostitutes outside the jurisdiction in which they serve. In police school they are counseled about personal finances, especially the importance of saving. Personal appearance must be sober at all times, hair is not to be worn long, and civilian clothes must be subdued in color and conservative in style.

24. For example, see Christie W. Kiefer, "The Psychological Interdependence of Family, School, and Bureaucracy in Japan," *American Anthropologist*, February 1970, p. 71.

Even in informal groups of officers there is an acknowledged leader who, by virtue of rank or seniority, is responsible for the behavior of the others. If an accident occurred or an individual behaved badly, the leader would be ashamed for failing to discharge his responsibilities. To give an illustration, four police superintendents on a study-tour of the United States were teasing one of their number about wanting to run away with an actress. One officer commented ruefully that if that did in fact occur, he would be disgraced because he was senior among the group.

Japanese police officers constantly exhort one another to live up to the ideals of the organization. Signs are hung in every station, often framed in glass, bearing mottoes about conduct. The year's slogan in one prefecture was "Create a grass-roots police." The motto was not hung and forgotten, an empty ritual, but was continually referred to by all ranks of officers. Supervisors seize every opportunity—inspections, shift-meetings, athletic tournaments—to deliver short lectures about duty and responsibility. They hold an endless number of meetings devoted to the examination of conduct. The chief usually addresses the personnel of the station at least twice a month. Once a month a study meeting of the entire staff is held, leaving a skeleton crew on the street, which lasts a whole morning and is devoted to discussing new regulations and general problems. Some stations have regular "morale" meetings, which are attended by patrol officers and sergeants, focusing on problems of misconduct. There are also regular but more limited meetings of supervisory officers, of section leaders, of shift leaders, and of the personnel of each shift. Meetings are a fixture of life in Japan, reflecting compulsive concern with the prevention of improper as well as unsafe behavior.

There is a great deal of talk about the "police spirit"—attributes all police officers should display. Police officers pridefully say they are not "sararimen" (salarymen), working only for a wage. They are the new samurai, infused with *Nihon damashi*—Japanese spirit. The constant inveighing about duty and spirit sounds forced and artificial to an American, more appropriate to a Boy Scout meeting or a Sunday school class than to seasoned police officers. To the Japanese it is part of the style of the organization, as unremarkable as the air they breathe.[25]

25. In a leaf out of the Japanese book, several American police forces have recently developed "values statements," which are short, succinct statements of the principles that should govern police action. Publicized with considerable fanfare, such statements are promulgated to provide a rationale for police conduct, so that police officers can under-

The work group can legitimately and effectively play a larger role in maintaining responsibility in Japan because the organization is more than an instrument for accomplishing tasks; it is a community. Being a police officer is not just a job; it is a way of life. Long hours on duty in an unrhythmic shift-system separate police from the rest of the world. Opportunities for socializing outside the fraternity are limited, even with one's family. The work itself is conducted in groups. The koban assures this, though it is also true for administrative offices and detective sections. Police officers work together, eat and sleep together, and share mundane housekeeping chores. They relate to one another along many dimensions of activity, not simply the few associated with police tasks. Officers are encouraged to develop hobbies together; displays of calligraphy, flower arranging, and photography are fixtures in the lobbies of police buildings. Police officers describe the relations they want with one another as "wet" rather than "dry," indicating an empathic involvement.[26] Life in the police has the ambiance of an American army company, a touring theatrical troupe, or a college fraternity—people with a job to do requiring total involvement, multiple role playing, and intimate conduct.

Because group relations in the Japanese police are so distinctive, the number of hours spent on duty each week should be looked at differently than they would be in the United States. Indeed, it is misleading, psychologically, to compare them at all. Hours served in the United States are spent at work; hours served in Japan are spent living communally, producing a crucial nonwork consequence. Duty hours in Japan help to form and develop a community of a particular sort. Though the workweek is long, it would feel much longer if served in the American way.

Group bonding also transforms the way Japanese police officers view their careers. Officers will observe sadly that they have only eight or ten more years until retirement or that they recognize that they will be able to serve in only three or four more posts. This is in sharp contrast to the

---

stand what they must do in general terms, whatever their specific assignment and without reference to a voluminous book of rules. Such statements are a long way from the terse "serve and protect" that has long been the motto of American policing. See, for example, Houston Police Department, *Neighborhood Oriented Policing* (Washington, D.C.: International Association of Chiefs of Police, 1988), Appendix I.

26. Americans would say "warm," but more than warmth is involved. "Wet" connotes moistness, stickiness. Americans consider these unpleasant in human relations; Japanese do not.

way American officers look forward with pleasure to retirement, counting the days until they can leave. Policing in Japan is a consuming way of life; in the United States it is a job to get done.

Japanese police officers often live together off duty. This is more than the coincidence of private residence that occurs in the United States. All Japanese police officers are required to live in a dormitory during the year in police school, even if they are married. Furthermore, dormitories are provided for bachelor officers after police school. They must live in them during the first six months on the job, though many stay for longer periods because of the high cost of procuring food and housing privately. In the dormitories curfews are maintained; officers must get permission if they want to stay out past 11:00 P.M. Since most patrol officers are young and therefore unmarried, it is common for as many as half the personnel of a shift to live together in a dormitory. Housing is provided for about half of all married police officers, mostly in large apartment houses. Occupancy is sometimes limited to a fixed term, during which officers are urged to save enough money to cover the cost of a down payment on a house or an apartment.

Athletics play an important part in knitting the police community together. Even though space is scarce, every police station sets aside a large room for practicing judo and kendo.[27] Time is reserved during duty hours for practice of one or the other. Stations reverberate all day with the thump of bare feet, shouting, and the hollow sound of the judo drum. Officers fight, sweat, and bathe together before going back on duty. This is one way of promoting what are graphically referred to as close "skin relations." In midsummer and again in midwinter two weeks of competition are held within each police station and prefectural headquarters, culminating in an intramural tournament. At these times all officers, often including chiefs of sections and stations, practice daily with their men. Some stations also have baseball teams that play in a police league. It is common to see police officers, together with civilian staff, playing volleyball or badminton outside on warm days. In large office buildings deskbound workers are invited by loudspeaker to rise and participate in calisthenics as a midafternoon break.

The intensity of community spirit is dramatically expressed during the annual prefectural judo-kendo tournaments. These are really three tournaments in one: station against station, section against section

---

27. Kendo is derived from traditional sword fighting. Combatants dress in helmets, body-armor, and ankle-length blue skirts. They fight barefoot, dealing hard blows to the head and body with bamboo staves about four feet long.

from headquarters, and company against company from the riot police. Teams practice daily for months under the eyes of police coaches. During the tournaments, which are held in large municipal arenas, the galleries are packed with spectators, mostly nonparticipants from the work group and some families. Top officers from the prefecture are on hand, accompanied by distinguished guests. Long signs and banners are hung over the balcony railings. Men and women, the latter usually traffic aides, stand in the crowded aisles and lead cheers by means of complicated arm and body movements. The noise is deafening and keeps up all day long. Partisanship among participants is intense: they lose their tempers, refuse to quit when injured, and hang their heads in shame when they lose. Winning teams celebrate by throwing their coaches and chiefs into the air. One hardbitten coach, fifty years old, admitted to me that when his team lost he felt like crying. To an American the atmosphere is identical to a traditional college rivalry—the same emotion, identification, and single-mindedness.

Symbols augment group solidarity. Stations create their own mottoes and hang them on the walls. Every prefecture has its own police song. So too have various training schools, units of the riot police, some of the larger police stations, and occasionally a bachelor dormitory.

The immediate work group also does a great deal of socializing together outside of duty. Though for the most part informal—a spur-of-the-moment drink or meal after work—senior officers deliberately contrive occasions for fostering "wetter" relations among members of the group. Overnight trips are arranged for hiking or fishing, or to seaside resorts and famous gardens. Groups stay at inexpensive police hotels at which they eat and drink together wearing traditional kimonos (*yukata*) after bathing communally in large tubs. They sleep three and four to a room on movable mattresses (*futon*) on the floor. Boisterous, lighthearted, noisy, and ribald, such groups develop the kind of camaraderie that is found on a hunting trip among close friends in the United States or at a professional convention.

Supervisors make a point of taking bachelor officers home for a meal and sometimes a bath. To be entertained in a Japanese home is very unusual, and the bath is a symbol of total hospitality. Or they organize a party at a restaurant or a bowling alley. Social occasions are organized quite calculatingly, senior officers saying to one another, "It is time for a party" or "We haven't had a section party in two months." More is at stake than simply avoiding friction among workmates; the purpose is to develop a special intimacy, a climate of emotional trust.

Group parties, especially if they involve drinking, serve to foster closer communication among ranks. This is important because where hierarchy is pervasive, candor may be inhibited. The Japanese compensate in an interesting way. What an individual says when he has been drinking is by accepted custom forgiven; it is not to be remembered. Japanese get "high"—loud, happy, bawdy—more quickly than Americans, who, by comparison, seem controlled and inhibited in their drinking. The apparent susceptibility of Japanese to alcohol is psychological rather than physiological. The whole point of drinking is to obliterate the constraints of hierarchy. There is no virtue in "holding one's liquor" when the purpose of drinking is to create unstructured interaction. Police officers recollect many instances when hidden feelings were revealed during a drinking party, an unburdening that benefited group relations later on. Two young officers spoke fondly about carrying their gruff sergeant home one night after a drinking bout. Now they felt they knew him as a person; he had entrusted himself to their care. Where an American sergeant would be embarrassed, the Japanese sergeant undoubtedly felt that the evening had served its purpose.[28]

Japanese police officers view Americans as being too homebound, too private, and neglecting to develop "wet" relations with workmates. A person who does not socialize with his colleagues is guilty of "my home shugi" (*mai homu shugi*)—antisocial privacy. Note that the phrase has incorporated English words into Japanese: this kind of isolation is associated with the United States. Japanese do not entertain colleagues at home, at least not commonly. They do not invite acquaintances to meet their wives, see their children, "make themselves at home." Consequently, the Japanese do not understand that when an American goes home, socializing with colleagues is not precluded. The Japanese are right, however, in appreciating that the demands of home and work may conflict, but while a Japanese police officer is concerned that home will threaten the work community, the American police officer is concerned that work will threaten home life.[29]

The intensity of involvement with the work group is not unique to the police, nor its centrality of moral tone. Most large-scale organizations—banks, ministries, laboratories, factories, insurance companies—have work communities much like the police. Industrial firms have

28. Socially expected drinking can be a burden to senior officers. One commented ruefully to me that he had twenty-two years of training in becoming a drunk.

29. A revealing story is told in Japan about a newly married woman who asked her husband worriedly whether his job was going well, because he was coming home for dinner every night.

company songs, flags, and lapel pins. They arrange marriages, provide free bathing facilities, and organize classes in birth control, dressmaking, calligraphy, and budget management. They provide an assortment of fringe benefits, including housing, vacation accommodations, and health care. Work affiliation in Japan is the basis of life's most crucial rewards—affective as well as material.[30]

The police community is an intensely male world. Women as police officers—2 percent of the force in 1989—pose a more perplexing problem for the Japanese than for Americans precisely because the organization is totally enveloping. Even though the Equal Opportunity Law of 1986 prohibits discrimination in the workplace on the basis of sex, policewomen are given only a few limited jobs, such as working with juveniles, making crime-prevention presentations to schools and community groups, working undercover against shoplifters and bag-snatchers, and impounding illegally parked vehicles. They invariably serve tea to male officers and visitors. Osaka even has a miniskirted drum-majorette corps composed of policewomen. Women receive less academy training than men and they do not carry firearms. Police-women have not even been integrated into koban activities, which would seem to be a protected environment where a woman's touch might be very useful in dealing with the public. The argument usually given is that such assignments would require living together too intimately for the sake of appearance, since a koban is not just a place to work but also a place to eat and sleep.

At the same time, women display the same pride in their work and the same totality of commitment to the police that men do. And they flock to the police in higher proportions than do their male counterparts. Perhaps this is because Japanese policewomen do not expect anything more, a failure of consciousness. It may also be that in Japanese organizations work is valued, whatever it is. Japanese policewomen are pampered but they are also appreciated. Some officers do grumble, however, that women are paid equally for less-demanding work. Overt sexism in one respect occurs less among the police in Japan than in the United States: I have yet to see pinups of scantily clad women in police facilities, even behind the scenes.

American police officers too are conscious of belonging to a distinct

30. For a marvelous description of life in a Japanese business, see Thomas P. Rohlen, *For Harmony and Strength* (Berkeley and Los Angeles: University of California Press, 1974). Rohlen observed that Japanese organizations are "a collectivity, constituted of emotionally satisfying personal relationships, working in the spirit of concord for the general interest" (p. 50).

group. But there is a crucial difference. The Japanese police community has been deliberately created; identity, entailing distance from others, has been fashioned to augment pride. Community spirit is fostered to facilitate the carrying out of organization tasks. In the United States, identity is accidental and based on estrangement and sometimes rejection. American police officers have been driven inward against their will; their communitarian spirit is defensive, like that of a persecuted minority group. The basis of community among the police in the United States is uncertainty.

In generating responsible police behavior, Japan and the United States have emphasized different strategies. In Japan reliance is placed primarily on the police community itself. The police are self-disciplined. In the United States the burden of achieving responsible behavior is placed upon mechanisms of constraint external to the police organization. When scandals occur Americans reflexively think of providing better external supervision, through elected representatives, civilian review boards, or courts. This is not to say that external mechanisms do not exist in Japan or that internal disciplinary procedures are nonexistent in the United States. But faith in each strategy differs substantially between the two countries.

The readiness with which Americans resort to external constraints to achieve responsible police behavior can be counterproductive. External intervention in police affairs is viewed by police officers, justifiably, as a threat to the autonomy of the organization. Defenses are erected against these intrusions, which have the effect of making the organization more resistant in the future. As in the case of innoculating a living organism, infection generates an immune reaction. One indication that this has occurred in the United States is the "blue power" movement in which police officers, feeling embattled against the outside world, have organized for political action. They have campaigned for the election of officials sympathetic to them, lobbied for stricter criminal legislation, mounted campaigns for the abolition of civilian review boards, publicly criticized other agencies in the criminal justice system, and condemned special investigations of police misbehavior. This is unheard of in Japan. There is no "blue power" movement because there is no object to organize against. Discipline comes from within; it is not the result of probings from outside. Japanese police officers see their environment as benign.

American police often reject outside criticism as being ill-informed; they continually argue that no one can appreciate police work except another police officer. Japanese officers too become irritated when they are criticized publicly, but their irritation is tinged with pride. They realize that high public expectations are a mark of respect, and they want to keep it that way. On the other hand, Japanese police are less willing than American police to be candid about their mistakes. They are afraid that any crack in the image of excellence will undermine public confidence. Therefore, where American police are relatively forthright about mistakes, but argumentative in the face of criticism, Japanese police are closemouthed but hypersensitive.

Comparing Japan and the United States, certain characteristics pertaining to conduct and discipline in the police form strikingly contrasting patterns. In the United States where police scandals are recurrent, public respect for the police is low, police officers feel invidiously exposed to public gaze, their self-esteem is precarious, they are defensively assertive in politics, and their sense of group solidarity is based on feelings of rejection. In Japan where scandals are infrequent, public regard for the police is high, police officers pridefully accept the applicability of high standards to their conduct, their self-esteem is solid, they have not organized in defense of their autonomy, and solidarity is founded on pride. Is it a coincidence that these patterns respectively are associated with very different practices for achieving responsible police behavior? It is at least worth asking whether so great a reliance on external checks in the United States is not in some measure responsible for the disciplinary problems so often deplored.

The implications of this discussion for the United States are tragic in the classical sense that the future is inevitably contained in an unchangeable past. The way each country addresses the problem of ensuring responsible police conduct reflects deeply rooted beliefs, practices, and values. Americans could not give up their faith in the efficacy of external checks any more than they could manufacture the tightly disciplined work communities in Japan. Indeed, as long as distrust in police performance is pronounced among Americans, an act of perverse courage would be required to entrust them more fully with their own discipline. Current circumstances and American culture inhibit a shift in emphasis between internal and external mechanisms. Therefore, if the American strategy of accountability is counterproductive, the United States will continue to sow the seeds of the behavior it wants so much to eradicate.

The Japanese model for achieving responsible police behavior has much to commend it. But approval should not be unqualified. An organization that so effectively shapes and manages individuals could be massively irresponsible without fear of dissent within or exposure without. This potentiality must be examined.

Because the work community is so dominating economically and emotionally, officers must consider carefully any action that could jeopardize their standing in it. Occupational mobility is much lower in Japan than in the United States, which makes the consequences of losing one's job even more catastrophic. Choosing an occupation in Japan is like choosing a wife in a society that regards divorce as a sin. Moreover, where mild rejection, let alone ostracism, can be emotionally shattering, the primary ethical injunction easily becomes "Don't rock the boat."[31] But the inhibitions against dissent are even more subtle. Decisions are made collectively in the police, as in other Japanese organizations. Before a decision is made, extensive consultations take place between a superior and his immediate subordinates. Every senior officer feels obliged to discuss alternatives and solicit opinions extensively. Every person has his say. After consensus has been reached, any act of dissent seems ungracious and lacking in magnanimity. If, therefore, misbehavior is the result of policy or is tacitly condoned by the group, the chances seem slight that an officer would step outside the group to condemn what is taking place.

Loyalties within the police are personalistic. They are particularly intense between an officer and his immediate superior, and they undercut attachment to universalistic norms. Senior officers speak eloquently about the need to protect subordinates who make mistakes. They refer graphically to the need for "maintaining a strong stomach"—Americans would say "guts"—in such a situation, having the courage to take responsibility themselves. By showing they understand the predicament of the subordinate and protecting him from the consequences of his mistake, the superior forges a bond of obligation between the subordinate and himself. One effect of such bonds is that junior officers think twice about exposing superiors to censure for their own mistakes; they become cautious. Another effect is to thicken the silence around mistakes. Personal obligations overwhelm the requirements of accountability.

There has been a sharp debate in police circles about the need to develop a greater sense of individual responsibility in rank-and-file officers. Most believe that even though some misdeeds are hushed up, even from senior officers, most errors are known by supervisors, corrective

31. Referring to Albert O. Hirschman's provocative analysis in *Exit Voice, and Loyalty* (Cambridge: Harvard University Press, 1970), Japanese officers cannot exit. Though they can voice dissent, they do so at the risk of seeming disloyal.

action is taken, and the obligation forged through protection is so intense that the chances of further impropriety is dramatically reduced. What concerns some, however, is that the traditional practice of holding senior officers responsible for the misconduct of juniors inhibits the development of individual initiative and responsibility. Group responsibility transfers obligation away from the rank and file. At the same time, Japanese police do not believe, as Americans tend to, that misconduct is the result of a few "bad apples." Organizations determine behavior; the buck stops there. So the problem for the Japanese is to preserve group responsibility by punishing supervisors and making formal apologies to persons harmed, while insisting within the organization that individuals bear the primary obligation for avoiding improper conduct.

Some thoughtful Japanese officers have also questioned whether the community of the police is not too self-contained. Police officers are recruited young, trained intensively for a year, monitored closely during a probationary period, and imbued with the peculiar customs of the organization. Though officers so trained have an almost intuitive grasp of the needs of their workmates, they have not had much opportunity to develop an empathic sense for others. It would be easy for them to become righteous about the values extant within the police, dismissing without reflection the perspectives of others.

There are persuasive reasons, then, for believing that the dynamics of Japanese social organization can discourage candid testimony about what goes on within the police. But this is true for other societies as well, though for different reasons. In the United States the defensiveness of the police certainly discourages individual officers from assisting outside critics. They run as great a risk of being regarded as traitors by their colleagues as Japanese officers do. Moreover, the police in the United States, like those in Japan, are organized along authoritarian lines. A career can easily be wrecked if a police officer becomes known as a troublemaker. It is not clear on a priori grounds that internal dissent is more inhibited in Japan than in the United States. Damaging revelations about police behavior by police officers are more common in the United States, but this may simply reflect a different incidence of misconduct. Unless an observer participates for a long time in the life of each organization, judgments about duplicity are bound to be vague and unsatisfactory.

Responsibility encompasses more than ensuring that individual officers adhere to appropriate standards of conduct, the kind of responsibility amenable to discipline and exhortation. The larger notion is that an organization like the police should achieve the objectives entrusted to it by society. In Japan and the United States this means preserving a safe social environment through means that do not conflict with human rights. Although the police in Japan have an exemplary record with respect to individual performance, American police have been far more open and self-critical in meeting this larger responsibility.

Police operations in the United States have been open to outside inspection and evaluation since the President's Commissions on Law Enforcement and the Administration of Justice, 1967. Hundreds of academic studies have been made of the efficacy of fundamental police strategies, as well as the tactics employed by individual officers.[32] Nothing like this has been done in Japan. Only one study exists of the impact of the koban system on crime and public attitudes.[33] No controlled experiments testing the efficacy of different strategies have been tried. The National Research Institute of Police Science, a unit of the National Police Agency, does research for the police, but concentrates on forensics and problems the police face. It does not evaluate competing strategies for delivering police services. Only two Japanese scholars have done empirical work on the police.[34] Indeed, the police establishment is keenly suspicious of academic scholars. Their suspicion is not unfounded: since Japanese social scientists lack a tradition of empirical research into bureaucratic behavior, they tend to approach the police with strong ideological predispositions.

Although the Japanese police have unparalleled capacity to produce information about their activities, their knowledge of the impact of these activities is confined to data about reported crime and arrest rates. Neither the police nor other government agencies have been interested, after an initial study in 1969, in undertaking victimization surveys that measure the amount of crime people have experienced rather than the amount reported to the police. The prime minister's office publishes yearly studies of public opinion, in which a few items apply to general

32. Herman Goldstein, *Policing a Democratic Society* (Cambridge, Mass.: Ballinger, 1977); Jerome H. Skolnick and David H. Bayley, *The New Blue Line* (New York: Free Press, 1986).

33. K. Hoshino, "Police Activities to Raise the Level of Public Safety from Crime," *Reports of the National Research Institute of Police Science*, 1976–77.

34. S. Miyazawa, "The Attitudes and Behavior of the First Line Detectives Concerning Criminal Investigation: A Study with Observation and Survey Methods," *The Hokkaido Law Review*, 1979–82, and M. Murayama, "Patrol Police Activities in Changing Urban Conditions—The Case of the Tokyo Police" (Paper prepared for the annual meeting of the International Sociological Association, 1988).

attitudes toward the police. The police know a great deal, then, about what the organization does, but little about what the organization achieves. In the jargon of American social science, the Japanese police know a lot about their outputs but little about their outcomes.

The police themselves have no regular programs for assessing the satisfaction the public has in their efforts. Unlike many police agencies in the United States, they do not routinely do follow-up calls to victims or leave self-addressed cards that people who have called the police may use to evaluate police performance. The Japanese police do, however, receive information about problems the public thinks should be addressed, through the regular residential survey.[35] Finally, Japanese police do not welcome observers of police operations. There are no ride-along or walk-along programs available to citizens, as there are in the United States. To some extent, this is offset by the accessibility of the koban to public view and by the prevalence of foot patrols.

All in all, American police are one of the country's most studied institutions. The Japanese police, by contrast, are one of the most closed. Where American police are learning to achieve their social objectives through systematic evaluation, the Japanese police achieve theirs through heroic effort. They mobilize vast resources, plan with infinite precision, practice with masochistic diligence, and sacrifice home life and health to faultless performance.[36] This is sometimes described as Japanese perfectionism, and to Americans it often seems excessive. It is more than that. Exaggerated effort, individually and collectively, is a way of demonstrating commitment to the organization. It is a group rite, like climbing a mountain or fasting for peace. Thus police operations often seem to be ends in themselves rather than rational undertakings for specific objectives. For example, during security preparations for the Emperor's funeral in 1989, contingents of police were sent from every prefecture, no matter how remote, to demonstrate solidarity. The Tokyo Metropolitan Police Department mobilized 32,000 police for the funeral and ordered patrol personnel to go on alternate-day, twenty-four-hour shifts for the six weeks leading up to it. The London police, in contrast, mobilized only 6,000 officers for Prince Charles's wedding in the face of a much more tangible terrorist threat from the IRA. And

35. This will be discussed in chapter 5.
36. A poll in 1982 by Japan's national television network found that the word most liked by Japanese was *doyoku*, effort. The next, in descending order, were those for patience, thanks, sincerity, endurance, love, harmony, kindness, friendship, and trust. Robert Whiting, *You Gotta Have Wa* (New York: Macmillan, 1989), p. 61.

during funeral week itself, many officers in nonoperational units slept overnight at Tokyo police headquarters even though any need for them was vanishingly small.[37]

Total commitment, as opposed to calculated investment, serves another purpose. If things do go wrong, the police can say that they did all that was humanly possible. The problem with this mind-set is that it is appropriate for short-run crises but not for long-term operations. Managing by zeal is intelligent when a clearly discernible objective is to be achieved. When, however, the objective is more diffuse, such as maintaining public safety while not infringing on human rights, effort is not a guarantee of accomplishment.

In short, the Japanese approach to managing their responsibilities is more instinctive, less pragmatic, than the American. So one confronts a paradox: although the propriety of the behavior of the American police is probably worse than the Japanese, American police are more open; the Japanese police, who have much less to hide, are more closed.

The conclusion to be drawn from this comparison of Japanese and American practices for ensuring responsible police behavior is that a too exclusive reliance on the Japanese model would be as mistaken as a too exclusive reliance on the American. The approaches are complementary. External checks are needed in both countries to ensure that police standards of propriety are coincidental with those of the society at large. External checks reduce the danger that either police force becomes hermetically sealed—the one out of pride, the other out of alienation. The point that Americans must reflect on is whether the Japanese have been more successful in providing external accountability than Americans have in creating internal responsibility. The point the Japanese must reflect on is whether Americans have provided more pragmatic openness in implementing police programs that ensure that the social responsibilities of the police are met.

37. Robert Whiting found the same approach in Japanese baseball, which he describes as emphasizing "endless practice, iron-handed discipline, and the belief that good players are made, not born" (*You Gotta Have Wa*, p. 317).

5

Community Relations

Twice a year uniformed patrol officers knock on the door of every residence in Japan and ask questions about the people living there. How many people live there? Are they related to one another? What are their ages and sex? Are they employed? If so, what kind of work do they do? Do they own a car? What are its make, model, and license number? The answers to these questions, usually supplied by women, since calls are made during the day, are written down on printed forms. The police invite residents to list especially valuable items of property with the police, so that they may be identified in case they are stolen. The police elicit information about happenings in the neighborhood generally. Have new people come to the block? Has the resident noticed any people acting suspiciously? What crimes have occurred recently? They encourage people to discuss problems of living in the neighborhood, such as the quality of municipal services or troublesome neighbors. Police officers visit small businesses as well, obtaining a roster of employees with information about their background. A special point is made of discovering the hours of work of the business and whether someone stays overnight on the premises.

These visits by the police are referred to as the residential survey[1] and are a fundamental part of Japanese police work. Japanese officers are

1. *Junkai-ren.*

surprised that American police do not do the same. They cannot understand why Americans might find such visits distasteful. To the Japanese
the residential survey is as natural as rain, and they are critical if it is not
done regularly.[2] It is a dramatic indication that the role of the police in
Japanese society is not the same as in the United States. Though both
police forces have the same general responsibilities, they relate to the
people in intriguingly different ways. Two features are especially striking. First, Japanese police officers penetrate the community more extensively than American police officers, but they do so in a more routine,
less formal fashion. Second, police and public in Japan share tasks more
fully than in the United States; the boundary line between the police
and the citizen is more permeable in Japan. I shall examine each of these
features in turn.

The Japanese force is neighborhood-centered. Its personnel are deployed in fixed posts—koban—scattered throughout every community.
The residential survey is a device for extending the koban's knowledge
of its community, for demonstrating the availability of police service,
and for developing personal relations between police officer and citizen.
The information collected through the residential survey is used almost
exclusively by local officers. It is not filed or collated at some central
headquarters, not even at the level of police stations. The bound note-
books that officers carry, which seem so ominous to Americans, are
kept in a locked case in the koban. They are used primarily for locating
people and premises. Indexing of the files is primitive, usually only by
name and address. If these files are to be used in criminal investigations
or intelligence operations, koban staff must be told what to look for in
them. The residential survey provides a decentralized memory that has
to be jogged by directive in order to be exploited. The information is
not shared with other government agencies, a point which officers stress
with residents.

Today, unlike the prewar period, residents are not required to answer questions of police officers calling at their homes. Officers frequently simply leave the form and ask that it be filled out and returned
to the koban. Most people cooperate readily; outright refusals are uncommon though not unknown. Refusals in principle come, according
to police officers, primarily from left-wing people—a point that may be
inferred from a refusal and duly noted on the information card. By and
large, resistance can be overcome by persistence and affability on the

2. H. Nishimura and S. Suzuki, "Citizen-Helping Role of the Police and Inhabitants
in the Community," *Bulletin of the Police Research Institute* 27, no. 1 (July 1986): 54–63.

part of individual officers. Lists of topics that might generate easy conversation are sometimes posted in koban and regularly updated. A more serious impediment than ideology is the attenuation of community that has occurred in some neighborhoods. Officers complain particularly about the difficulty of carrying out the survey in the large apartment complexes of the burgeoning "bedtowns." Working wives are common and no one is left at home for the police to contact. They have to come back in the evening or leave the form in the mailbox. Apartment residents take less interest in one another than people do in older neighborhoods composed of detached homes and they are not well informed about community happenings.

The residential survey is usually carried out in the morning or afternoon when emergency demands on the police are slight. It is not a chore police officers enjoy. There is no sorrow in a koban if the pressure of work is so great that rounds cannot be made to each residence, as the National Police Agency suggests. Because of the decline in patrol personnel over the last twenty years, the standard has in fact been hard to maintain. The number of visits assigned to officers also varies considerably throughout Japan. In busy urban centers officers may have about three hundred residences and businesses to visit; in less built-up places they may have over one thousand. Senior officers are aware of the distaste with which the residential survey is regarded and have sought to maintain enthusiasm by stressing its importance in criminal investigations and the surveillance of dangerous people. Special merit points, for example, may be given by police stations to officers who turn up solid criminal intelligence through the residential survey. Officers who carry out the survey with particular skill are honored with special awards. The residential survey will undoubtedly remain a fixture of Japanese policing.

The work of the residential survey is slow, dull, and sometimes awkward. Rarely do residents notice anything either intrinsically interesting or relevant to the serious side of police work. They complain about a neighbor's loud radio, inefficient public services, or harassment by door-to-door salesmen. They imagine suspicious behavior without being able to provide specific details. Conversations once begun are often difficult to shut off, especially if the people are old, retired, or simply lonely. Officers occasionally accept a cup of tea or a cold drink. Though this deepens contact, it slows the officer down and establishes future obligations. Visiting officers volunteer to inspect the locks on doors and windows and give advice about crime prevention.

American police officers frequently complain that most of the people their work brings them in contact with are unpleasant and unsavory individuals that the rest of society wants to ignore—crooks, perverts, alcoholics, the homeless, prostitutes, and thugs. The residential survey is an antidote to this. It forces officers to meet normal people in home surroundings on occasions not marred by stress or demands. Officers meet the respectable people they are protecting rather than the sordid people they are protecting society from. The survey helps the Japanese police officer, as well as the Japanese citizen, recognize the humanity in the other.

In the 1980s American police too began to recognize the critical importance of developing closer relations with communities outside the crisis atmosphere of emergency calls for service. The "community policing" movement, as it has come to be known, features several elements: encouragement of community-based crime-prevention, emphasis on providing non-law-enforcement services to the public, decentralization of operational decision-making, and development of grass-roots accountability.[3] Although its implementation is very uneven across the country, some observers believe that it represents an entirely new model of policing and will dominate American policing for the forseeable future.[4] Some of the concrete programs that are designed to create closer community contacts are increased foot patrols, establishment of neighborhood police offices or ministations, liaison with groups that have troubled relations with the police, and assignment of officers to neighborhoods, with the responsibility to address ongoing nonemergency safety and security needs. Until ten years ago Japan and the United States followed fundamentally different philosophies in designing police practices. Now they are converging, and Japanese practices are being studied carefully by American police.

The Japanese police have long been aware that they are in a unique position to provide advice and assistance to people about a host of personal matters. Few people know where to turn to obtain help in solving their problems. Since the police are the most pervasive government agency, advice from them can save people agonizing steps. Accordingly, all prefectures have set up general counseling offices. They go under

    3. Jerome H. Skolnick and David H. Bayley, *The New Blue Line* (New York: Free Press, 1986), and *Community Policing: Issues and Practices Around the World* (Washington, D.C.: National Institute of Justice, 1989).
    4. George L. Kelling and Mark H. Moore, "From Political to Reform Community: The Evolving Strategy of Police" (Paper prepared for the Executive Session on Police, Harvard University, May 1987).

various names: Komarigoto Sodan (Trouble Counseling), Keisatsu Sodan (Police Counseling), Kaji Sodan (Domestic Affairs Counseling), and Oideyasu Corner (Welcome Corner). All police stations assign at least one experienced older officer to general counseling. The larger prefectures, as well as some police stations, have special offices or telephone services for juveniles.

The Osaka police estimate that they received 120,000 requests in 1988 that were referred to counseling offices. Most of these came from people who appeared in person at police stations. Its Welcome Corner in central Osaka was getting about 100 per month. The Tokyo police handled 43,000 in 1988, 6,000 at headquarters and the rest at police stations. In many cases the counselors simply refer people to appropriate nonpolice offices. Other cases lie within the police purview, such as missing persons, traffic regulations, delinquent children, harassment, and the progress of investigations. Indicative of the acceptance of the police counseling role is the fact that a large number of people want advice about personal problems that do not involve law enforcement at all—marriage, divorce, debts, wayward children, and disputes with neighbors.

Counseling of a general sort is something that American police officers do too. Studies have repeatedly shown that most calls made to the police in the United States do not involve law enforcement.[5] Police officers spend most of their time advising, mediating, referring, listening. What is different is that American police organizations have not adapted as willingly to the performance of this function. The nonenforcement part of police work is considered a recent discovery in American police circles, giving rise to clichés about police being "peace officers" rather than "law officers." In Japan the first family counseling office was set up in 1919 in Tokyo. Though Japanese officers do not consider counseling a glamorous part of police work, they have not resisted shaping the organization to accommodate it. They do not grumble, as American officers do, that police are not social workers. Counseling has been accepted as an inseparable part of police work.

Another dimension of routine nonemergency contact between police and public involves crime prevention. The Japanese police have devoted attention to it longer than the American. At the present time the

5. The President's Commission on Law Enforcement and the Administration of Justice, *Task Force Report: The Police* (Washington, D.C.: U.S. Government Printing Office, 1967), p. 13; David H. Bayley, *Patterns of Policing* (New Brunswick, N.J.: Rutgers University Press, 1985), chap. 5.

amount of crime prevention may be about the same, although generalizations about the United States are always tricky because of the lack
of national data. Crime prevention has been a major field of specializa-
tion within the Japanese police for many years. This is reflected in the
fact that organizationally it has the same status as criminal investigation,
security, patrol, and traffic. The comparison between Japan and the
United States is somewhat misleading because crime prevention in
Japan also covers what Americans know as vice control and juvenile
counseling, with more personnel devoted to these than to enhancing
the public's ability to prevent crime. Plans are now afoot to separate vice
from crime-prevention units, leaving at its core juvenile counseling and
the development and supervision of programs designed to produce that
ounce of prevention that will make an emergency response unnecessary.
American police have long had vice and juvenile units, while an explicit
concern with community crime-prevention began in the early 1970s
with the development of Neighborhood Watch. The last survey of the
distribution of police personnel by assignments in the United States, in
1981, mentioned vice and juvenile counseling but not crime prevention.[6]

Every year since 1977 the Japanese police have mounted a national
crime-prevention campaign in October on a selected topic, such as
automobile theft or household burglaries. These feature a blitz of publicity, rallies, demonstrations, and the distribution of informational materials. In the same year they began designating areas with high rates of
burglary as "special prevention districts." There were 818 of these in
1988. Police work intensively with those communities to devise plans
to meet the problem. The police also select 70 to 80 areas nationally to
be Model Territories each year, each distinguished by signs at the pe-
riphery, like Neighborhood Watch in the United States, where special
efforts are made to develop new crime-prevention programs.

Police officers regularly consult with homeowners and businesses
about security. Technicians are provided by the police to install pick-
proof locks for doors. Koban officers couple crime-prevention checks
with the residential survey, making on-site inspections and leaving
printed pamphlets. If a resident is not at home when an officer calls, he
often leaves a printed card on which he has noted defects in security—
doors unlocked, inadequate safety-catches on windows, valuable property left unattended in the yard. Very well trained teams from headquar-

6. Police Executive Research Forum, *Survey of Police Operational and Administrative
Practices, 1981* (Washington, D.C.: PERF, 1981).

ters, often composed of policewomen, present dramatic skits to schools and community groups to illustrate points about protection from purse-snatchers, unscrupulous door-to-door salesmen, and vehicle traffic. Films are circulated about molestation, street safety, and household security. With appropriate fanfare the police award medals and plaques to citizens for outstanding assistance or timely telephone calls to the police emergency number. Signs about crime prevention are seen everywhere in Japan. Notices reminding people to use the police emergency number are tacked in public places, stuck on the front of private homes, and placed on banners across major streets. Notices are erected on beaches, warning couples about sexual attacks by hoodlums.

Koban have created a curious kind of folk literature in connection with crime prevention. Many of them circulate single mimeographed sheets filled with admonitions, information, and hand-drawn cartoons designed to teach lessons about crime prevention. Each koban adapts to local circumstances the directives sent down from prefectural headquarters. The circulars may note that summer is coming and more children will be playing in the streets; that alcoholism rises at New Year's; that purse-snatching has become common at a particular shopping center. Information is also included about local events and meetings. When koban personnel change, new officers may be introduced through short biographies. Koban take great pride in their creations, and national and prefectural awards are given for the most original bulletins. Newsletters like these have been tried in several American cities during the last decade, but they are by no means general.[7] They are controversial because it is feared that publicizing information about the incidence of crime locally will raise more fears than will be allayed through tips about crime avoidance.

The Japanese police work constantly with other government agencies and community organizations to reduce those conditions that generate crime and disorder. For example, they may urge the construction of a pedestrian overpass, consult with the sanitation department about picking up abandoned bicycles and automobiles, or work closely with the owners of games arcades about not admitting children during school hours. Koban officers in an area frequented by poor casual laborers advise government agencies about neglected refuse collection,

7. Anthony Pate, Mary Ann Wycoff, Westley G. Skogan, Lawrence W. Sherman, *Reducing Fear of Crime in Houston and Newark* (Washington, D.C.: The Police Foundation, 1986).

improper sanitation, and patterns of illness requiring medical attention. They also advise the owners of flophouses and bars about keeping their facilities cheerful and healthy. They prevailed on a city government to replace sidewalks with asphalt so that broken concrete could not be ripped up and thrown during labor agitations.

Such programs are very much like what is being called "problem-oriented policing" in the United States. In both countries police are aware that crime prevention, in the long run, involves addressing enduring conditions within local communities. The difference, however, is that in Japan such an approach is not an innovation of the 1980s. Moreover, problem solving, based on an analysis of recurring incidents, is not a special program; it is something that commanders, assisted by koban officers, consider their responsibility all the time. It is not seen as a managerial tool for redefining the role of patrol officers.

In sum, then, police penetration of the community in Japan is more routine and personal than in the United States and it is more active in ways unrelated to law enforcement. Deployment in koban forces police officers in Japan to play a role in the community as known persons, not like American police officers, who are seen as anonymous faces flickering by behind a facade of steel. A koban is an active force in community life; it is not simply a passive source of police assistance. In the United States the justification for contact between police and citizen, apart from criminal activity, is overwhelming need, and initiative belongs to the citizen. An American policeman is like a fireman—he responds when he must. A Japanese policeman is more like a postman—he has a daily round of low-key activities that relate him to the lives of the people among whom he works.

The second point of contrast in the ways in which Japanese and American police relate to their respective communities has to do with the permeability of the boundary between police and citizen roles. In Japan private persons are mobilized in explicit ways to assist police officers in the performance of their duties, creating a cooperative relationship between police and public, which is rare, although growing, in the United States.

Every neighborhood in Japan has a Crime Prevention Association composed of resident volunteers who work closely with the local police station. Activities of the associations vary considerably from place to place, depending on the imagination and enthusiasm of members. They erect signs in public places—such as "Beware of pickpockets"—and distribute leaflets about home protection. They bombard the community with reminders about the importance of calling 110, the police emergency number. Small, square 110 notices are one of the most common items of graffiti in Japan. No pretext is too trivial for a call to the police; seeing a "suspicious person," as association literature puts it, is sufficient justification. Associations publicize and sell improved locks and window catches. They contribute money to police stations to purchase crime-prevention vans or publish crime-prevention booklets. Association members are on the alert for situations that can cause accidents— open trenches, unguarded canals, or defective playground equipment. They maintain informal surveillance over troublemaking people, especially gangsters. One association distributed signs to businesses as part of the "three don'ts movement: don't fear gangsters, don't give them money, and don't use their help." They counsel managers of parking lots about protection from car thieves. They flood communities with posters and pamphlets about the evils of amphetamine use. Intimidating door-to-door salesmen are frequently warned away by association members. Lists and pictures of wanted persons are circulated through neighborhoods, as are checklists for evaluating home security.

Crime-prevention associations organize their own street patrols, each member wearing an armband, which sometimes accompany the police but most often go on their own. Patrols are most common during special campaigns and at New Year's time, when businessmen transport substantial amounts of cash and public drunkenness is a major problem. Many patrols specialize in juvenile delinquency and concentrate on entertainment and shopping areas, where they watch for truants and runaways, caution against unseemly behavior, and admonish youths under eighteen who are smoking. They take the names of juveniles and notify school authorities and parents about their behavior. Civilian patrols augment police coverage during emergencies. After a rash of fires suspected to be the work of an arsonist, members of a local association walked the streets during the night carrying lanterns, like a medieval watch. School children in groups of thirty were enlisted by another association to patrol in the early evenings chanting "Lock up your home" and "Watch out for fire." When a series of crimes of a particular sort occur, most associations walk and rally to alert people about precautions they might take.

Crime-prevention associations are intertwined with a system of informal local government that reaches into every household. The smallest unit of formal government is the *ku* (township) in cities and the *buraku* (hamlet) in rural areas. Under these, like spreading vines on a forest floor, are centuries-old institutions of unofficial neighborhood governance called the *han* and the *cho-kai*.[8] A han consists of twenty to thirty adjacent households.[9] Several han form a cho-kai. Membership in the han and the cho-kai is automatic. Their vitality varies from place to place. In most places notices from government are circulated to heads of the cho-kai and then through the community. Message-boards are passed from house to house containing information of all kinds—the fire season has arrived, water will be stopped on the day after tomorrow, the crime-prevention association will hold a meeting, and so forth. Households are obligated to participate in projects undertaken by the cho-kai. For example, each household may be asked to send one person on a designated day to help clean out the drains of the neighborhood. The cho-kai leaders make sure that the neighborhood garbage box is cleaned twice weekly by members of each household in rotation. A household that fails in its duties to the community atones by sending a small gift to the other houses. The cho-kai collects money for services not provided by formal government, such as maintaining a pump that supplies the neighborhood's water. The head of the cho-kai, like the head of the han, is called on to mediate disputes, as when two neighbors quarrel over the placement of a wall or a branch that overhangs a property boundary.

All of Japan is covered by crime-prevention institutions linking the citizen and the police. At the bottom are 647,000 "contact points." Originally created by action of the prefectural police, they have been taken over by the crime-prevention associations. A contact point is a residence or a business, designated usually by a narrow vertical sign fixed near the door, where people may solicit police help or obtain information. In a rough calculation, there is about one contact point for every fifty households in Japan. Not all contact-point people are members of crime-prevention associations; many volunteer because of goodwill to the police or because the signs may deter victimization. Crime-prevention associations are usually organized on the basis of police station jurisdictions. There are 1,260 constituent associations in Japan, the same number as police stations. Some prefectures have crime-

---

8. David W. Plath, *The After Hours* (Berkeley and Los Angeles: University of California Press, 1964), p. 142, says that neighborhood government associations are six hundred years old. Because the system was exploited by Japan's military government during the war for purposes of regimentation, the Occupation tried to discourage its continuation.

9. Names differ from place to place: *kumi* in some rural areas; *tonari-gumi* in Osaka; *han* in Tokyo; *chonaikai* in Kochi.

prevention branches, an organizational layer between the station-level groups and the contact points. These may coincide with elementary school districts or local governments. When a cho-kai becomes a member of a crime-prevention association, as some do, they are referred to as branches. There are also several thousand specialized crime-prevention associations composed of occupations and workplaces. They too are members of station-level associations. For example, there are crime-prevention associations for pawnshops, restaurants, bars, banks, rice sellers, public bathhouses, and gas stations.

The geographical and functional crime-prevention associations are federated on a prefectural basis. In some places there are intermediate city associations. The forty-seven prefectural associations are members in turn of the All Japan Crime Prevention Association headquartered in Tokyo. Thus Japan is linked from top to bottom, central government to neighborhoods, by a network of crime-prevention institutions that can be used to inform citizens about crime and its prevention at great speed and very little cost.

Although almost everyone in Japan is touched by the work of the crime-prevention associations, membership is impossible to determine because membership criteria vary. In some places every resident who accepts the authority of the cho-kai, which means almost everyone, is automatically counted a member; in other places membership refers only to the active leaders of the organization. It is like trying to determine membership in Neighborhood Watch in the United States. Would that refer to the leaders who mobilize participation or to the members of the public who are enlisted? What one can say is that several hundred thousand people are actively involved as leaders of crime-prevention associations in Japan or hosts for contact points.

Financing is equally unstandardized. In many places the cho-kai contributes some of its resources to the local crime-prevention association. Thus all residents, whether they know it or not, make some financial contribution to crime prevention.[10] Amounts vary considerably, from Y30 to Y400 per year ($0.25 to $3.00). Dues from voluntary members are not standard either. A large part of association income comes from business enterprises either as voluntary donations or as membership fees. General tax revenues also find their way into crime-prevention work. Just as cho-kai often contribute to local associations, so other

10. Receipts for the payment by households to the crime-prevention association are pasted to the doorposts, along with metal disks showing payment of fees for radio license, water, Red Cross, and Community Chest.

units of government, such as cities and prefectures, make grants to the federations. The largest source of income for the national federation is the national government. There is a delicious element of poetic justice in this gift. A foundation has been established into which a fixed percentage of the profits from legalized gambling are paid. Operating under a mandate to promote the public welfare, the foundation's governing board has repeatedly selected the All Japan Crime Prevention Association as one of its beneficiaries. Proponents of legalized gambling in the United States should take note.

Leaders of crime-prevention associations tend to be elderly, male, and conservative. Women and youth are seriously underrepresented, although there are usually women's units within the associations that are active in youth counseling. Retired people are the backbone of the associations. Leadership appears to be self-perpetuating, though the mechanisms are unclear. Social status as well as the ability to support activities financially are undoubtedly important elements. So too is an active sympathy for the police. The police rarely influence the selection of local leaders, apart from warning associations away from people who have criminal records or undesirable business connections.

The police are undoubtedly the dominant partner in the relationship with the crime-prevention associations. Associations are viewed, by their own leaders as well as the police, as auxiliaries. Associations submit plans for crime-prevention campaigns to the police, taking their cues from police perceptions of public need. In every police station, as well as at higher levels, officers are assigned to work with the associations, providing information, coordinating activities, and informally monitoring performance. In many places office space for associations is provided in police buildings. Secretarial assistance for local associations is provided by police station staff. Retired police officers monopolize salaried positions in prefectural and national federations; they are also prominent, though not paid, in local associations.

But the associations are not completely passive. They are conduits for community input into police policy, especially when matters of local implementation are involved. The process of consultation seems to be informal, founded on personal relations rather than institutional procedures. Since association leaders are prominent people locally, their opinions are important to the police. On occasion, personal and community interest may not be easily distinguishable. Police officers testify that association leaders sometimes protest to the police about the enforcement of parking regulations, usually asking that the police be more lenient. There is general agreement that certain areas of police activity are out of bounds for association commentary—for example, criminal investigation. It appears that associations are reluctant as well to criticize the behavior of individual officers. Being protective of the image of the police, they do not want to be the agency for publicizing police misbehavior.

The police value the work of the crime-prevention associations and encourage their growth. Evaluation of the impact of the associations on crime have not been done, nor would they be easy to do given the low incidence of crime. Police view the associations as valuable instruments for developing a sense of neighborhood identity, a need the police view as acute in the suburbs of modern Japanese cities. Individual officers display genuine appreciation for the work of the associations. Like professionals in any line of work, they occasionally find the volunteers underfoot. Nonetheless, they do not deprecate association activity nor patronize their members. The public as a whole is probably not as favorably disposed toward the associations as the police.[11] Left-wing political parties have sometimes criticized the assertiveness of crime-prevention associations in particular places. Even people who are conservative politically sometimes criticize the associations for being cliquish and ingrown. Sometimes individual members anger people by throwing their weight around too much. The police occasionally have to restrain volunteers who think they have the authority of full-fledged police officers.

Extensive though cooperation is between police and public through the crime-prevention associations, they represent only the tip of the iceberg. Most neighborhoods also have Traffic Safety Associations. Like the crime-prevention associations, they are embedded in institutions of local government and integrated upward into federations. They do various good works, such as organizing traffic safety campaigns, putting up signs about avoiding accidents, and serving as traffic wardens to assist in rerouting traffic around dangerous situations. In addition, Japanese society is honeycombed with committees made up of private citizens and officials that consult on matters of public safety. In most prefectures, for example, there are committees on juvenile delinquency, child welfare, violence, outdoor advertising, construction hazards, and gas-main explosions. There are hundreds of private organizations representing al-

11. I know of no public opinion surveys on this. Items about crime-prevention associations have not been included in the periodic surveys on crime and police conducted by the Prime Minister's Office.

most any role a person can play in society that petition the police about matters affecting their members. There are organizations of mothers, taxi drivers, high school teachers, attorneys, automobile-driving instructors, owners of bars, theaters, and so forth. All in all, the police operate within an intricate network of civic associations, all of which insist on being consulted on matters of mutual concern.

Only in the last decade or so have private groups in the United States given the kind of assistance to the police that is routine in Japan. The American tradition of law enforcement has not been hospitable to the development of private groups to assist the police. Law enforcement was considered a task which was to be carried out by formal agencies of government. The private citizen, though enjoined to obey the law, was not encouraged to play an active role in catching lawbreakers. Invidious words have been invented to describe such people—snitch, tattletale, fink. People should cooperate with the police when asked but they were not expected to take initiative themselves, unless of course they were victims. Encouragement of private people to share responsibilities with the police was considered dangerous to liberty, an invitation for people to intrude into other people's lives. The only time Americans considered banding together for law enforcement purposes was when official agencies had lost control. Citizen assistance did not supplement police efforts; it replaced them. This is the vigilante tradition, which is regarded very suspiciously by Americans for good reason: vigilantes are creations of desperate circumstances, unrestrained by ordinary processes of law.

To some extent this is what is happening now. The United States is boiling at the moment with community-based crime-prevention programs aimed especially at the problems of burglary, drugs, and juvenile crime. There is an atmosphere of desperation. Crime-prevention programs are being promoted and carried out by a host of agencies: government, business, private foundations, civic clubs, and ad hoc community groups. The problem with these efforts is not lack of creativity and action but lack of system. Although the programs are extensive, they are often neither coordinated nor inclusive. Nor is it clear that they will endure long enough to make an impact. They suffer from the besetting problem of waning enthusiasm and declining commitment. In the United States, the wheel of community crime-prevention has to be reinvented again and again.

In almost every community in the United States, but especially in the large cities, stories could be told of citizens taking action against crime. It began with Neighborhood Watch in the early 1970s, targeted on household burglaries. By the late 1980s the crack-cocaine epidemic had produced a frenzy of activity, not all of it reassuring. Sometimes citizens have taken the law into their own hands, burning down crack-houses and attacking street dealers. People have gotten hurt in such confrontations, and some have themselves been charged with criminal offenses. In some areas drug dealers have retaliated, especially against people known to be informing the police. As a result, police and community groups are now stressing discipline and training. The lesson being reiterated across the country is that the public should not think of themselves, no matter how desperate the situation gets, as substitute police.

The point about the United States, then, is that policy-makers and much of the public have become convinced that communities at the grass roots must be enlisted if crime, especially drug trafficking, is to be reduced. Though America's efforts are imaginative and extensive, they are scattered, fragile, and uncoordinated. Unlike those in Japan, they are the result of exigency rather than tradition.

Since colonial times Americans have been preoccupied with limiting governmental authority. Governmental power is created reluctantly to accomplish particular purposes. People invested with these extraordinary powers must be carefully specified; private citizens cannot be entrusted with public authority. Similarly, the powers themselves must be carefully delineated so that officials can be held accountable in law. In Japan, on the other hand, government is not an explicit creation of society. In philosophical terms, there is no social contract. Government is an expression of community just as parenthood is an expression of family. Government is not a separable function grafted onto preexisting communities. Therefore the dividing line between police officer and citizen is more vague than in the United States. The responsibilities of the citizen are not eclipsed by the creation of police officers. Though the police officer is designated in law to preserve public safety, the citizen bears a moral obligation to do as much. In the same way, the police officer's duties are not exhausted by what is specified in law. Police officers are moral, not just legal, actors. They are expected to play an informal role in creating a consensus within the community about right behavior. That the Japanese people actively assist the police in law enforcement is the obverse of the active unstructured role the police play in community. Because the line between government and society is unclear, both police officer and citizen are responsible for law enforcement and both police officer and citizen are moral actors.[12]

Because of the service orientation of the Japanese police, its deployment in neighborhood police posts, and the traditional involvement of the community in crime prevention, many Americans regard Japan as a model of community policy. So, too, do the Singapore police, who adopted the Japanese koban system wholesale betwen 1984 and 1989.[13] The Japanese police, curiously enough, are not so sanguine. They do not doubt the efficacy of their system, but they have become seriously concerned that it has lost its vitality. Their confidence, and complacency, was shaken in 1987 with the publication of a survey showing that the police were the least well regarded among government agencies with respect to their reception of citizens.[14] Senior officers also knew that the public heartily disliked finding koban unattended when the police were patrolling or out on call, a practice that was increasing in residential areas with small koban.

In response, the National Police Agency ordered all its functional divisions to devise means of improving responsiveness to the public. Prefectural forces were to do the same. A special committee was created in Tokyo to coordinate the process of reexamination and planning. By 1989 several initiatives had been launched and final approval was pending on new practices throughout the police.

In general, it was thought that the police were not sufficiently in touch with the enforcement priorities of the public. Because of the reward system, patrol personnel were devoting too much time to the enforcement of minor laws that the public found irritating and unimportant. The example most frequently cited was enforcement of regulations governing bicycles. What the police should have been doing instead was to concentrate on truly significant serious crime as well as the unique disorder problems of different areas.[15] The police also were agreed that

---

12. See also comments by Albert Craig in Asahi Shimbun, *The Pacific Rivals* (New York: Weatherhill-Asahi, 1972), p. 303; Richard Halloran, *Japan: Images and Realities* (New York: Alfred Knopf, 1969), pp. 100–101; and Masao Maruyama, *Thought and Behavior in Modern Japanese Politics* (London: Oxford University Press, 1963), chap. 1.

13. David H. Bayley, *A Model of Community Policing: The Singapore Story* (Washington, D.C.: National Institute of Justice, 1989).

14. *White Paper on Police, 1988,* pp. 50–51. The survey was done by the Management and Coordination Agency of the Japanese government and was published in August 1987.

15. Curiously, American police conjuring with "community policing" have thought that their need was to deemphasize serious crime, which was relatively rare in most neighborhoods and difficult to prevent in any case, and attend to more trivial matters closer to the felt needs of the public, such as noisy neighbors, disorderly teenagers, drunkenness in

the attitudes of officers toward the public needed to be adjusted. Rather than regarding themselves as morally superior, perhaps in a too heroic warrior tradition, they needed to learn to be solicitous, welcoming, and sympathetic. They needed to view the public as genuine partners and valued clients. Revealingly, the National Police Agency launched a new magazine for all personnel entitled "Community Policing: Polite Meeting of Citizens."[16] Taking advantage of the enormous popularity of adult comic books in Japan, it also distributed 100,000 copies of its own comic book to patrol officers, dramatizing the importance of becoming more efficient and friendly in dealing with the public.

More specifically, the police are considering the simplification of paperwork in handling lost-and-found items, having determined that 35 percent of the people who come to koban do so in that connection. The feasibility of creating a national recording form and computer-linked data base is being studied. So too is a single national telephone number for police counseling. Personnel at reception counters at police stations are to be trained to guide people more efficiently to the assistance required. Traffic police are reexamining the balance between enforcement, especially in reducing speed-related accidents, and congestion relief. Koban officers who make house visits in the evening are being asked to telephone ahead instead of simply dropping by. Procedures are being simplified for obtaining police permission for a host of activities, such as owning hunting rifles, blocking roads, and undertaking construction.

A key element in this fine-tuning of the koban system is the development of more adequate liaison between patrol personnel and the communities they serve. Although the Japanese police have been a more pervasive presence in communities than the American, they have assumed that the koban and foot patrols were sufficient. They have not set up explicit liaison mechanisms. This task was left, by and large, to crime-prevention officers or the chiefs of police stations. Both groups

---

public, vandalism, and nighttime hot-rodding. Although the point of departure of Japanese and American police would seem to be different, the goal is the same, namely, the reshaping of police activities away from priorities set by the police to those perceived by the public in particular localities.

16. Ironically, the Japanese police are looking to the United States for inspiration and direction in refining their koban system. The phrase "community policing" here and in conversation among police is taken directly from the English and transliterated. A monograph on community policing around the world—Skolnick and Bayley, *Community Policing* (n. 3 above)—was translated into Japanese and serialized in the new magazine.

had their own networks of contacts, primarily with prominent citizens and the leaders of the crime-prevention associations. Recognizing, however, that "the commonsense of the police may not be the commonsense of the public," each koban has been ordered to set up liaison meetings with community leaders at least twice a year.[17] Some koban are meeting monthly. The informal community government associations—the cho-kai and tonari-gumi—are being used to sponsor periodic public discussions with local police. In Osaka koban officers have been urged to stop and talk informally to groups of housewives and other residents on the streets in order to solicit suggestions about needed police activity. These have been called "mini-ko-cho-kai."

All of this implies that koban will be encouraged as well as trained to develop their own plans for meeting local problems. This has not been the case in the past. By and large, koban personnel performed the same routines according to the same schedules throughout Japan, regardless of local circumstances. Police managers are beginning to realize that responsive policing means transforming koban sergeants from supervisors into managers. It requires koban to become active problem-solvers, an approach several police forces in the United States have been actively exploring.[18]

Only the elderly in Japanese society have been singled out for special outreach by the police. For many years, police officers have regularly telephoned elderly people living alone to check on their well-being. Some koban and several prefectures schedule "Silver Days" when personnel stop at the homes of elderly people. Particular effort is being made to bring them into crime-prevention organizations. In 1987 each prefectural force was asked to develop plans for addressing the needs of the elderly. And ninety districts with high concentrations of elderly were pinpointed for coordinated planning among the police and other government agencies.

But the Japanese police, unlike the American, have made no efforts to develop consultative links with minority groups in society. Minorities make up only a small proportion of the population. The largest group is the Koreans, numbering about 680,000, followed by the Chi-

17. This apt phrase was coined by Y. Sakiguchi, former director of training of the National Police Agency, in an article for senior officers. The regulation about koban liaison committees was in fact enacted in 1981 but was implemented in a rather mechanistic way. By 1987 about 4,000 such committees were in existence.

18. John E. Eck and William Spelman, *Problem-Solving* (Washington, D.C.: Police Executive Research Forum, 1987).

nese, at 75,000.[19] Together they constitute one-half of 1 percent of the population. In addition, roughly 2 percent of the population may be *burakumin*, traditional outcasts who are ethnically Japanese.[20] Discrimination against such groups is known to exist and relations with the police are sometimes strained. Nonetheless, there is no crisis, by Western standards, in ethnic relations, although the true extent of minority disaffection is difficult to gauge because Japanese regard minorities as a taboo subject. Japan is beginning to experience a significant amount of illegal immigration, which concerns the police very much. This topic will be discussed in chapter 9.

In sum, Japanese as well as American police are engaged today in self-conscious reorientation of their police operations. Both are doing so under the slogan of "community policing." For the Japanese, the effort amounts to fine-tuning: they have the structures, and they need to instill into them a more enthusiastic community-oriented spirit. For the Americans, "community policing" is more dislocating because appropriate structures of deployment and community interaction need to be developed for the first time. The decentralized system in the United States also makes the process of reform less systematic and more haphazard. Both forces have the same objective in mind, but they begin at very different places. At the same time, senior leaders confront the same problems of implementation: resistance among the rank and file, counterproductive reward systems, competing claims on resources, and unimaginative first-line supervisors. Both are also aware that if innovation is to succeed it cannot depend upon the personality of particular leaders. It must become an accustomed part of the mind-set of the organization. In the jargon of reform, innovation must become institutionalized.

Talking about "community policing" in Japan and the United States is like listening to two groups of people singing the same song but from different places in the score. American police have much to learn from Japan about concrete programs of community involvement. Japanese police have much to learn from America about monitoring and evaluating the effects of change.

19. Foreign Press Center, Tokyo, *Facts and Figures of Japan* (1987 edition), p. 12.

20. George A. De Vos, *Japan's Outcasts* (London: The Minority Rights Group, 1971), p. 3.

6

The Pursuit of Pleasure

In both Japan and the United States police must deal with a special category of offenses commonly referred to as victimless crimes or vice—gambling, prostitution, the drinking of alcohol, pornography, and drug addiction. Victimless crimes have peculiar features compared with other criminal offenses. First, there is generally no complaint. Because no one feels victimized, police intervention is not impelled by a specific request. Cooperation in prosecution is invariably low, since neither buyer nor seller has an incentive to complain. Because the police must obtain information from uncooperative participants about what is essentially a private transaction, questions of infringement of individual rights continually arise. Search and seizure issues are common in narcotics cases; enticement in prostitution; wiretapping in gambling; and freedom of expression in pornography. Second, most people involved in victimless crime, whether seekers or purveyors, think of themselves only technically as criminals. They may be ashamed but they think of their acts as no one's business other than their own. When legal prohibition is coupled with substantial demand as well as a fitful sense of moral guilt, corruption becomes inevitable. Police scandals in the United States have chronically involved the regulation of vice.[1]

1. Roger Lane, *Policing the City: Boston 1823–1885* (Cambridge: Harvard University Press, 1967); James F. Richardson, *The New York Police* (New York: Oxford University Press), chaps. 7 and 9.

Third, the number of people involved in victimless crime is enormous. In the United States 20 percent of all arrests made by the police are for victimless crime.[2] Isn't it odd that at a time when crimes against persons are rising disturbingly, a very substantial portion of police resources are being devoted to offenses in which there is no aggrieved party? Fourth, demand for illegal pleasures creates a clandestine world where the ordinary protection of the law ceases to exist and huge amounts of money are generated for invisible purposes. In the United States organized crime has fed on prohibited pleasures.

How have the Japanese handled this vexing set of enforcement problems? Have they devised distinctive measures for regulating the pursuit of pleasure? Have they been able to insulate their police from the corroding effects of having to regulate what many want but the law prohibits? In order to answer these questions, I shall examine police enforcement of laws pertaining to drinking, gambling, prostitution, and drug addiction.

Drinking

Proportionate to population six times more Americans than Japanese are held by the police for drunkenness.[3] Furthermore, drunkenness accounts for a larger proportion of people detained by the police in the United States than in Japan. In 1987, drunkenness accounted for 7.7 percent of Americans taken into custody by the police; in Japan, 0.2 percent. The legal status of drunks held by police is also different. In the United States, people are arrested for drunkenness; in Japan, they are not arrested but "protected," as are lost children, the mentally deranged, and sick and wounded persons, until they can take care of themselves or be entrusted to other auspices.[4] Drinking alcohol is not an offense in Japan, not even in public. Japan has no "dry" areas.

2. *Sourcebook of Criminal Justice Statistics, 1989*, p. 480. This includes arrests for drunkenness.

3. In 1987, 77,800 persons were "protected" by the police in Japan, compared with 828,300 arrested by the police for drunkenness in the United States. The rate of persons detained for drunkenness in Japan was 62.7 per 100,000, and 346 in the United States. *White Paper on Crime, 1988*, p. 5; *White Paper on Police, 1988*, p. 38; *Sourcebook of Criminal Justice Statistics, 1989*, p. 482.

4. "Law to Prevent Drunkards from Giving Nuisance to Other People," Article 4. In 1987 there were 608 of these. When people are taken into protective custody, relatives or an appropriate court must be notified.

Japanese police officers show an almost exaggerated solicitude for drunken people. They stand by impassively when teased by them, sometimes enduring a bleary baiting that would anger most American officers. Unless an individual is sodden or wild, they will allow him to go his befuddled way. Japanese drunks tend to be "happy drunks"; they are neither mean nor surly. On the street they are usually found in small groups, arms around one another's shoulders, reeling, staggering, singing, and joking. Police officers treat drunken people according to the general view that they are children and not responsible for what they do and say. The duty of a police officer is to protect them from their own excesses. Censorious law enforcement would be very unjust since, as was noted in chapter 4, a major purpose of drinking is to relax tensions among a people always conscious of interpersonal status and obligation.[5] The object of drinking is to create ties of personal warmth and sympathy; to "hold one's liquor," to fail to show its effects, amounts to the wasting of a precious opportunity.[6] So the police show endless patience in dealing with drunks, maintaining a light touch so as to sustain happiness. It is no wonder that Japanese police officers often lament that Japan is a "paradise for drunkards."

While Japanese society excuses drunkenness, it does not excuse all behavior that results from drinking. Drinking to excess is tolerable as long as it does not encroach on duty. A man would be strongly condemned if drinking forced his family into bankruptcy or caused him to miss work. Similarly, verbal indiscretions in one's cups are forgiven, but not negligence that endangers others. The Japanese are exceedingly strict, for example, on drunken driving. The police regularly set up checkpoints on major roads late at night as the bars are closing. As cars are stopped, each driver is made to say a few words so that officers, leaning in the driver's window, can smell whether he has been drinking.[7] Police also watch for the driver who keeps his face averted, trying to hide his "sake flush."[8] If they have been drinking, drivers are given the choice of pleading guilty to a charge of drunken driving or submitting

5. Chie Nakane, *Japanese Society* (Berkeley and Los Angeles: University of California Press, 1970), pp. 124–26.
6. David W. Plath, *The After Hours* (Berkeley and Los Angeles: University of California Press, 1964), pp. 87–88.
7. Because this duty is unpleasant, an electronic gadget has been invented that makes a beeping sound in the presence of alcohol. It is about as big as a three-cell flashlight.
8. Many Japanese react in a unique physiological way to the consumption of alcohol. Their faces become flushed, turning quite distinctly red. Some find this so embarrassing that they refrain from drinking.

to a breath-analyzer to determine the quantity of alcohol in the blood. Conviction for drunken driving carries a penalty of immediate license revocation and up to two years imprisonment at hard labor or a fine of not more than Y100,000.[9] Japanese standards for the proportion of alcohol in the breath indicative of being drunk are the most stringent in the world.[10] An ounce of whiskey, if the test is administered immediately, will produce a reading of drunk. Many Americans and Europeans have bitter memories of being caught driving in Japan with an amount of drink in their systems that would not have caused a flicker of concern at home. There are three outcomes for the driver who has submitted to the breath-analyzer at a drunk-trap: if drinking has been in small amounts, the driver will be given a warning; if moderate, the driver will be given a citation and told to rest in his car beside the road for an hour or so; if heavy, he will immediately be arrested and taken to jail.

Most social drinking in Japan is done in public accommodations concentrated in almost unbelievable numbers in well-known entertainment areas. In the Minami area of Osaka, which is hardly more than a quarter-mile square, there are 3,700 establishments serving liquor.[11] It is like a rabbit warren. Bars, nightclubs, and cabarets are tucked into corners, upstairs, downstairs, and behind one another. Narrow alleys branching off small streets are completely lined with miniscule bars, sometimes arranged in tiers two stories tall. Entire floors of large buildings are given over to separate bars. Yet if all one wants is a quick drink of beer, it is not even necessary to go inside: throughout Japan beer is dispensed on the street from sidewalk vending machines, like soft drinks in the United States.

The entertainment districts of Japanese cities are like adult versions of Pleasure Island from Walt Disney's version of Pinocchio. Built close to mass transportation terminals, they are brightly lit areas covering several square blocks interlaced with pedestrian malls and covered arcades. Every kind of entertainment imaginable is provided—movie theaters, bowling alleys, restaurants, bars, Mah-Jong parlors, department stores, strip shows, nightclubs, electronic games arcades, snack bars,

9. $800.
10. In Japan 0.25 milligrams per liter of exhalation, 0.8 in Canada, 0.35 in Britain, and 1.0 in the U.S. The Road Traffic Law, Article 65, stipulates that these standards are to be set by cabinet order. Information provided by the Traffic Bureau Section, Tokyo Metropolitan Police Department.
11. Information provided by the local police. Distinctions among liquor-serving businesses will be explained below.

and dusky hotels. Like the midway at Coney Island, the sights are dizzying in profusion and glitter: glass elevators that rise gracefully on the outside of buildings, vast underground shopping arcades linked to the surface by moving stairs and decorated with tinkling water fountains, cabarets three stories tall built to resemble turreted castles complete with inset stained-glass windows, sleazy nightclubs bedecked with enormous cutout figures of half-clad women, ice cream parlors large enough to have a mezzanine and an arched ceiling sixty feet high, restaurants displaying in glass cases plastic imitations of their food so real as to make the mouth water, and stunning women in beautiful kimonos and high black wigs standing discreetly inside the glass doors of posh cabarets. The air throbs and shimmers with tantalizing pleasures.

Every city has these pleasure islands; the larger the city, the greater the number. Location and clientele give each one a distinctive character. The Ginza in downtown Tokyo is for the well-to-do. Chauffeured limousines jockey for position along tree-lined streets, waiting for their owners to be deposited unsteadily in the backseats by nightclub hostesses. Kabukicho, near Shinjuku station in Tokyo, is for the middle class and for young adults. The crowds are more diverse than in the Ginza. T-shirts and blue jeans mingle with business suits and ties. Dating couples are common, walking hand in hand amid the swirling throng. Many young men carry bowling bags and families with small children spill out of movie theaters to enjoy an ice cream before going home. The automobiles nosing slowly along the crowded streets are sporty and bright, crammed with grinning young men. Garish floodlit signboards tower over the street advertising risqué movies. The crowd's pleasure seems to come as much from inspecting itself as from actually buying. Life is outdoors, on the street, rather than shut discreetly behind closed doors. There are lower-class entertainment areas too, such as Nishinari in Osaka and Asakusa in Tokyo. Men in open-necked shirts and workers' knickers squat in groups along the sidewalks. Many have battered, puffy faces, bruised from work or recent fights. Stand-bars are crowded with people, and cases of beer bottles are piled to the ceiling. Refuse is heaped in piles and pedestrian underpasses smell of urine. Shops draw down their shutters early in the evening; streets are more shadowed. Grimy merchandise is sold from the sidewalk by peddlers, forcing pedestrians to push together to get by. Late at night, wheeled food stalls provide cheap bowls of noodles and fish to weary revelers.

For the police, fights are the major problem arising out of drinking. On Friday and Saturday nights especially they are called out repeatedly to remove quarreling drinkers from bars and cabarets. When drinkers become violent or helplessly sodden, the police take them to special cells, aptly called "Tiger Boxes," where they are held overnight.

Regulation of drinking involves more than holding people responsible for the consequences of their actions. The places and hours of drinking are strictly controlled. Establishments that serve alcohol, along with dance halls, Mah-Jong parlors, and pachinko houses, must close at midnight. Drinking places require some prodding, so patrol officers make spot checks after closing hours. They are not unreasonable, usually allowing leeway of about half an hour, long enough for patrons to finish their drinks. The police have a unique and powerful ally in the enforcement of closing hours. Public transportation throughout Japan shuts down during the middle hours of the night. Buses stop as early as 10:30 P.M. and most trains and subways close by shortly after midnight. Since the proportion of car owners is much lower in Japan than in the United States, closing public transportation at night leaves most people stranded. They are forced to stay overnight in a hotel or take a taxi home at extortionate rates. Between ten and twelve o'clock at night streams of people hurry toward homeward-bound buses, trains, and subways; public transportation drains people out of the entertainment districts like water from a leaky barrel. The police do not enforce closing hours so much as they preside over them.[12]

Commercial establishments that are allowed to sell alcoholic drinks come in a variety of types, and the distinctions among them are subtle.[13] First, traditional Japanese restaurants, which are usually walled houses with a garden, a diminutive fountain, and raised floors of tatami mats. Food is served by kimono-clad women, usually middle-aged, who participate in the conversation. Second, cabarets are Western in decor and allow dancing with the hostesses. Some of them are large enough to hold several hundred people. Third, nightclubs, which are smaller versions of cabarets, forbid dancing with hostesses. Floor shows are not standard at either night clubs or cabarets. Most make do with a small

12. Closing public transportation at night causes particular problems for employees of night-entertainment establishments. Cabarets and nightclubs sometimes band together to provide private bus transportation for their employees, especially their hostesses. A common sight in entertainment districts around midnight is tired women boarding buses while a few male patrons cluster around the doors and windows for a last few words before the evening ends.

13. Interviews with crime-prevention officers. Also *White Paper on Police, 1988*, pp. 71–75. Regulations are set down in the "Entertainment Standard and Regulation Law," 1985.

band or a piano player. Foreigners are frequently disappointed because Japanese nightclubs seem more like glorified cocktail lounges. Fourth, bars, which come in Western and traditional styles. Oddly, it is the Western ones that have hostesses; in Japanese-style bars hostesses are optional. Neither kind allows dancing.

Drinking places, especially bars, are small by Western standards. Many have room for scarcely a dozen people. Prices are high, probably a function of high overhead costs and low turnover. In the posh entertainment areas, the cost of a night's drinking can be astronomical. An hour in a Ginza cabaret for three men drinking only beer and nibbling hors d'oeuvres can easily come to eighty dollars. Hostesses are a substantial part of the cost. At some cabarets they are provided in relays every twenty minutes, always one hostess to each man. They sing, joke, make light conversation, and invite patrons to dance. Expense accounts are the foundation of the nightlife economy. All large firms, including government ministries, provide money for lavish entertainment. Wining and dining at the expense of one's employer is a prized perquisite of promotion. Expense-account entertaining is so common that cabarets and their hostesses present monthly bills to regular customers rather than itemizing each evening's cost.

The enforcement of drinking hours calls for considerable judgment on the part of the police because different kinds of establishments are subject to different rules. The great division is between places that serve alcohol and also food—like bars, cabarets, and nightclubs—and those that serve food and also alcohol—like restuarants and "snacks."[14] The first group must observe the midnight curfew; the second group can stay open later, precise hours being determined by each prefecture. There were 343,500 of these in 1988.[15] The problem for the police is that many "snacks" are indistinguishable from bars and small nightclubs. How is a patrol officer to determine accurately whether food complements drink or drink complements food? Duplicity can be quite blatant. Some "snacks" advertise "Snack and coffee" on illuminated signs picturing a bottle of White Horse scotch and do not close until 5:00 A.M. Furthermore, early closing hours must be observed by all places that serve alcohol and have hostesses. But many "snacks" employ waitresses. Moreover, in 1,700 of them waitresses are advertised as wearing "no panties." Police shrug their shoulders about these matters

14. "Snacks" is the word the Japanese use.
15. National Police Agency, 1989.

and follow a policy of being stern with only the most indiscreet offenders.

Though the police officially deny it, closing hours for drinking establishments are enforced with varying degrees of strictness in different places. In skid rows, which are not numerous in Japan, closing the bars can lead to a riot. The police are more concerned with bars that open too early in the morning as the day laborers are collecting for work, rather than too late at night. Parts of some cities gain a reputation for having lenient closing hours or for fudging the distinction between bar and "snack," so that the dedicated night-owl can continue to drink into the small hours of the morning. There are well-known migration patterns among night-people as one area closes and another stays open. Closing policies are set by prefectures but implementation rests with the chiefs of police stations. If nonenforcement becomes too notorious, prefectural headquarters may suggest to a station chief that standards should be tightened. The Crime Prevention Division has plainclothes squads, operating out of prefectural headquarters, that monitor such matters. Enforcement that is too strict can lead to the transformation of bars into snacks. This weakens the control of the police over them, since they are then licensed by the Board of Health instead of the Public Safety Commission. If an establishment is licensed by a Public Safety Commission, a threat of license-suspension by the police is more credible than if it is licensed by the Board of Health.[16] Though closing hours are observed more often than not, they are stretched in some places, depending on three factors: the historic traditions of the area, demands of a peculiar clientele, and competition felt by businessmen from other parts of town or other businesses providing similar services.

The police also try to discourage various rackets associated with drinking. Though customers cannot be solicited on the street, in most entertainment districts "catch girls"[17] are often seen enticing men to come drink at a particular place. Price gouging is notorious and almost impossible to stop. Some bars change prices at different hours of the evening, raising them according to demand. Others charge separately for entry, service, food, drink, hostesses, and the table. Police officers

16. Public Safety Commissions license other places where men and women mix under commercial auspices, notably dance halls and dance schools. Mixing of men and women is considered "morals" business, hence the preserve of the Public Safety Commissions. National Police Agency, Tokyo, *Crime Prevention Police*, p. 11.

17. Americans would call them "B-girls."

repeatedly advise the inexperienced to be wary, but sympathy is about all they can give to the disgruntled customers who flock forlornly to koban late in the evenings.

Gambling

In the United States the major form of victimless crime, at least in terms of money spent, is gambling. In Japan as well, gambling and running a lottery are offenses under the Penal Code.[18] Yet gambling is a much smaller problem in Japan than in the United States, the incidence of gambling offenses running less than one-sixth the American rate.[19] In Tokyo, which has a population larger than New York, there are about 400 gambling offenses each year.[20] The explanation for the low incidence of offenses in Japan is simple: gambling is allowed under state auspices; only private gambling is prohibited. The government provides enough outlets through authorized channels to assuage the public's gambling itch. This is no small accomplishment in a country that has been characterized as a nation of plungers.[21] The government runs horse, bicycle, car, and boat races, including the gambling on them. The state also sponsors over 500 lotteries a year, some of them enormously rich.

The major participant-betting sport is Mah-Jong.[22] Though prohibited, a lot of quiet betting undoubtedly goes on, generally for small stakes. The police occasionally make raids, but, as the statistics show, the police are not very attentive.

Probably the most popular game of chance is pachinko. In 1988 it grossed over $60 billion, which is three times the value of Japanese auto sales and half the budget of the national government. Very much like pinball, the game involves injecting a small steel ball into a maze; as the ball falls through, bells ring and lights record a score. The ringing, clat-

18. Penal Code of Japan, Chapter XXIII, Articles 185–187.
19. In 1987, 2,122 gambling offenses were reported in Japan; in the United States there were 25,400. *White Paper on Crime, 1988,* p. 5; *Sourcebook of Criminal Justice Statistics, 1988,* p. 481. The respective rates were 1.7 and 10.4 per hundred thousand.
20. Tokyo Metropolitan Police Department, 1987.
21. Kazuo Akasaka, "Wanna Bet? A Nation of Gamblers," *East* (April 1971): 32–35.
22. Mah-Jong parlors are licensed by Public Safety Commissions. They cannot admit people under eighteen years of age and must be located more than a certain minimum distance from schools or temples.

tering noise of pachinko machines is a fixture of most entertainment districts. Pachinko machines are crammed by the score into narrow rows in sleazy, smoke-filled halls. No skill is required to play as patrons merely turn a knob, sending a cascade of balls through the machine. Pachinko narrowly avoids being gambling because prizes and not cash are awarded. But there are ways around these rules that put pachinko on the border of legality. Though pachinko parlors cannot buy their own prizes back, private persons can. In some cities there are even licensed stores for buying pachinko winnings. The National Police Agency condemns this practice. Dealing in pachinko winnings is complicated by the fact that cigarettes are the most common prize, but dealing in cigarettes is illegal without a tobacco license, and authorized tobacco dealers are prohibited from buying pachinko cigarettes. Nonetheless, late at night in back streets near pachinko parlors people can be seen darting into ill-lit doorways to trade winnings, including cigarettes, for cash. Once in a while the police crack down, but by and large they consider it too insignificant to bother about.

Prostitution

For the first time in Japanese history prostitution fell under legal censure in 1958 when, amid considerable public controversy, the "Anti-Prostitution Law" was enacted.[23] To many observers, especially foreign ones, it appeared as if Japan had overthrown a historic tradition of legalized prostitution. Famous red-light districts three hundred years old, such as Yoshiwara in Tokyo, Shinmachi in Osaka, and Shimabara in Kyoto, were closed. The reality is significantly different from the impression.

The famous law of 1958 does not prohibit prostitution in terms that Americans expect. The law prohibits three acts: public solicitation, provision of facilities, and management of prostitutes.[24] The law does not

23. The year 1958 is commonly associated with passage of the law, but this is wrong. The law is No. 118 of 1956, May 24. It was enforced for the first time April 1, 1957, but had no punishments for offenses. The law was then revised, Chapter Two being added. These portions came into effect April 1, 1958. Though the law was passed in 1956, it is fair to say that it did not become effective until 1958.

24. Specific provisions of the law punish streetwalking, acting as a go-between, furnishing accommodations for purposes of prostitution, inducing a person to become a prostitute, and participating in the earnings of a prostitute.

prohibit private sex acts for money.[25] A man and a woman may legally negotiate a price for sexual services and go to a hotel to consummate the arrangement. As long as everything is discreetly done, neither party is punishable. It is not commercial sex that the law enjoins but public display and knowing facilitation by third parties. A prostitute and her clients cannot be punished, but a landlord who knew her trade could be. The prostitute herself is liable to legal sanctions only if she solicits publicly.[26] In the United States, where prostitution is illegal everywhere except a few counties in Nevada, participation in sex for money is the key prohibition. In Japan neither the act of sex nor the commercial nexus is punishable.

This explains why, compared with the United States, antiprostitution enforcement is much less a burden on the police and the rate of arrests per unit of population is one-seventeenth as much. In 1987, 3,196 persons were prosecuted in Japan for offenses under the law, compared with 110,100 who were arrested in the United States.[27] Most offenders in Japan are apprehended for pimping, followed by streetwalking. Since 1959 the number of persons prosecuted has declined most years. There were about one-third as many arrests in 1971 as in 1959 and two-thirds as many in 1987 as in 1971.

Decline in apprehensions does not mean that prostitution is withering away. Patrol officers will point out that a particular area is an "ex-red-light district," adding with a smile that perhaps it is not so "ex-." Though Yoshiwara in Tokyo has had its name changed, the area is still widely identified with prostitution. The most flagrant disguise for prostitution is the Turkish bath. According to the police there were 1,471 in 1988, but they are no longer called Turkish baths. After repeated complaints from the Turkish government in the early 1980s, their name was officially changed to "Soapland." Soaplands feature private rooms appointed for hot baths, massages, and sudsy sex. A few are theme-parks for prostitution, the premises rigged up to look like jumbo jets, with the women dressed as hostesses, or like hospitals with nurses, or girls'

25. The law does condemn prostitution as being "against the dignity of human beings, sex morals, and good manners of the society." Article 1. The law articulates a high moral standard, then, but does not enforce it.

26. The law refers to "persons," not just "women," as I have implied. Male prostitutes are subject to the same restrictions as women.

27. *White Paper on Police, 1988*, p. 76; *Sourcebook of Criminal Justice Statistics, 1989*, p. 481. The offenses covered in the American statistics are: prostitution, managing a brothel, pandering, procuring, transporting, or detaining women for immoral purposes, and attempts to commit these offenses.

schools with demure students.[28] Although prefectures may prohibit Soaplands, only five had done so by 1988.[29]

Prostitution also flourishes through "telephone clubs," where men pay $20–$30 to receive calls at private phones in the "club's" premises from women who have been recruited to offer sexual services.[30] They make their own arrangements concerning place and payment. Advertisements for women to call designated numbers appear in magazines, on handbills, and in sample packets of facial tissues handed out on the street.

Because commercial sex acts are not punishable per se, Japanese tactics against prostitution differ considerably from American. Plainclothes police officers are not sent out to pose as customers, making an arrest either after the solicitation or the occurrence of an overt act indicating willingness to participate in sex. Thus the legal problems of entrapment are avoided altogether. Japanese antiprostitution squads operate against women behaving indiscreetly in public, accosting men on the street or bargaining openly. They round up the "catch girls"—most of them are middle-aged women—who solicit for prostitutes. Many stations have photograph albums with pictures of the most notorious "catch girls." Police officers question prostitutes and their clients about third parties who abet their arrangement—landlords, pimps, procurers.

The police in Japan, as in the United States, know quite well where prostitution is going on. The great difference is that there is legal justification in Japan for ignoring it. Keeping prostitution out of public sight in the United States, which is all that police forces really do, is the same as winking at prostitution; officers are conscious that they are acting contrary to law. Keeping prostitution discreet is precisely what the Japanese law enjoins. Therefore, Japanese police officers are not conscious of doing wrong when they point out to an observer where prostitution is being practiced—though they may be willfully ignoring the extent of complicitous involvement by third parties. They are also increasingly concerned about foreign women, mostly recruited in Thailand and the Philippines, who are held in virtual slavery as prostitutes. If these women complain about their treatment, prosecution is difficult but their own deportation is certain.

28. Ian Buruma, *Behind the Mask* (New York: Pantheon, 1984), chap. 6.

29. Prohibition may occur under the 1985 "Act to Control Businesses Tending to Affect Public Morals." Soaplands have been prohibited in Aomori, Gunma, Nagano, Toyama, Nara, and five areas of Hokkaido. Information from the National Police Agency.

30. *Japan Times,* 7 March 1989, p. 3, and police officials.

The strictness of antiprostitution enforcement varies from place to place. Around the harbors of major ports regulation is often lax, the police recognizing that sailors have fierce expectations on this score. In lower-class entertainment areas streetwalking can be found fairly openly. The phone numbers of prostitutes are pasted by pimps in public telephone booths; more brazenly, they pass out printed cards to automobile drivers stopped in traffic. Certain areas are known historically as being centers of prostitution. In one area there are 150 small brothels along narrow streets and alleys, each looking like a traditional two-story shop with sliding front doors and a raised, carpeted platform inside. An elderly woman, dressed in a kimono and seated on the platform, quietly invites passersby inside. A younger, pretty woman, also traditionally dressed, sits farther back facing the door, her eyes discreetly downcast. With the sliding doors drawn back on a cold winter's evening, both women are swathed in woolly lap-robes often woven with homey pictures of animals. The robe of one attractive girl, sitting close to a twinkling kerosene heater, was the replica of an American flag.

The police may reason, though this is conjecture, that since commercial sex is not illegal per se, it is better to contain it within designated locations than to drive it underground and perhaps disperse it over a wider area. From time to time the police undertake campaigns to curb flagrant practice. The impetus usually comes from prefectural headquarters, which, in turn, has been prompted by reports from its own plainclothes patrols, local police stations, or citizens' groups complaining about unseemly behavior. But because police manpower is not unlimited, antiprostitution work must be balanced against other needs. Since discreet behavior of a freelance sort is what the law allows, regulation within the bounds of decorum—a standard that varies from place to place—is what the police in fact provide.

Around major entertainment areas patrol officers quickly learn to recognize habitual prostitutes and their protectors. They may even be able to address them by name. Police and prostitutes are both street people and they exchange banter like opponents in a well-understood athletic contest. Verbal exchanges are often quite matter of fact: "Why are you sitting down?" spoken to a group of women at an intersection; to a single girl on a corner, "Are there any new ones in your group?" As a patrol approaches, loitering men can be seen giving hand-signals, warning prostitutes down the street to walk purposefully and not stand around. One summer night patrol officers saw two suspected prostitutes standing at the far end of a dark city block; tucking their caps under their arms and hiding their batons behind them, they sauntered slowly down the street. Too late the girls realized the ruse and tried to run away. They were caught and given a lecture. Officers from a patrol car saw a saucy young woman with red hair talking to two men on a street corner. As she walked away one officer stopped her and asked questions while his colleague talked to the two men. The men refused to implicate her and she volubly protested her innocence: "If people ask me directions, I can answer them if I want to!" "I wasn't *standing*, I was *walking*." There are moments of humor in these relations. A patrol car in which I was riding drove up quietly behind a tall, short-skirted young woman in the middle of a bar-lined street. Though we could not hear her, she was saying something to two men walking away. Turning around and seeing the patrol car stopped immediately behind her, she gasped in surprise and her hand flew ingenuously to her mouth. Appalled at the narrowness of her escape, she did a slight knee-bend like a curtsy and gave a smile of mingled relief and embarrassment.

Cultural mores shaping the law and police practices pertaining to prostitution are very different in Japan and the United States. In Japan a sexual double standard is socially sanctioned. Infidelity is not a source of guilt to men; they do not suffer a bad conscience from being sexually incontinent. Nor do wives feel that infidelity necessarily threatens their marriage. Going with a prostitute is spoken of as being therapeutic, a way of releasing tensions, much as drinking is. A man's duty to his wife and family is not conceived in sexual terms, apart from siring offspring. Standards of acceptable conduct are breached only when extramarital sexual activity is allowed to impinge on the husband's performance of nonsexual duties to his family.[31] As long as infidelity does not lead to public indiscretions and profligacy, morality is not considered to have been violated.

Marriages have customarily been arranged because marriage was viewed as an institutional relationship between families, not simply an emotional attachment between individuals.[32] Although virginity is assumed in a bride, it has never been a part of Japanese custom among good families to demand proofs, nor have illegitimate children been

---

31. Ruth Benedict, *The Chrysanthemum and the Sword* (Boston: Houghton Mifflin, 1946), chap. 9.

32. Tadashi Fukutake, *Japanese Rural Society* (London: Oxford University Press, 1967), pp. 44–45.

stigmatized in law.[33] There was often a trial period in marriage to determine whether the woman fitted into the new household. Even today, there is sometimes a delay between the ceremony of marriage and notification of the government, without which the marriage is not legal. Divorce by mutual consent has always been possible in Japan and never for infidelity on the part of the man.[34] When the penal code was redrafted after World War II, Occupation authorities recommended that adultery be included as grounds for divorce for the woman as well as for the man. The Japanese legislature objected, with the ironic result that adultery by either party was eliminated as an offense under the code.[35]

The climate within which prostitution is tolerated may be becoming less hospitable. The agent of change is the growing presence of love in marriage. Though families still play an important role in bringing prospective partners together and in investigating the other party, young people by and large insist on the right of veto.[36] While they may not insist on prior emotional attachment—though that is not uncommon—they do want a partner with whom the formation of an emotional bond is possible. The tendency of young people to reject the traditional saying "Those who come together in passion stay together in tears"[37] may have important effects on the way in which infidelity is regarded. Marriage based on passion, or the possibility of passion, leaves less room for extramarital dalliance. Sex assumes a more central place in the definition of the marriage relationship, with the result that sexual continency becomes a duty of the husband. Since love is a reciprocal relationship, marriages based on it weaken the acceptability of a double standard.

Furthermore, women are becoming more assertive socially, less willing to accept limited sex-determined roles. This was reflected in popular

33. R. P. Dore, *City Life in Japan* (Berkeley and Los Angeles: University of California Press, 1958), pp. 107–8. Until 1948, the Civil Code referred to two categories of illegitimate births—"recognized illegitimate" and "strictly illegitimate." A child was "recognized illegitimate" when the father assumed responsibility for it even though he could not or would not marry the mother. The status of "recognized illegitimate" was eliminated because it was considered demeaning to women, implying the status of a concubine. Shirley Hartley, "The Decline of Illegitimacy in Japan," *Social Problems* (Summer 1970), p. 81.

34. Yozo Watanabe, "The Family and the Law," in *Law in Japan*, ed. Arthur T. Von Mehren (Cambridge: Harvard University Press, 1963).

35. Chalmers Johnson, *Conspiracy at Matsukawa* (Berkeley and Los Angeles: University of California Press, 1972), p. 37.

36. Dore, *City Life*, chap. 11; Ezra F. Vogel, *Japan's New Middle Class* (Berkeley and Los Angeles: University of California Press, 1963), chap. 8.

37. Fukutake, *Japanese Rural Society*, pp. 44–45.

disgust, especially among women, at the revelations of unbridled sexual liaisons by senior members of the ruling Liberal-Democratic party and the political capital made of this by the female leader of the Socialist party in the elections of 1989. It would appear that the subservience of women is declining with the intensification of romance in marriage. Perhaps women's militancy against prostitution is encouraged by an intensification of the emotional basis of marriage because this may be one aspect of the development of a less compliant role for women.

The fact that sex outside marriage is widely excused is part of a larger pattern. Entertainment for men is centered primarily outside the home and it does not involve wives. Social activity is based on workplace friendships supplemented by lingering ties to school and university friends. Men do not generally entertain one another at home; they go to public facilities. Such places then provide female companionship. In effect, the feminine element is provided impersonally by the marketplace. The ambiance of this form of socializing is unfamiliar to Americans, indeed almost unimaginable.

There are different styles to the way in which female companionship is provided. In high-class traditional restaurants the women are often well over fifty; in cabarets and nightclubs they are young, the emphasis being on physical attractiveness. In both settings parties can become quite bawdy. With older women it takes the form of verbal suggestion, innuendo, and double entendre. There is elaborate playing on words, rather like Elizabethan humor. With the young women, bawdiness is physical as well as verbal. Distributed among a table of men, the women deliberately intrude into the physical space of men. They hold hands, press knees together, rest a hand on the knee or thigh of the man. The men put their arms around the women, allow their hands to drag across breasts, or rest their hands on thighs. Conversation is suggestive and not too subtle. Men pretend to unzip their flies in response to imagined invitations; the physical endowments of the women are openly complimented.

For the young hostesses the work is tiring and degrading. Their faces, caught unawares, frequently register disgust or boredom. At the same time, there is no question about who is in control: it is the women. They ply the men with food and drink, ordering without being asked; they make sure that the men do not spill on themselves, spreading napkins and cutting food into bite-sized bits; they restrain the men's hands, keep tempers calm, and guide unsteady patrons to the men's room and to the street at evening's end. Responsibility belongs to the hostesses, which is why the men can relax. Sexually there is no ambiguity in the situation at all. The night spots are for the most part well lit, unlike American cocktail lounges. Flirtation is vigorous but thoroughly ritualized. A man can try to arrange a rendezvous and the hostess is free to accept or reject. The men are not engaged in seductions; at most they enter into a business transaction under cover of stylized risquéness. The hostesses are being used but they are not helpless.

The contrast between behavior in an American cocktail lounge and a Japanese cabaret is striking and revealing. In the Japanese case flirting is open, not arch or furtive, and there is no ambiguity about outcome. Both parties are free to offer and refuse. The presence of a man's wife or date is unthinkable. In an American cocktail lounge flirtation is less open, more furtive, and outcomes are uncertain. Wives and dates are encouraged.

Japan has another unique institution that throws light on sexual customs—the "Lovers' Hotel." Clustered on the fringes of entertainment areas, they look like small modern hotels, neon lit, multistoried, shadowy in appearance. Illuminated signs advertise rooms for rent by the hour or the night. No questions are asked, no registers are signed. Many have covered parking places, which make coming and going more private. At some hotels parking attendants place placards against the front and rear of the cars so that license plates are obscured. Parents know that these are not hotels for families; should they be unobservant enough to enter, they would be turned away. Japan has solved at a stroke a problem that plagued generations of American lovers. Until the recent revolution in sexual mores, Americans either had to be rich or use disreputable motels in order to arrange assignations. The Japanese approach was more straightforward, recognizing a difficult problem made more acute by small houses and fewer motorcars. "Lovers' Hotels" undoubtedly facilitate prostitution but the police say that problems of disorderly conduct are few; all parties are eager to avoid publicity.[38]

Private prostitution is tolerated in Japan because it is not considered an insidious social force. Male sexual activity before as well as outside marriage has been legitimized, subject to the one qualification that the family must be protected. There is a parallel between the Japanese handling of sex and alcohol. Both indulgences are allowed under regulation so long as the duties of one's station do not suffer. Contrary to what Americans believe, stable family life and prostitution are not incompatible. Divorce rates are very low by international standards, even though

38. According to the National Police Agency, there were 10,011 "Lovers' Hotels" in 1988.

divorce is obtainable by mutual consent or by suit of either party.[39] In comparison with the Japanese, Americans appear to have overemphasized the influence of sex outside marriage on social life; they see in it an insidious social force. In the name of the family they have sought to prevent infidelity under commercial auspices. Because sexual practices and beliefs about the social impact of sexual practices are tightly interlocked, the role of the police with respect to sex in any society cannot be easily changed. The Japanese see no social need for the police to act as sexual censors; Americans do. Japanese results would seem to belie American belief, but then Americans are not Japanese. Perhaps Americans would be unable to buffer the social effects of legalizing prostitution. It is important to bear in mind when dealing with culture that what is real is what people believe—things are indeed what they seem.

Lack of censoriousness about the practice of prostitution applies to homosexuality as well. Homosexuality is not a crime in Japan, unlike the United States where in many states until quite recently it was a felony. Homosexuality is subject to precisely the same rules that apply to heterosexuality—prohibition of solicitation and performance of indecent acts in public places. A movie theater, for example, that becomes the haunt of homosexuals will be patrolled by police in plainclothes to prevent indecent behavior. There are "gay bars"[40] in most cities, some of which have hostesses who are "blue boys," meaning female impersonators. Some of these bars have become famous and are visited by the general public; "blue boys" have appeared on national television and some have become celebrities. Police encounters with homosexuals, both male and female, are unstrained; they are not marked by the contempt and covert baiting found in the United States. Even in tough neighborhoods among derelicts and hardened day-laborers, "blue boys" can be seen mixing, talking, and drinking without attracting hostility.

Drug Addiction

The pattern that emerges from this examination of Japanese policy toward victimless crimes is that acts themselves are not prohibited. Outlets have been allowed for adults, especially men, for

39. In 1984, Japan had 1.5 divorces for each 100,000 persons, the United States 4.9, Sweden 2.4, and France 1.9. Foreign Press Center, Tokyo, *Facts and Figures of Japan* (1987 edition), p. 16.
40. A Japanese-English expression.

drinking, gambling, and sex as long as indulgence is discreet, does not harm others, and compulsion is avoided. Japanese and American policies toward the pursuit of pleasure are, therefore, substantially different. The keynote in Japan is regulation; in the United States, prohibition.

This conclusion is compelling only so far, for there is one form of victimless crime where prohibition is strict and the police unrelenting in their enforcement. This is the area of narcotics addiction and drug abuse. Using and dealing in narcotics, hallucinogens, and stimulants are subject to stern criminal penalties. There is no movement toward legalization of any forms, including marijuana, excepting of course for licensed medical purposes. Nor are there any programs for maintenance of addicts on drugs under medical auspices, as in Great Britain. The only acceptable goal of treatment is permanent abstention. Hallucinogens are classified as narcotics and penalties for marijuana use are almost as severe as those for use of opium derivatives.[41] Punishments allowed under Japanese law tend not to be as stiff as those in the United States, if federal and New York State statutes are representative. In Japan possession and use of narcotics are punishable with jail sentences up to seven years—five years in the case of marijuana.[42] Possession of stimulants in Japan can earn an offender ten years in jail. In New York State possession of as little as two ounces of heroin or cocaine is punished with from three years to life imprisonment; four ounces and over, fifteen years to life.[43] Federal law punishes possession only if there is an intent to sell. In both countries selling, distributing, and possessing drugs for gain is regarded more seriously than possession for personal use. The punishment for dealing in opium and cocaine derivatives in Japan is a jail sentence of from one to ten years. In New York State sale of as little as one-half ounce of heroin or cocaine is punishable with from three years to life in prison; two ounces and above, fifteen years to life. Under federal law, selling or possessing with intent to sell of 100 grams of heroin, 500 grams of cocaine, and 5 grams of crack are punishable with prison sentences of from five to forty years.[44] If the quantities respectively are 1 kilogram, 5 kilograms, and 50 grams, the prison sen-

41. The penalty for possession of marijuana for use is imprisonment up to five years; for opium, up to seven years. National Police Agency, *Comprehensive Strategies for Drug Control in Japan* (Tokyo: All Japan Crime Prevention Association, 1987). Written in English, this booklet provides a very complete summary of drug enforcement in Japan.

42. Narcotics Control Law, 1953, Article 66; Opium Law, 1954, Article 52; Cannabis Control Law, 1948, Article 24(2).

43. Information provided by the New York State Police, 1989.

44. Drug Abuse Prevention and Control Act, 21. U.S.C. Title 841 (a)(b) (1989 Supp.).

tences rise to a minimum of ten years and a maximum of life. Japanese law provides for compulsory hospitalization of addicts, including marijuana users, for periods up to six months.[45] Though procedures vary a great deal in the United States, the federal government and most states have some measures for compelling persons dependent on drugs to undergo treatment.

The Japanese have had remarkable success in dealing with drug problems. The number of people arrested for hard-drug use declined sharply during the 1960s, after rising steeply through the 1950s.[46] This is not because the police adopted a more tolerant policy or because arrests became more difficult to make. Arrests for heroin use peaked in 1962 at 2,139 before falling to between 30 and 50 arrests per year after 1966. A slight rise to 252 occurred between 1971 and 1973 but quickly disappeared. In 1988, 105 persons were arrested throughout Japan for heroin possession or sale. Use of cocaine continues to remain almost nonexistent. Crack is unheard of. Violations involving opium are also negligible, not more than 57 a year back through the late 1950s and now running less than 10.[47]

In numbers of persons involved, the major postwar drug problem has involved amphetamines.[48] By 1955 amphetamine use had risen to what the Japanese thought was epidemic proportions. In that year, 55,664 persons were arrested for stimulant violations. Three years later only 271 arrests were made. Through the 1960s the number of arrests remained stable, about 800 a year. In 1970 the numbers rose sharply and have been increasing gradually since. The peak was reached in 1984 with the arrest of 24,022 persons. Since then the number has declined marginally each year, to 20,399 in 1988. The Japanese continue to be alarmed and refer to the new "stimulant boom."

Marijuana arrests too have risen since the mid-1960s, from 39 persons arrested for use or sale in 1965 to 712 in 1975 and 1,144 in 1986. By American standards marijuana use is clearly a negligible problem.

And that of course is the point. Drug problems in Japan and the United States are incommensurable. In 1987 Japan arrested 22,337 persons for drug offenses, but only 1.4 percent in connection with hard

45. Narcotics Control Law, Article 58, paragraphs 6–10.
46. All information on drug trends in Japan comes from the National Police Agency, *Comprehensive Strategies for Drug Control in Japan, 1987,* and *White Paper on Crime, 1989.*
47. Total offenses under the Opium Law ran over a thousand in the 1960s but the great majority were for cultivation only. In 1986, for example, 362 arrests were made under the Opium Law but only 4 for use or sale.
48. "Speed" in the United States, "kokusaizai" or "hiropon" in Japan. Chemically, phenil-amino-propane or phenil-methyl-amino-propane.

drugs. Stimulant arrests constituted 91 percent. Marijuana made up the remainder. In the United States, with a population not quite twice as large as Japan's, 937,400 persons were arrested in 1987, 46 percent in connection with heroin or cocaine. Seventy-four percent of the American arrests were for possession, 26 percent for sale. In Tokyo 2,589 persons were arrested for stimulant offenses in 1987, 317 for marijuana offenses, and only a handful in connection with hard drugs. In New York City, with a population about two-thirds of Tokyo's, there were 43,953 felony narcotics arrests in 1988. With respect to arrests for sale of narcotics, 58 percent were for cocaine, 24 percent for heroin, and 14 percent for marijuana.[49]

The impact of drugs is also dramatically different in both countries. According to the National Household Survey on Drug Abuse in 1985, 9.4 percent of the U.S. population twelve years of age and older smoked marijuana in the month preceding the survey, 2.9 percent used cocaine, 0.9 percent inhalants, 1.3 percent stimulants, and less than 0.5 percent hallucinogens.[50] In round numbers this means that if the survey was representative, as was claimed, approximately 18 million Americans twelve years old and older smoked marijuana during a single month in 1985, 5.5 million used cocaine, 1.7 million sniffed inhalants, and 2.5 million took stimulants. In Japan there are only estimates of drug use. The police cite the international rule of thumb that the number of people using drugs is usually about ten times the number of arrests. If this applies to Japan, then about 225,000 people could be involved.[51]

Drug use in Japan does not play a significant role in crime, as it does in the United States. One hundred and fifty-five persons were arrested for stimulant-related crimes in 1987, 105 because of their pharmacological effect and 50 by persons trying to get stimulants. No figures are available for hard-drug involvement in crime, obviously because the numbers are vanishingly small. The United States government estimates that at least 60 percent of all men arrested in 1988 tested positive for drug use, excluding marijuana.[52]

49. Information furnished by the New York City Police Department.

50. *Sourcebook of Criminal Justice Statistics, 1987,* table 3.72.

51. An expert on drugs at the National Research Institute of Police Science in Japan estimates that there are as many as 400,000 users of stimulants, less than 10,000 of marijuana, almost none for heroin and cocaine, and none for crack. Private communication, February 1989.

52. National Institute of Justice, U.S. Department of Justice, "Drug Use Forecasting (DUF): April–June 1988 Data," p. 6. For cocaine use alone, 83 percent of males arrested tested positive in New York City, 65 percent in Los Angeles, 57 percent in Chicago, 55 percent in Washington, D.C., 54 percent in Houston, and 45 percent in Detroit.

What is the secret of the Japanese success? How have they been able to reduce the incidence of drug use so dramatically during the past twenty years? A definitive analysis of the causes of drug addiction and its responsiveness to official policy is beyond the scope of this study. It is instructive, however, to examine what the Japanese themselves say are the reasons for their success, comparing that with American experience. Japanese experts attribute their enviable record to two factors: strict law enforcement and a climate of public opinion implacably hostile to drug use.

The claim by the Japanese that narcotics enforcement is particularly strict is not true in relation to the United States. As we have seen, statutory penalties for narcotics use and dealing are less severe than in the United States. However, in evaluating the strictness of law enforcement, one must go beyond statutes and examine implementation, particularly the kinds of penalties imposed. Seventy-seven percent of persons sentenced in U.S. federal district courts in 1986 for drug offenses were incarcerated and the median term was three and one-half years.[53] The average prison term for possession was three years and nine months, for distribution or manufacture five years, and for "general trafficking" sixteen years. In American state courts the same year 64 percent of those tried for drug trafficking were incarcerated for a median term of two years.[54] Unfortunately, sentence information is not available in state courts with respect to possession. Presumably, terms would be less than for trafficking. In Japan, on the other hand, courts incarcerated only 27 percent of those convicted of hard-drug offenses, possession and dealing together—54 percent of stimulant offenders, and 19 percent of marijuana offenders.[55] The rest had their sentences suspended, some with and some without police supervision. Of the twenty-five persons incarcerated for hard-drug offenses, thirteen were sentenced to three years or less. For stimulant offenders, only 4 percent were sentenced to more than three years. Twenty-two percent served six months or less. As one would expect, marijuana offenders were treated most leniently of all: 2 percent were sentenced to more than three years, 12 percent to one year or less.

Although the comparisons are not exact, it appears that a larger proportion of drug offenders convicted of either possession or trafficking

53. U.S. Department of Justice, Bureau of Justice Statistics, "Special Report: Drug Law Violators, 1980–86."

54. *Sourcebook of Criminal Justice Statistics,* p. 562.

55. General Secretariat, Supreme Court of Japan, *Annual Report of Judicial Statistics for 1987,* vol. 2, p. 215.

go to prison in the United States than in Japan and that their sentences tend to be longer, especially at the federal level.

Japanese police enforcement is more restricted than American. Because of strict interpretation of the law against entrapment, Japanese police never make an undercover offer of drugs for sale and only arrange "buys" by providing money to informants who indicate that they have been approached by a willing seller. The police themselves almost never pose as buyers. And they never send undercover officers to become part of drug-dealing organizations. Moreover, because customs law requires drug shipments to be seized, police cannot conduct clandestine surveillance of transshipments through Japan in order to provide information to foreign countries about networks and contacts. They may tap the phones of willing informants, but they have rarely applied to the courts for permission to do so against uncooperative targets. It is not surprising, therefore, that the great majority of drug arrests in Japan are for simple possession, and they are made by uniformed patrol officers acting on suspicion that someone has been using and may be carrying drugs. American police officers undoubtedly would feel seriously handicapped if they were asked to fight the "war on drugs" under similar rules.

The Japanese police do have one important advantage. They can punish people for the use as well as the possession of drugs. For example, users of stimulants may receive up to ten years imprisonment and users of opium up to seven years. Heroin addicts may not be punished for use, but people who have knowingly administered heroin to them may be. Marijuana use is not punishable.[56] Furthermore, the police may take blood and urine samples under court order to determine whether suspects have been using drugs. Such requests to the courts are rarely rejected. In current American law, this would amount to an illegal search and seizure under the Constitution's guarantee against self-incrimination. Finally, people who are determined by medical and psychological examination to be drug addicted, meaning unable to control their desire for drugs, may be compulsorily hospitalized. In 1988, 98 people were compelled to enter hospitals for treatment, 95 stimulant suspects and 3 narcotics suspects. Treatment consists of going "cold turkey," that is, having all drugs withdrawn. Methadone therapy is not used.[57] Civil commitment of addicts was popular in the United States during the 1960s and early 1970s but was gradually given up as ineffective. It remains to be seen whether the hardening of attitudes against users of drugs in the United States revives this practice.

56. National Police Agency, *Comprehensive Strategies for Drug Control in Japan* (1987).
57. Ibid., p. 127.

The Japanese enforcement approach, then, is to target users in order both to dry up the market and to obtain information about sellers. Drug users are not viewed tolerantly in Japan, either as private participants in victimless crime or as victims exploited by circumstances beyond their control. There is a paradox here. This approach can only work when the number of users is still relatively small. The number of drug users in the United States is so large that facilities are lacking even for people who want to be treated, let alone for all users. Ironically, then, such a draconian strategy might be accepted in the United States when the problem of drug abuse seemed to be out of control, but that is precisely the time when it could not be implemented successfully because of the massive size of the using population. Japan, in contrast, has identified the user as the culprit from the start, before the problem outran treatment resources. The daunting size of the American drug-abuse problem is what is now causing public consideration of the merits of decriminalizing drug use and monopolizing its sale under government auspices.

Japanese experts also argue that enforcement efforts are facilitated by Japan's being an island, therefore making access easier to control, and by the fact that its organized criminal gangs have been reluctant to engage in drug dealing. Although they may be working with foreign dealers in transshipping, they have not sought to develop a Japanese market.[58] This is certainly true with respect to hard drugs. The only small exception is with respect to stimulants. And there the major consumers appear to be the gangs' own members or people on the fringes of their activity, as in the entertainment industry.[59]

The second major reason cited for Japan's success in meeting the drug problem has to do with the climate of public opinion. Drug use in Japan is not considered a private matter, like drinking or going with a prostitute. It is an offense against the community, an antisocial act that weakens the nation. A drug addict is not a private sinner; he is a subversive.[60]

The effectiveness of social pressure at work in the Japanese commu-

---

58. David E. Kaplan and Alec Dubro, *Yakuza* (Reading, Mass.: Addison-Wesley, 1986). Japan's criminal gangs will be discussed in chapter 9.

59. This seems to be accepted opinion among police as well as civilian experts on Japan's drug scene.

60. The link between patriotism and condemnation of drug use may be based on memories of the Opium Wars in China. China's penetration by European powers and her ultimate prostration are attributed in part to the wholesale importation of opium. The Japanese themselves took a leaf out of the European book in the 1930s and exported huge quantities of opium from Manchuria into China as a means of expanding Japan's empire.

nity can be seen dramatically in the case of smoking. Though the Japanese are heavy smokers, they have effectively enforced a prohibition against smoking in public by persons under twenty years of age.[61] Smoking is considered a presumptive sign of juvenile delinquency. Teenagers discovered smoking will be admonished by the police, their names taken, and parents and school authorities notified. Police officers as well as civilian juvenile counselors demand that adolescents destroy their packs of cigarettes on the spot. I have seen teenagers taken out of dance halls by the police and made to shred their cigarettes one by one on the street. A patrol car cruising one evening in a residential neighborhood suddenly made a U-turn and dashed back half a block to where two teenage boys were lounging on a low wall. The driver had noticed one of the boys throwing a cigarette end away. The officers found the stub and confiscated a pack of cigarettes. The boys were taken to the home of the younger, where the mother apologized for their behavior and thanked the officers for being so attentive. A report was made to the juvenile delinquency office. It is intriguing to speculate on the reactions of American parents in the same situation. Would they respond as gratefully as the Japanese mother did or would they be inclined to mutter about police officers with nothing better to do? The smoking prohibition is enforced only against teenagers still in high school. Once they have gone to work, they are considered of age and the police wink at their smoking as they do at their drinking. College students are also exempt. American teenagers in Japan are unaware of the impact they have on Japanese who see them smoking on the street. To the Japanese it appears brazen, and though police and private citizens are generally too polite to say anything, they resent this disregard of Japanese custom. If Japanese public opinion supports—not just tolerates—this kind of enforcement in the case of smoking, is it any wonder that drug problems among youth are minimal?

Public opinion about drugs is not only adamant, it is united. Japan is probably the largest homogeneous nation in the world. There are no large racial, national, or linguistic subgroups that can form pockets of deviance because of the mechanics of cultural domination. Class barriers too are relatively permeable, lessening even further the possibility that alienated groups will seek to develop identity or assuage frustration by consuming drugs.

61. This policy goes back to the Meiji period. Baron Kanetake Oura, "The Police in Japan," in *Fifty Years of New Japan*, ed. Count Shigenobu Okuma (London: Smith, Elder, 1909), vol. 1, p. 291.

In conclusion, Japan's success with stemming drug use is not due to more severe prison sentences, though it may be tied to stricter enforcement against users, especially in the form of compulsory hospitalization. The primary reason for success undoubtedly is near-unanimous public hostility to drug use, an antagonism that is acted out in informal ways and clothed in the sentiments of national pride and identity.

If we look at victimless crime as a whole, it is apparent that the Japanese have avoided many of the problems that strain law enforcement in the United States. The police have not been corrupted or demoralized by having to enforce laws against victimless crime. The number of offenses committed each year is not large. Since this is not due to indifference on the part of the police, the law and public opinion would seem to be in substantial harmony. Few people are brought into conflict with the law in their pursuit of pleasure. What are the lessons that can be drawn from Japanese experience that might help Americans as they wrestle with this unique category of offenses?

Success in managing the pursuit of pleasure does not depend on the harshness of criminal penalties. Without the reinforcement of an active public opinion, police enforcement cannot be effective, unless the populace will tolerate draconian enforcement measures. Conversely, the more adamant the public is against a particular form of victimless crime, the less reliance need be placed on official instruments of regulation. Therefore, the development of enforcement policies must involve an assessment of public opinion toward particular indulgences. The key feature about public opinion to assess is whether the act involved is perceived as a private vice or a public menace. That is, is its indulgence viewed as compatible with the performance of necessary social obligations? If it is viewed as not inevitably harming others, then its unpleasant effects should be contained through regulatory supervision and not through prohibition. Japan has criminalized an act of vice only in the one instance where there is an overwhelming consensus that the act is antisocial—namely, drug addiction. The United States prohibits many kinds of vice—prostitution, gambling, narcotics, and sometimes alcohol—regardless of whether the public considers them inherently antisocial.

The harmful social effects of the pursuit of pleasure may be eliminated in various ways. The choice is not, as many Americans think, between prohibition or license. There are in fact four alternatives.

First, prohibition—that is, penalizing the indulgence itself.

Second, regulating the circumstances under which indulgence is permitted. This was the tack taken in the United States with respect to alcohol after the repeal of the Volstead Act. It is the policy the Japanese apply to alcohol, prostitution, and gambling. Indulgence is allowed so long as it does not transgress the rights of others.

Third, not acts themselves, but consequences arising from indulgence may be penalized by criminal sanction. Such a policy recognizes that indulgence does not always compromise responsibilities but only sometimes does so. The Japanese tolerate drinking but are implacable toward drunken driving. Americans, on the other hand, though they once tried to prohibit alcoholic consumption, are comparatively lenient toward the drunken driver. Similarly, the Japanese, who tolerate prostitution, look with enormous misgiving at the emotional promiscuity involved in the so-called sexual revolution and have preserved very stable families; Americans, who prohibit prostitution, accept the sexual revolution almost with enthusiasm and tolerate high divorce rates. The Japanese are more responsible in their indulgence; they do not act as if they believed that indulgence and duty are incompatible.

Fourth, informal sanctions can be developed that help to reduce unpleasant consequences from private indulgence. These informal sanctions may supplement as well as exist in lieu of legal prescriptions. One problem with any criminal regulation or prohibition is that it thrusts responsibility onto official agencies. It tends to blunt public discussion of what is right and proper. In a new version of Gresham's Law, legality drives out reasonableness. Consider the case of marijuana. People in the United States who oppose criminal penalties for private use spend so much time speaking for decriminalization that they give little attention to the desirability of marijuana smoking. Few people seem able to argue that penalties for marijuana smoking are too severe and at the same time that smoking is harmful in general and that marijuana smoking is intoxicating and should be avoided as much as possible. Similarly, the American approach to containing sexual immorality is to prohibit prostitution. Few people discuss circumstances in which infidelity may be inevitable, possibly justified, and ways to cushion those effects. Informal social sanctions constraining the manner in which infidelity is indulged may be more salutary in terms of human effects than banning prostitution entirely. In the United States, unfortunately, being a libertarian often does sound very much like being a libertine.

The difficulty with the precept that enforcement policies must fit concepts of social effect lies in knowing when to shift from one mode to another. Just as public opinion legitimizes enforcement, allowing it to work, so legal prescriptions help set community norms about what is proper. Laws have a pedagogical function; they are a useful standard of appeal. Attempts to prohibit drinking in the United States through the criminal law were founded on a widespread view that society was in grave and immediate danger. It is clear that advocates of prohibition misassessed the opinion of the general public. Most people did not believe that drinking was incompatible with the performance of social duties. The alcohol-prohibition experience shows that there is no quicker way to determine the moral context of an offense than to criminalize it. If alternatives to prohibition are recognized, the criminalization of indulgence can be looked upon as a controlled experiment, the implication being that if it fails, repeal should be immediate and other policies substituted. This should not be a cause for anguish. Shifting from prohibitory to regulatory modes and informal sanctioning is not capitulation. Indeed, such a shift may be the only successful way to contain the harmful effects of the pursuit of some pleasures. Minimization of harmful effects is much more important than moralizing through prohibition.

The Japanese experience suggests a last sobering thought. The relation between what a society believes about a particular form of pleasure and how it chooses to supervise it may be self-fulfilling. A society that believes a vice is containable through regulation without dissolution of the community may be more effective in containing that vice than a society that believes the vice can be contained only through prohibition but is ineffective in doing so. Even narcotics addiction can be stemmed and its social effects limited by means of regulation if the community as a whole reinforces the norm that containment is necessary. Conversely, a society may be effective in prohibiting indulgence in a vice if people believe that this is necessary to save society even though in fact they are mistaken. The point is that effectiveness in regulating the pursuit of pleasure depends on a community's conception of the social effects of indulgence. The community's conception varies from pleasure to pleasure, so policy must be discriminating. Unfortunately, attitudes such as these are rooted deep in popular culture; they change very slowly. It follows that enforcement difficulties may be as peculiar to different countries as views of morality.

7

The Individual and Authority

One Sunday afternoon a man of about forty years old, dressed in a neat suit and tie, was brought to a koban by two patrol officers. He had parked illegally on a narrow residential street. He was thoroughly chastened, and the officers, after talking to him for several minutes, decided that instead of issuing a parking ticket, which would require payment of a fine, they would have him send a formal letter of apology to the chief of the local police station. So the man sat down at a koban desk and wrote out a letter in longhand. After giving his name, address, age, occupation, and nature and date of the offense, he wrote as follows: "I am very sorry for the trouble caused by illegal parking. I will be very careful in the future that I will never repeat the same violation. For this time only please I beseech your generosity." After signing his name and adding his seal,[1] he was allowed to go on his way, justice having been done in the minds of all concerned.

Variations of this quaint little drama occur frequently in relations between the Japanese police and public. Police officers freely adapt their responses to misconduct according to the personal background and demeanor of offenders. The most important basis for doing so is a display of contrition by the offender. Apology is one form repentance takes.

---

1. A seal (*hanko*) is a small wooden stylus imprinted with a Japanese character. It is legal authentication of a signature.

Written apologies, as in this case, are widely used by police officers in connection with relatively minor offenses where an automatic fine is levied.[2] The letter written by this man was copied from a form kept in the koban under a clear plastic cover. Some offenders, knowing about the procedure, ask to be allowed to give an apology in lieu of the fine. The decision depends totally on the judgment of the officers involved. Unless they believe that an offender is truly contrite and will not offend again, they insist on due punishment. To Americans, giving an apology would seem a minor price to pay. One can imagine them being irate at not being allowed to apologize, and wondering about what kind of favoritism was involved. To the Japanese, however, apologizing can be acutely embarrassing—so much so in fact that often the police simply warn the offender rather than demanding a formal apology.

Late one night koban officers were summoned by a young woman to save her from a man who, she said, had tried to force her to come to a hotel. It turned out that they had had an affair some time before and he, meeting her by accident, wanted to resume it on the spur of the moment. The woman was both furious and scared. The man, flashily dressed in a pink shirt and white slacks, was very embarrassed and steadfastly maintained that he had only asked her to come for a cup of tea. Discounting his denials, they lectured him sternly about using threats. Then the officers arranged that if he apologized to the woman and wrote a letter saying he would not do this again, the woman would sign an undertaking that she would not press charges. Taken into the room where the woman was, he shuffled his feet reluctantly and with bad grace mumbled "Sumimasen ne"—"I'm really sorry." Drunken men who relieve themselves outdoors are often let go if they are cooperative and apologetic; if they try to run away, they are fined. Youths under twenty found smoking in public may have their parents or teachers notified, but not if they voluntarily destroy their cigarettes on the spot and apologize.

Late one evening two patrol officers on bicycles stopped a man for drunken driving; he tried to escape by reversing his car, which narrowly missed one officer and punched a hole in the side of a small wooden house. A breath test showed he was drunk and he was marched on foot to a koban. The police wrote up the incident in detail and asked the man extensive questions about himself. As the interrogation dragged

2. Automatic fines are not paid to the police; they are collected for government by banks and post offices.

on, the driver became progressively more clear-eyed, subdued, and finally penitent. One of the young bike officers and the senior patrol officer of the koban disagreed sharply about the appropriate penalty to assess. The patrol officer wanted as severe a punishment as the law allowed—after all, it was he who had almost been run over—and the senior patrol officer wanted leniency, arguing that the man was a respectable businessman from out of town, that he could make amends to the homeowner directly because he owned a construction company, that he had a good driving record, and that he was very sorry for what he had done. Two full hours after the accident, the officers agreed that the case would not go to court but that the man would have to repair the damage under police supervision and would be given a ticket for drunken driving. The exact charge would be determined by traffic specialists at police headquarters.

The police, who are seldom surprised about human behavior, are well aware that contrition can be feigned and their goodwill abused. The police response is suitably cynical. Some kinds of chronic offenders—such as streetwalkers, bar owners who do not close on time, and women who solicit for striptease shows—are allowed to sign formal apologies precisely in order to create a file of admitted offenses. When the police then do decide to prosecute, the collection of apologies clearly demonstrates that they are habitual offenders and deserve no leniency.

The Japanese recognize that it is difficult in practice to separate discretionary treatment based on a calculation of the genuineness of contrition from treatment based on pure sympathy. But this possibility does not disturb them as it would Americans. With disarming candor Japanese police officers explain the importance of showing sympathy for people enmeshed in the law. Only by letting the "warm blood flow," as they say, will offenders eventually learn to respect both the law and its agents. There are many instances of this. The police discovered that a bicycle being ridden without a light had been stolen. The owner of the cycle, who lived near where the young thief worked, refused to prosecute a "child," though the thief was sixteen years old. Because the boy was very contrite, the police too refused to press the matter. Charges were dropped by the police against a university student caught shoplifting 9,000 yen worth of phonograph records, because he had no previous criminal record, and was very repentant. A taxi driver parked illegally in front of a small store. The police discovered that because he had many previous violations, notification of this offense would cause his license to be suspended. Already bearing heavy expenses from a recent divorce, the taxi driver was on the brink of financial ruin. The police prevailed on the store owner to write a letter saying he had given permission for the taxi to park there, thus shifting the blame for the offense. Knowing that their sympathetic impulses may get in the way of performing their duties, officers sometimes take steps to protect themselves. For example, chauffeured limousines habitually double-park outside cabarets, waiting for their owners to finish the night's carouse. Near one koban, chauffeurs were usually given a fifteen-minute grace period before the police ordered them to move on. Orders were given through a loudspeaker because, said the officers, if they went in person, they would have trouble being stern with the drivers, who were only following orders. Though police officers acknowledge that sympathy occasionally causes them to forget duty, they consider the risk worth running in order to establish a personal bond between citizens and the police, subject to the qualification that serious or chronic misconduct is not to be forgiven.

The Japanese language reflects the acceptability of molding law enforcement to individual characteristics. *Giri* and *ninjo* are the significant words for explaining the moral obligations of life. *Giri* refers to duty, the obligations of conscience. *Ninjo*—sometimes translated "fellow-feeling"—refers to sympathy felt by one person for another; it connotes empathetic sensitivity to the needs of the other. A moral person embodies both *giri* and *ninjo*. *Giri* without *ninjo* lacks warmth; *ninjo* without *giri* lacks principle. An exquisite dilemma is created—one repeatedly treated in Japanese literature, drama, and cinema—when *giri* and *ninjo* conflict. In Japan, as in the United States, *ninjo* prompts an individuating response, but unlike the United States, duty—*giri*—does so as well. Though the Japanese acknowledge universalistic standards, *giri* is not a matter of abstract principle. At its core are considerations of dyadic human relationship; that is, reciprocal obligations between specific people or between an individual and a specific group. The importance of this for the police is that by knowing the personal circumstances of an offender, they can draw conclusions about the network of personal obligations in which the individual is lodged. They can judge whether *giri* is likely to constrain the individual, whether, therefore, he is likely to do what he says. *Giri* provides a basis for intellectually individuating, since it provides a way of discussing the sanctioning power of social bonds. This is similar to an American police officer deciding that because an offender is a respectable doctor and dutiful father, he can be excused for a violation because he would not want to jeopardize his reputation.

Americans know that personal relationships can create constraining obligations, but their moral vocabulary does not recognize it explicitly. Japanese police consider personal circumstances openly because their morality—and their language—stresses the primacy of such networks, thereby making the assessment of the consequences of individuation more predictable.

Police officers in the United States also exercise discretion on the basis of demeanor and background of offenders. The difference is that they deny that they do. They pretend that they mechanically apply the law to all offenders, regardless of personal characteristics, leaving punishment entirely up to the courts. To Americans, unequal enforcement on the basis of individual attributes smacks of favoritism, prejudice, or corruption. Though the police do it, recognizing that offenders vary as to the chances of again committing the same offense, they know they run a substantial risk of public censure. The use of discretion has not been legitimated in the United States as it has in Japan. And because its use is hidden, there are few opportunities for police officers to work out, even among themselves, appropriate grounds for its use.

When the Japanese adapt their behavior to the attitude of an offender, they are reinforcing strong ethical norms that require people to acknowledge guilt. This includes acknowledging responsibility for duties unfulfilled. The great injunction erring Japanese must obey is to say publicly, "I'm sorry." A patient in a hospital died three weeks after being transfused mistakenly with blood of the wrong type. While the doctor in charge was absolved of legal responsibility, the incident was not considered settled until the doctor agreed, prompted by a senior official in the public prosecutor's office, to send a letter of apology to the parents.[3] When a military plane was involved in a crash with a commercial aircraft, the director-general of the Defense Agency resigned after apologizing publicly for failing in supervision. Hikers in the mountains of northern Japan were asked to write out formal apologies if they were caught taking rare alpine plants.[4] An aliens registration office refused to process a renewal application for an American professor until the professor had apologized in writing for appearing after

3. Tsuneo Horiuchi, "The Civil Liberties Bureau of the Ministry of Justice and the System of Civil Liberties Commissions," in United Nations, *Effective Realization of Civil and Political Rights at the National Level—Selected Studies* (New York: UN, 1968, ST/TAO HR/33), pp. 74–75.

4. *Japan Times*, 29 August 1972, p. 2. Four thousand three hundred people were warned during late summer; one hundred ten wrote apologies.

the expiration date. Another professor, who could not produce his pass-
port when asked by the police, had to write a letter of apology to the
local police station. Three men got caught in an elevator that stopped
between floors in a multistoried bar. The police were called when the
men created a scene, shouting and arguing, because the management
refused to accept responsibility and apologize. After the massacre of
passengers at Lod Airport in Israel in 1972 by radical Japanese youths,
the Japanese government published a formal letter of apology to Israel
and to the relatives of the victims. To Americans this act appears to be
similar to expressions of condolence American presidents automatically
send when there has been a natural disaster abroad or a foreign states-
man has died. To the Japanese, however, it had a more profound meaning. It was a symbolic act of national atonement. The burden of responsibility may sometimes be too great to be met through apology, as
when the father of a radical terrorist hanged himself after seeing his son
in police custody on television.[5]

An apology is more than an acceptance of personal guilt; it is an undertaking not to offend again. This theme is strikingly confirmed in
Japanese folktales, which are an important though little-used indicator
of cultural values. Professor Betty Lanham surveyed a selection of
popular folktales from the United States and Japan.[6] She found that half
the Japanese stories stressed forgiveness for evil behavior acknowledged. In only one popular American folktale was forgiveness asked
and given—Cinderella. Even more revealing were the changes that the
Japanese wrought in Western folktales when they were translated into
Japanese. In a Japanese version of "Goldilocks and the Three Bears" the
story ends with Goldilocks apologizing for her rude behavior and the
bears forgiving her and inviting her back. In the American version,
Goldilocks runs away, relieved at the narrowness of her escape. In one
version of "Little Red Riding Hood" the Japanese have made a change
that is almost too good to be true. The wicked wolf captures Little Red

5. *Japan Times*, 29 February 1972, p. 2. The custom of apology has deep roots.
Harumi Befu, "Village Autonomy and Articulation with the State," in *Modern Japan*, ed.
John W. Hall and Marius B. Jansen (Princeton: Princeton University Press, 1968), p. 310,
notes that verbal and written apologies were traditional sanctions employed by villages in
Tokugawa Japan.
6. I am indebted to Professor Betty Lanham for bringing this information to my attention. The following discussion is based on her delightful article, written with Masao
Shimura, "Folktales Commonly Told American and Japanese Children: Ethical Themes
of Omission and Commission," *Journal of American Folklore* (January–March 1967),
pp. 33–48.

Riding Hood and her grandmother, puts them in a sack, and carries them off. Confronted by a hunter responding to their calls for help, the wolf falls on his knees and tearfully asks forgiveness, saying "I won't ever do anything bad again. Please forgive me."[7]

These stories suggest that Japanese and Americans differ profoundly in their views about the mutability of character. The Japanese believe that behavior patterns can be permanently remolded. An act of contrition is not a hollow ritual but an undertaking with respect to the future that can succeed. When police officers accept written apologies—except in the special case of habitual offenders—they do so in order to constrain subsequent behavior. In the United States contrition is not so strongly linked to reform; Americans are skeptical that the past can easily be transcended. It is instructive that in the American version Goldilocks runs away; she never admits her thoughtlessness. Maybe this is why there are so many stories in the United States of offenders who outdistance their past by moving to new communities. They do not apologize and remain; they pay a formal penalty and "start again" by physically going someplace else. The Japanese believe that the network of human obligations within which individuals live will produce reformed behavior. The society, in its constituent groups, supports the erring individual in forming new behavior patterns. Apology is the sign that obligations are accepted; forgiveness is the sign that the promise is accepted. Unless character is considered mutable, neither act is meaningful.

If the web of informal human relations is more constraining in Japan than in the United States, more effective in producing reformed behavior, it would be reasonable to expect that recidivism rates would be lower in Japan than in the United States. This is probably the case among offenders as a whole—that is, all who have been discovered committing a criminal offense—but it is not true for persons imprisoned and then released—the usual basis for computing recidivism in the United States. In Japan 47 percent of all persons released from prison at the end of their sentences were reimprisoned for further offenses within three years and 57 percent within five years.[8] In the United States 41 percent of prisoners released from state prisons were imprisoned again within three years.[9] The great majority of American prisoners (92 percent) were held in state facilities in 1987.[10] About 61 percent of persons sen-

7. Translation provided by Professor Lanham.
8. Study by the Mininstry of Justice, 1982.
9. *Sourcebook of Criminal Justice Statistics, 1988,* p. 658. This figure is based on an eleven-state study in 1983.
10. Ibid., p. 619.

tenced to Japanese prisons have been there before, while in U.S. state prisons only 37 percent of adults and 6.5 percent of juveniles have had a prior commitment.[11] According to American criteria for judging the effectiveness of a criminal justice system, the Japanese system is less effective than the American.

The explanation for the paradoxical relation between recidivism and beliefs about the mutability of character—changeable in Japan, unchangeable in the United States—is that formal sanctions against criminal behavior, especially imprisonment, are used more sparingly in Japan than in the United States. Japan appears to divert a larger proportion of offenders away from court adjudication, where they might be sentenced to prison, than is the case in the United States. For example, 32 percent of Penal Code defendants in 1987 were sent to summary courts where the maximum penalty could be a fine; 28.5 percent had their prosecution suspended; 26 percent were referred to family courts; and only 8.5 percent were formally tried.[12] Although hard data are lacking in the United States, there is general agreement that prosecutors file charges before courts in about 50 percent of cases submitted to them. Furthermore, once defendants get to courts, Japanese defendants are less likely than American to be imprisoned, at least for serious offenses. For example, 44 percent of people tried for Penal Code offenses in 1986 were given prison sentences.[13] In county courts in the United States, which handle the bulk of all criminal convictions, 71 percent of serious felony offenders were sentenced to prison.[14] Because Penal Code offenses cover more than the serious felony offenses examined in the United States, it is important to examine sentences for comparable offenses. Seventy-eight percent of convicted Japanese murderers were sentenced to prison, compared with 95 percent of the American; 66 percent of Japanese rapists, 86 percent of American; 86 percent of Japanese robbers, 87 percent of American; 73 percent of Japanese thieves, 65 percent of American; and 50 percent of Japanese who committed bodily injury versus 74 percent of Americans who committed aggravated assault. With the exception of larceny, American courts are more likely than the Japanese to send people to prison. The supposition that a larger proportion of offenders go to prison in the United States than in Japan is further supported by the fact that a much larger proportion of the

11. Ministry of Justice, 1989, and *Sourcebook of Criminal Justice Statistics, 1988*, p. 622.

12. *White Paper on Crime, 1988*, p. 14.

13. Ibid., p. 17. These figures are for prison sentences that were not suspended. They are for 1986.

14. Bureau of Justice Statistics, *Bulletin: Felony Sentences in State Courts, 1986*, p. 2.

total population is in prison in the United States than in Japan, even allowing for differences in crime rates. The incarceration rate for Americans is 5 times greater than for Japanese (228 vs. 44.2 per 100,000), despite the fact that the serious crime rate is only 3.2 times as high.[15]

Recidivism is higher, therefore, in Japan, not because the criminal justice system is not effective, but because it is primarily the more serious offender who is sent to jail. Jails are a last resort in Japan; in the United States they are a generalized response.

Shaping official response in accordance with the background and demeanor of offenders, especially sincere repentance, is not unique to the police; it is a characteristic of the Japanese criminal justice system as a whole. Prosecutors, for instance, have almost unlimited discretion with respect to decisions to prosecute. The Code of Criminal Procedure states that prosecutors are to consider "character, age, and situation of the offender," as well as "conditions subsequent to the commission of the offense."[16] In the past few years, prosecutors have chosen not to prosecute about 36 percent of the suspects submitted to them for commission of serious Penal Code offenses. In about 81 percent of these cases, the decision was based on criminological reasons, not insufficiency of evidence.[17] The more serious the offense, of course, the more likely it is that prosecution will take place. In murder cases, prosecution is more or less mandatory. Appeals against a prosecutor's decision not to prosecute are possible but rarely made.[18]

Criminological considerations affect prosecution in the United States

15. *White Paper on Crime, 1988,* p. 108, and *Sourcebook of Criminal Justice Statistics, 1988,* p. 613. Figures for 1987. For the calculation on respective serious crimes rates, see chapter 1.

16. Article 248 reads: "If, after considering the character, age, and situation of the offender, the gravity of the offense, the circumstances under which the offense was committed, and the conditions subsequent to the commission of the offense, prosecution is deemed unnecessary, prosecution need not be instituted." Japan, Ministry of Justice, *Criminal Statutes,* vol. 1.

17. The proportion of cases in which prosecution was not made in 1987 was 9.2 percent for all offenses; 34.8 percent for all Penal Code offenses excluding bodily injury or death resulting from traffic-related professional negligence; 19.3 percent for special law offenses; and 3.2 percent for traffic offenses. *Summary of the White Paper on Crime, 1988,* pp. 15 and 96.

18. Committees composed of eleven private persons are empowered to hear appeals from a decision not to prosecute and to recommend prosecution if necessary. Law for the Inquest of Prosecution, 1948. Aggrieved persons or third parties may complain to the courts if they are dissatisfied with a prosecutor's decision, and the court can order prosecutions, appointing its own lawyer as prosecutor. In 1986 there were 1,248 appeals against decisions not to prosecute out of about 400,000 such decisions. Ministry of Justice, 1989.

as well, but it is impossible to tell how much. By and large, American prosecutors are not required to prosecute, even when evidence is sufficient for conviction. Estimates of how many cases are actually dismissed are very impressionistic. A common figure is 50 percent.[19] If the proportion is so high, and therefore larger than in Japan (50 percent as opposed to 35 percent), it is possible that relative to all offenders the proportion in which criminological considerations play a role in determining prosecution is as great as in Japan.

In both countries the behavior of the offender also influences the severity of the sentences handed down by the courts. Whether there is a significant difference in the operation of this factor between the two countries cannot be determined without comparing statutory provisions against actual sentences and without knowing what was going on in the minds of the judges. It is clear, however, that sentences in general are lighter in Japan than in the United States. Not only are fines awarded more commonly but prison sentences are significantly shorter. In 1987, 40 percent of Japanese prison sentences for Penal Code offenses were for less than one year. Ninety-six percent were for three years or less.[20] In the United States in 1987, the average prison sentence for felony convictions in state courts was over six years.[21] Like many states in the United States, Japan has a death penalty. It is imposed exclusively for murder.[22] In both countries defendants who cooperate and confess their guilt are treated more leniently than those who demand trial and are then convicted.[23] Similarly, prior criminal record also influences sentences.

In both Japan and the United States, therefore, prospects for rehabilitation are assessed and allowed to affect the response of the criminal justice system. What is striking about Japan is the extent to which individuation has been accepted explicitly, certainly much more than in the United States where the word "rehabilitation" has a bad odor among the general populace. In Japan, police officers, prosecutors, and judges

19. Frank W. Miller, *Prosecution* (Boston: Little, Brown, 1969), chap. 8. Donald M. McIntyre and David Lippman, "Prosecutors and Early Disposition of Felony Cases," *American Bar Association Journal* (December 1970), pp. 1154–59.

20. *Summary of the White Paper on Crime, 1988,* p. 99.

21. *Sourcebook of Criminal Justice Statistics, 1988,* p. 562. The average sentence imposed by U.S. district courts in 1987 was five years and three months. *Sourcebook,* p. 558.

22. Penal Code, Articles 199–200.

23. Japanese evidence comes from the testimony of prosecutors. U.S. data are very clear on this point. Mark Cunniff, *Sentencing Outcomes in 28 Felony Courts, 1985* (Washington, D.C.: Bureau of Justice Statistics, 1987), p. 26; Alfred Blumstein, et al., *Research on Sentencing: The Search for Reform* (Washington, D.C.: National Academy Press, 1983), vol. 1, p. 18.

openly discuss whether the attitude of an offender and his personal social environment are conducive to improved behavior. The norms governing differentiated responses, whether by police officers or others, are matters of explicit consideration, thereby ensuring that actions of the system are consistent with the public's view of justice.

The legitimation of discretionary uses of authority by police officers enhances their identification with the rest of the criminal justice system. Appropriate to their tasks, they make choices in terms of the same goals and values that shape decisions at higher levels. The police are not aware of being subprofessionals to the extent that police officers are in the United States. This is an important reason why relations between police and courts, as well as police and prosecutors, are less hostile in Japan. American police officers bitterly and publicly assail prosecutors and courts for failing to support their efforts to curb crime. In a favorite word, they complain of being "handcuffed." Japanese detectives display less of this. The major impediments to criminal investigations which detectives cite are lack of resources and declining public cooperation. Though they can be pressed into discussing changes of legal procedure since World War II that have limited investigatory authority, there is no emotional intensity to the discussion. Criminal investigations have been made more difficult, but manageably so. Even though Japanese courts have authority to determine the proper application of police powers, acting in accordance with procedural safeguards very much like those in the United States, the police feel part of the same community of justice.

The Japanese police officer can devote so much more time to considering appropriate treatment because he need devote less time, compared with American police, to determining guilt. The reason for this is that the characteristic stance of a Japanese confronting the police is submissiveness. More than simply being polite or deferential, Japanese are willing to admit guilt and to accept the consequences of their actions. The approved reaction of a suspect in the face of authority is compliance; he must not feign innocence or seek to avoid punishment. In an apt phrase, the suspect is not to act "like a carp on the cutting board." The offender places his fate in the hands of society's authoritative agents, cooperating with them in setting the terms of his reconciliation with the community. Japanese police officers who have dealt with American suspects—mostly around military bases—are shocked at their combativeness. Even when Americans are caught red-handed, say police officers, they deny their guilt. They display no contrition and immediately begin constructing a legal defense. They insist on talking to lawyers, remain uncommunicative, and act as if being accused is an infringe-ment of their civil rights. Japanese suspects readily sign interrogation records; Americans never do. From the Japanese viewpoint, Americans are unwilling to accept responsibility for wrongful actions.

Not all Japanese, of course, are submissive before the police. Some people talk back, though more rarely than in the United States, espe-cially if they feel that the police have not been respectful enough. When people are angry or frustrated they sometimes scold the police or threaten them with superior authority. Rudeness and verbal resistance comes most commonly from hardened street people, such as hoodlums and day laborers, drunks, and politicized students. The most common insults, apart from omitting "san" in "Omawari-san," are *pori-ko* and *zeikin dorobo*.[24] Many other people treat the police as objects of fun. This is most common among young people who have been drinking. For example, a young man suddenly intruded between two strolling police officers; he was bent over as if in pain and holding his crotch. He asked breathlessly if they knew where he could find a toilet. Then he straight-ened up quickly, laughed at the officers' surprise, and walked away with his friends.

The cooperativeness of the Japanese people with the police and pros-ecutors is indicated by one stunning fact: four-fifths of suspects are prosecuted without arrest. The great majority of suspects cooperate voluntarily in their own prosecution. In 1987, for example, 78 percent of all suspects for Penal Code and other serious crimes were examined by officials without being arrested.[25] Only 19 percent were held for longer than three days. In the United States, on the other hand, arrest is the beginning of a criminal case; it is the way in which prosecution is instigated. And arrest is tantamount to detention in jail, at least until a judge has heard the charge.

Of the relatively small number of Japanese suspects who are bound over for trial in district courts because they do not plead guilty and prosecution is not suspended, about 25 percent are released on their own recognizance and another 17 percent are granted bail. In effect, approximately 54 percent of suspects submitted for trial are detained.[26]

24. The literal meaning of *pori-ko* is "policeman despise"; it is insulting only by cus-tom. *Zeikin dorobo* means "tax robber."
25. *Summary of the White Paper on Crime, 1988*, p. 94. Prosecutors examined 481,154 people; 114,642 were arrested either by police or by prosecutors.
26. About 84 percent of Summary Court suspects are detained, with another 9 per-cent granted bail. *White Paper on Crime, 1988*, p. 104.

Most of these people are held for three months or less. In the United States, passage of the federal Bail Reform Act in 1966 has reduced the number of people held in jail pending trial, even though a far larger portion of American suspects still experience jail temporarily.[27] It is estimated that only 39 percent of people awaiting trial were held in jail in 1983 compared with 52 percent in 1967.[28]

The mark of accomplishment for a police force is the number of offenses known to the police in which a suspect is found and sent for prosecution. This is known as the clearance rate. American clearance rates are indicated by the proportion of crimes in which a person has been arrested—"cleared by arrest." The rate for serious crimes in the United States in 1987 was 20.9 percent.[29] If arrest figures were used to compute the Japanese clearance rate for all Penal Code offenses, the figure would be 26 percent. If, however, the clearance rate is based on the proportion of cases in which a suspect was submitted for prosecution, then the rate in 1987 was 59.8 percent.[30] The Japanese clearance rate for serious crimes similar to the American was 98 percent for homicide, 78 percent for robbery, 87 percent for rape, 93 percent for assault, and 60 percent for larceny.

The difference that a compliant population can make in the performance of a criminal justice system can be dramatically demonstrated by pulling together a few facts from each country. In Japan suspects are found by the police in a much larger proportion of offenses than in the United States—60 percent versus 21 percent.[31] In Japan 65 percent of all suspects are prosecuted. This means that prosecution is instituted in 39 percent of all offenses known to the police. Similar figures are unavailable for the United States. If 50 percent of all suspects are charged, as is the common opinion among experts in the United States, then 10.5 percent of offenses known to the police result in criminal prosecu-

27. They are released either on their own recognizance (ROR) or through bail.
28. Samuel Walker, *Sense and Nonsense About Crime,* 2d ed. (Pacific Grove, Calif.: Brooks/Cole, 1988), p. 54.
29. *Sourcebook of Criminal Justice Statistics, 1988,* p. 510. The clearance figure is based on the "index crimes" of murder and nonnegligent manslaughter, forcible rape, robbery, aggravated assault, burglary, larceny-theft, motor-vehicle theft, and arson. The clearance rate for violent crimes against persons was 47.4 percent and for felonious property crimes was 17.7 percent.
30. *White Paper on Police, 1988,* pp. 128–29.
31. This comparison favors the United States, since the clearance rate in Japan is based on all Penal Code offenses and in the United States only on seven of the most serious crimes. The American clearance rate for all crimes would, presumably, be somewhat lower than 20.9 percent.

tion. According to the best estimates, a larger proportion of prosecuted suspects admit their guilt in Japan than in the United States—95 percent versus 50 percent.[32] It follows, therefore, that admissions of guilt are obtained in 37 percent of known crimes in Japan, compared with about 5.3 percent in the United States. Actual convictions as a proportion of known crimes would be slightly higher than these percentages, since some suspects who do not plead guilty are found guilty by courts. The Japanese criminal justice system is almost seven times more efficient than the American in matching determinations of guilt to criminal offenses. The dividends from crime are considerably less assured in Japan than in the United States.

Japanese offenders are more willing than American to throw themselves on the mercy of police officers, prosecutors, and judges because reconciliation is considered a more important objective of legal processes than vindication. This would seem to be true whether the contest is between an individual and the state—a criminal prosecution—or between two private individuals—a civil action. It has often been noted that private suits between individuals are much less common in Japan than in the United States.[33] Moreover, Japanese courts have long encouraged conciliation rather than adjudication, so that a high proportion of civil suits are really disguised negotiations.[34] Some observers are convinced that the relative absence of legal conflict is a product not of attitudinal preference but rather of institutional failure.[35] Court dockets are enormously crowded, delays are very long, remedies are limited, and lawyers are not plentiful. The issue to underscore, then, is that both cul-

32. Ministry of Justice, 1989, and Samuel Walker, *Sense and Nonsense About Crime,* p. 125. The American figure might be higher. In federal district courts, 1987, 71 percent of suspects plead guilty. *Sourcebook, 1988,* p. 540. A study of court proceedings in 28 U.S. cities in 1981 found that guilty pleas varied from 26 to 82 percent of cases brought by public prosecutors. The median was 63 percent. Barbara Boland with Ronald Sones, INSLAW, Inc. *Prosecution of Felony Arrests,* 1981 (Washington, D.C.: Bureau of Justice Statistics, 1986).

33. Hideo Tanaka, "The Role of Law in Japanese Society: Comparisons with the West," University of British Columbia *Law Review* 19, no. 2 (1985): 375–88, estimated that in 1981–82 California had a per capita rate of civil litigation nine times higher than Japan, and California is not an especially litigious American state. See also Dan F. Henderson, "Law and Political Modernization in Japan," in *Political Development in Modern Japan,* ed. Robert E. Ward (Princeton: Princeton University Press, 1968).

34. Henderson, p. 453.

35. John O. Haley, "The Myth of the Reluctant Litigant," *Journal of Japanese Studies* 4, no. 2 (1978): 359–90, and "Sheathing the Sword of Justice in Japan: An Essay on Law Without Sanctions," *Journal of Japanese Studies* 8, no. 2 (1982): 265–81. See also Susan Chira, *New York Times,* 1 September 1987, A4.

tural and institutional factors may be at work in explaining the practices of Japanese justice.[36]

That courts are institutions where one submits rather than fights is indicated by the small number of lawyers in Japan. There are twenty-seven times as many lawyers per capita in the United States as in Japan.[37] In Japan there are eighteen times as many police officers as lawyers; in the United States there are almost exactly the same number of lawyers as police. The small number of lawyers in Japan, like the absence of civil litigation, may be a result of institutional decisions rather than popular preferences. Training for a professional career in law, whether to become a lawyer, a judge, or a prosecutor, is monopolized by the Research and Training Institute of the Ministry of Justice. Many more young men and women aspire to such careers than are allowed places.[38]

Japanese criminal courts act as though truth is to be discovered through the diligence and fair-mindedness of the officers of the court rather than through a contest of two more or less equal parties. Though adversarial features were introduced into the criminal justice system by the American Occupation authorities, the ethos of the system remains inquisitorial. Justice involves more than determining guilt; it involves shaping legal processes to fit particular circumstances and personalities of defendants. Japanese judges play an active role in trials, clarifying issues and questioning counsel as well as witnesses. They even allow new charges to be framed by prosecutors as the evidence unfolds.

Conflict generally in Japanese society, whether with peers or superiors, is not met with assertiveness, argument, and protestation. Aggrieved individuals "bend like the willow," hoping that unprotesting compliance will generate sympathy and generosity. If this fails, and a dispute must be submitted to outside mediation, such restraint will be read as unusual good faith. Americans are often misled by the Japanese response to conflict. Finding that the Japanese smile when Americans think they should be angry, Americans conclude that no disagreement exists. They then further strain relations by pressing ahead, ignoring, from the Japanese point of view, both the substantive difference and the gesture of trust. Japanese who have lived in the United States report

36. Robert J. Smith, *Japanese Society: Tradition, Self, and the Social Order* (Cambridge: Cambridge University Press, 1983).

37. Japan had 13,339 lawyers in 1989, whereas the United States had 655,191 in 1985. Ministry of Justice and *Statistical Abstract of the United States*, 1989, p. 178.

38. In 1987 about 30,000 people competed for 500 places in the Ministry of Justice's school. Proportional to population, as many Japanese compete for this examination as Americans do for the Bar Examination. Haley and Chira.

being hurt repeatedly when they tried to meet disagreement in the Japanese way. Adopting a submissive posture, they have found their wishes ignored and their feelings bruised. Americans do not establish respect in others by going the last mile to avoid friction. Rather, they show that they are alert and can act forcefully, that they cannot be taken advantage of. Americans continue to march under the famous colonial flag that shows a coiled snake and the motto "Don't Tread on Me."[39]

Japanese police officers and prosecutors not only expect suspects to confess their misdeeds, they act in such a way as to reinforce that norm. If submission is judged to be sincere, the appropriate response of persons in authority is to display warmth and understanding and to ease the transition back to rectitude. Repentance, indicating compliance with authority, has the effect of generating *ninjo* in officials, thereby lessening the severity of punishment.[40] Consequently, when a suspect is obdurate, police and prosecutors indicate displeasure; when a suspect cooperates, they feel compelled to be generous. Undoubtedly, therefore, an element of calculation lies behind the compliant behavior of Japanese suspects. They have been raised to expect that submission mitigates punishment. Japanese mothers always teach their children to say "Gomen nasai"—a profound "I'm sorry"—whenever they do wrong, the understanding being that the child who says "Gomen nasai" will not be punished.[41] Though American parents reward honest admissions of error too, they often insist as well on punishment—"to teach them a lesson."[42] So guilt is admitted in Japan for a variety of reasons: because it is a moral imperative, but also because it is a quid pro quo for leniency.

In both Japan and the United States the characteristic stance of offenders in the face of authority complements the role-definition of the police. An American accused by a police officer is very likely to respond, "Why me?" A Japanese more often says, "I'm sorry." The American shows anger, the Japanese shame.[43] An American contests the accusa-

39. The so-called Gadsden Flag, after Colonel Christopher Gadsden of South Carolina; it was also used by the commander-in-chief of the fledgling American navy.

40. The psychology of this relationship is discussed by L. Takeo Doi, "*Amai:* A Key Concept for Understanding Japanese Personality Structure," in *Japanese Culture,* ed. Robert J. Smith and Richard K. Beardsley (Chicago: Aldine, 1962), pp. 132–39.

41. See Edwin O. Reischauer, *The Japanese Today* (Cambridge: Harvard University Press, 1988).

42. Since we know that Japanese parents do punish, research is needed on the circumstances in which submissiveness mitigates punishment of children.

43. As H. Minami points out in *The Psychology of the Japanese People* (Tokyo: Tokyo University Press, 1971), p. 5, the role of police is to scold; the role of the public is to apologize.

tion and tries to humble the police officer; a Japanese accepts the accusation and tries to kindle benevolence. In response, the American police officer is implacable and impersonal; the Japanese officer is sympathetic and succoring. Both sets of police adopt the tactics of the other only when their initial gambit fails: unable to overawe, American police officers feign personal sympathy; unable to gain submission, Japanese officers begin to shout.

Japanese police officers are not viewed by the community simply as agents of law. They possess enormous moral authority. Their role transcends, though it must not contradict, legal prescriptions. A Japanese police officer is more than a specialist in catching criminals and advising about crime prevention. He acts with the aura of a teacher shaping conduct to conform to community standards. There is a space between legality and propriety. Japanese police officers are not afraid to trespass there, their characteristic action being to exhort and admonish. They continually deliver lectures on duty and morality, often in place of making an arrest or issuing a citation. For instance, a young man caught driving considerably above the speed limit was let go with a warning after the patrol officer, no older than the driver, lectured him quietly in front of his friends about protecting the lives of people riding with him. A middle-aged man who had pushed his way into a neighbor's house to rebuke the son for dating his niece was admonished by a senior patrol officer for playing the role of police officer. A teenage boy who omitted the "Sumimasen"—"Pardon me for bothering you"—in talking to a police officer was given a lecture on manners. A drunk was told to "act like a Japanese man" rather than like a derelict. A street-tough was asked rhetorically what kind of a Japanese he was if he was ashamed to admit his occupation.

The moral authority of the police derives from their affiliation with government generally. The prestige of government servants is very high, and police are accepted as part of this establishment. The function of government, according to Japanese political culture, is to lead, shape, and tutor. Government is viewed as an in-dwelling function of society; it is inseparable from the existence of community. In Anglo-Saxon countries, on the other hand, government and society are distinct. Government is created by decision of communities; its authority rests on the adequacy of representation and adherence to fundamental principles. In the United States, law has authority only so long as it is just. By extension, agents of government are to be obeyed only when they reflect the will of the people. American police officers have the authority of man-made law; Japanese police have the authority of unspoken moral consensus. Government is more exalted in Japan because it is not considered an artifact, a creation of human design.

Admonitions are effective constraints on behavior in Japan because the opinions of police officers are weighty with community censure. Police need rely less on explicit sanctions; it is sufficient to indicate that a person has gone beyond the pale. Japanese visitors to the United States are often surprised at the explicitness with which threats of punishment are spelled out: fines for the return of library books, for walking on the grass, for littering, for parking illegally. Through Japanese eyes Americans appear as penalty-calculating machines, computing the risks of illegal actions. In Japan prohibitions are stated publicly but penalties are hidden. The threat of exclusion from the community, not the severity of formal punishment, is the basis of conformity. An individual's sense of well-being, indeed his very identity, depends on his place within groups—family, workplace, school, neighborhood, and nation.[44] Standing alone is intolerable, a lesson first implanted in childhood. Observers of Japanese culture have noted that youngsters are punished by being put outside the house; American children are punished by being kept in.[45] American mothers chase their children around the block to get them to come home; Japanese mothers are chased by their children so as not to be left behind. Children are rarely left with babysitters. Safety consists of being within the family circle; outside are strangers, uncertainty, dread.[46]

The feeling that security consists in acceptance is transferred from the family to other groups, allowing them to discipline members through the fear of exclusion. This accounts for the ability of the police to discipline their own members so effectively.[47] By enwrapping the officer in family-like solicitude, the organization raises the psychological costs of expulsion. Similarly, a Japanese accepts the authority of law as he would the customs of his family. The police officer is analogous to an elder brother who cautions against offending the family. In both situa-

44. Ruth Benedict, *The Chrysanthemum and the Sword*, p. 288: "All his life ostracism is more dreaded than violence. He is allergic to threats of ridicule and rejection, even when he merely conjures them up in his mind."

45. Ezra F. Vogel, *Japan's New Middle Class*, chap. 12.

46. Benedict, chap. 12.

47. See the discussion in chapter 4.

tions, the specter of separation is raised. Wrongdoing impinges directly on the individual's sense of security. As a result, Japanese have a heightened "sense of the fatefulness of their antisocial impulses."[48]

Awareness that they are a moral rather than just a legal force makes Japanese police officers sensitive to the intangible effects of what they do. They do not need to be told that their actions influence attitudes toward law, government, democracy, and ethical conduct. They recognize that how they do something is as important as what they do. Knowing they are more than legal instruments, they accept the obligation of moral tutors to be upright in word and deed. By contrast, American police officers are ambivalent about claiming a social role for themselves apart from the prescriptions of law. They are curiously self-denying. They want to believe they have moral authority, yet they shrink from the responsibilities entailed. Blamed so much as it is, they pretend to be no more than technicians mechanically applying the law. They seek to protect respect by acting as if their role was very circumscribed. Since it is not in fact, their pretense leads to neglect of their more diffuse responsibilities.

More than moral authority is brought to bear on Japanese who are suspected of crimes. Compared with Americans, they have many fewer procedural protections. Japanese law allows suspects to be detained for up to twenty-three days before a decision to prosecute is made. In effect, suspects may be detained during investigation. The Japanese police on their own authority may detain a suspect for forty-eight hours; the suspect is then turned over to the public prosecutors, who have twenty-four hours to apply to a judge for a detention order. Judges can then authorize as much as twenty days further detention under supervision of the prosecutors before a charge is filed.[49] All of this is in sharp contrast to the United States where suspects may be detained for only twenty-four hours unless a charge has been filed before a court.

In each of the past few years, between ninety and a hundred thou-

48. For this excellent phrase, I am indebted to Christie W. Kiefer, "The Psychological Interdependence of Family, School, and Bureaucracy in Japan," *American Anthropologist*, February 1970, p. 69. Great material cost is also involved in being excluded in Japan because occupational mobility is quite low. A worker commonly stays with the same employer throughout his working life. Occupational mobility is thus intertwined with penitence, rehabilitation within groups, and the forcefulness of informal sanctions.

49. Code of Criminal Procedure, Articles 203–208. The twenty days is granted in two successive periods of ten days. Detention can be extended for five more days if the crime committed is extraordinarily serious.

sand people have been held beyond forty-eight hours.[50] Most are detained for less than ten days.[51] Judicial approval of requests for investigative detention is virtually automatic, as less than 1 percent are denied.[52] Suspects are held in jails attached to police stations that are curiously referred to as "substitute prisons" (*daiyo kangoku*). Under Japanese law, people who are jailed for more than forty-eight hours or bound over for trial or sentenced to prison become the responsibility of the national corrections bureau, which is run by the Ministry of Justice. However, the law explicitly allows such people to be held in police jails when normal prisons are filled or inconveniently far away from where prosecution is to take place. The jails then become "substitute prisons," even though they are run by the police. And the fact is that the Ministry of Justice has never built enough prisons to house the large number of persons arrested and not yet tried, as well as the small number of people sentenced to incarceration.

When people are held beyond forty-eight hours in "substitute prisons" they may not apply for bail. Although the Japanese constitution guarantees the right of bail except in a few limited circumstances, bail is granted only after charges have been filed; it is not available during investigative detention.[53] Because a key purpose of precharge detention is to induce confession, confession in effect becomes a condition for bail. This is not the case in the United States, where the sole purpose of bail is to ensure that the suspect will appear in court. Cooperativeness cannot become a condition for bail.

Furthermore, during detention in "substitute prisons" access to legal counsel is wholly at the discretion of the police and prosecutors. Although access to counsel is a constitutional right in Japan, prosecutors

50. *White Paper on Crime,* yearly, and Karen Parker and Etienne Jaudel, *Police Cell Detention in Japan: The Daiyo Kangoku System* (San Francisco: Association of Humanitarian Lawyers, February 1989), p. 12.

51. In 1985, for example, 62.5 percent were held for less than ten days. Ministry of Justice, 1989.

52. In 1987, 91,966 requests were made, 143 denied. *White Paper on Crime, 1989,* p. 94. During the last twenty years the rate of approval has been increasing, from 95 percent in 1969 to the current rate, in excess of 99 percent. Lawrence Repeta, "Introduction to the First Five Issues of 'Citizens Human Rights Reports' by the Japan Civil Liberties Union," *Law in Japan* (1987) 20:20.

53. Between 1984 and 1986, about 18 percent of suspects undergoing trial were released on bail. Of the 82 percent held in jail, about 22 percent were held one month or less, 60 percent for three months or less, and 20 percent longer. *White Paper on Crime, 1989,* p. 103.

may set conditions, often on the advice of investigating officers.[54] Defense attorneys must travel in person to prosecutors' offices to obtain written permission, but police staff at the "substitute prisons" may deny access on various expediential grounds, such as the prisoner's being interrogated, moved, asleep, bathing, and so forth. Nor may prisoners refuse to be questioned unless their attorneys are present. This is a far cry from the American practice of requiring police to recite Miranda warnings to all persons arrested, advising them of the right to be silent and to the presence of legal counsel. Japanese suspects do have the right to remain silent, and they must be so advised by police when they are detained or brought before a prosecutor.[55]

These powers of detention and interrogation in Japan, which are so extraordinary by American standards, have become a highly publicized issue during the 1980s. Prompted by several celebrated reversals of conviction, some of persons sentenced to death and kept on death row for many years, members of the defense bar have published dramatic descriptions of conditions in the substitute prisons.[56] These have prompted international investigation as well as submissions to the U.N. Commission on Human Rights. The fundamental charge is that suspects are coerced into giving confessions through a combination of isolation from outside support, prolonged and harassing interrogation, demeaning physical conditions, and uncertain access to food, sleep, and bathing.[57]

All observers, including police and prosecutors, agree that the primary purpose of detention is to obtain a confession. "Confession is king," as a police training manual puts it, because it fits moral imperatives of Japanese society. Also, of course, it has some powerful instrumental effects. Confession powerfully influences whether prosecution will be suspended, as well as the onerousness of punishment after con-

54. Code of Criminal Procedure, Article 39.

55. Code of Criminal Procedure, Book II, passim. The right of protection against self-incrimination is guaranteed by the constitution, Article 38. The requirement to advise people of their rights has been provided by legislative action.

56. The death-sentence cases overturned on grounds of coerced confessions were of Menda, imprisoned for 30 years, Saitagawa, 31 years, and Matsuyama, 22 years. *New York Times*, 20 September 1988, p. A4.

57. Futaba Igarashi, "Crime, Confession and Control in Contemporary Japan," *Law in Context* 2 (1984): 1–30; also "Report on How Detainees Are Treated in Japan's Substitute Prisons," from *Irasuto Kangoku Jiten* (privately printed); and The Joint Committee of the Three Tokyo Bar Associations for the Study of the Daiyokangoku System, *Forced Confessions: How the Japanese Police Forced Thirty Innocent People to Confess* (Tokyo: no date).

viction, but it cannot affect the gravity of the charge.[58] Plea bargaining is not permitted under Japanese law. Confessions also help investigators in collecting evidence needed for successful prosecution, which is essential because a person cannot be convicted in Japan solely on the basis of a confession. Japanese police and prosecutors also cannot offer immunity from prosecution in exchange for cooperation. Investigators and prosecutors argue that they need longer periods of controlled detention in order to obtain the kind of information that American officials could obtain by horse-trading.

The effect both of Japanese confessions and of American plea bargains is to reduce the number of cases that go to trial. But there is a huge moral difference. Plea bargaining, as the name suggests, is a cost-benefit transaction; it is a mutually advantageous trade between the offender and the system. It involves no acknowledgment of moral guilt on the part of the offender. Indeed, it obscures guilt because the suspect is confessing to something less than what was done. The law connives with the offender in misrepresenting the nature of the offence. On the other hand, a plea bargain is an open transaction publicly validated by the judge. The suspect knows clearly what is exchanged. In a Japanese confession, leniency and fair-dealing must be taken on faith and on whatever conditions the prosecutor deems fit. The American plea bargain may seem crass, but it opens the process of individuation to public inspection.

The extent of intimidation of suspects during detention in the "substitute prisons" is hard to know. Although two international lawyers, working with the cooperation of the police as well as the Ministry of Justice, said that "Japan engages in widespread physical and psychological torture, cruel, inhuman and degrading treatment," the number of stories that have surfaced is scarcely more than a handful. Nor does it appear that it is the poor who are particularly at risk. Precharge detention is used on people who willfully commit crimes, whose acts seem brazen and calculated. Therefore, the most notorious cases of detention pressure have involved crimes allegedly committed for political purposes, like the bombings by radical students in the early 1970s. Gangsters fall into the same category. But so too do white-collar criminals, especially if they might destroy evidence pertinent to prosecution. Leading figures in the Recruit scandal in 1989 were invariably detained

58. John Haley, "Sheathing the Sword of Justice in Japan," p. 270.

for the full twenty-three days, despite having been pillars of the political and business worlds.

The coercion that is applied is not often physical, the notorious "third degree." While credible cases of physical coercion have emerged, pressure more commonly takes the form of isolation, lack of privacy, interrupted sleep, and complete dependence on custodial staff. Because the compulsion to confess is so strong in Japan, the notion of improper pressure is very subtle. Interrogators may provide a cup of tea, but special food would be regarded by the courts as an unfair inducement. Offering a cigarette is probably all right, say police interrogators, but they would think twice about it. In one case a confession was judged to be involuntary because, among other things, the chief of the police station visited the suspect in his bath and undertook to wash his back for him. The court thought this created too strong an obligation on the suspect to confess.[59]

At the same time, one does not want to minimize a situation where the potential for impropriety is both unlimited and secret. The Japanese criminal justice system has power over suspects that is unique among the world's industrial democracies.

After lengthy negotiations among police, prosecutors, and the defense bar about the problem of "substitute prisons," the government proposed legislation that will place "substitute prisons" under the regulation of the correctional authorities of the Ministry of Justice, prohibit their use for the incarceration of convicted persons, which was rare in any case, and gradually reduce the "substitute prison" capacity in police stations in favor of Ministry of Justice facilities. The major change, therefore, is in custodial responsibility for the detainees: it will be transferred from the police to personnel of the Ministry of Justice. From an American perspective, this seems an anemic solution. Although some zealous members of the bar wanted immediate transfer of suspects out of police facilities after forty-eight hours, there seems to be no support either inside or outside of government for the abolition of precharge detention, assured visitation rights of family and defense counsel, expansion of the number of lawyers so that counsel was more readily available, inspection of detention facilities by "jail visitors," or enactment of legal obligation to inform suspects repeatedly of their constitu-

---

59. In the celebrated Matsukawa case, on appeal to the Supreme Court. See Chalmers Johnson, *Conspiracy at Matsukawa* (Berkeley and Los Angeles: University of California Press, 1977).

tional rights. Furthermore, there seems to be little concern that the Ministry of Justice, which is responsible for prosecutions, might share a community of interest with the police. Since confessions must be made before a public prosecutor in order to be introduced into court, prosecutors can hardly have been unaware of past abuses committed in "substitute prisons."

The lack of enthusiasm for abolishing the precharge detention system, even among the radical bar, demonstrates that the system fits deep-seated attitudes toward authority. Precharge detention is an opportunity for moral suasion to be applied to erring individuals. Pressure to confess is only partly to obtain convictions. More important, it is applied to teach, to humble, to extract contrition and repentance.[60] Shouting and hectoring, then, are to be seen not as an abuse of authority, but as the frustration legitimate authority might feel in the face of pigheaded persistence in deviant and self-destructive behavior. It is what parents do when they are at their wits end with ill-behaved children. The precharge detention period is an opportunity for police and prosecutors to act like authority figures throughout Japanese society: to require deference, in the form of an acknowledgment of error, as a condition of acceptance back into society. Even less than in the United States, the Japanese suspect is not innocent until proven guilty. Arrest is tantamount to conviction, which is shown by the media practice of referring to suspects, even very prominent ones, by their surnames without the addition of the respectful suffix "san."

The primary purpose of Japanese criminal justice, unlike American, is not to exact punishment. Its actions are symbolic, indicating social exclusion. In psychological terms, the system relies on positive as well as negative reinforcement, emphasizing loving acceptance in exchange for genuine repentence.[61] An analogue of what Japanese police want the offender to feel is the tearful relief of a child when confession of wrongdoing to parents results in an understanding laugh and a warm hug. Japanese officers want to be known for the warmth of their care rather than the strictness of their enforcement. As one perceptive observer has writ-

60. Walter Ames, who wrote an excellent book on the Japanese police entitled *Police and Community in Japan* (Berkeley and Los Angeles: University of California Press, 1981), once characterized the role of the Japanese police as "humbling machines," the better to teach deference to moral order. Private communication.

61. The power of this approach has been explored by John Braithwaite in his excellent book *Crime, Shame and Reintegration* (Cambridge: Cambridge University Press, 1989).

Chart 1

VARIABLES	JAPAN	UNITED STATES
I. Police		
1. Discretion	Legitimated	Suspect
2. Authority	Moral	Legal
3. Enforcement	Individuated	Categorized
4. Relations with rest of criminal justice system	Collegial	Antagonistic
II. Sanctioning process		
1. Sanctions	Informal, not explicit	Formal, explicit
2. Outcomes	Repentance	Punishment
3. Approved behavior	Confession	Plea-bargaining
4. Agency	Community	Government
III. The individual		
1. Stance before authority	Submissive	Combative
2. Demeanor	Embarrassment	Anger
3. Character	Mutable	Immutable
IV. Political culture		
View of government	Organic	Artifactual

ten, "the Japanese law-enforcement system does not apply punishment to fit the crime, but rather to fit the demeanor of the culprit after the crime."[62]

The discussion in this chapter has shown that the behavior of the police is related in subtle ways to general patterns of value and behavior. Because analysis has been far-ranging, a summary is in order. Police behavior meshes in particular with views about the mutability of character, the nature of government, the utility of various kinds of sanctions, and the role of authority. The aspects of police behavior and culture that have been discussed are listed in Chart 1. Each aspect constitutes a dimension of variation, and the position of Japan and the United States with respect to each has been characterized.

Though the chart suggests it, Japan and the United States are not the obverse of each other. Dichotomization exaggerates differences; varia-

---

62. Karel van Wolferin, *The Enigma of Japanese Power* (New York: Alfred A. Knopf, 1989), p. 88.

tion is actually a matter of degree. The crucial point is not that countries differ. Of course they do. What is instructive is the patterns in the variation peculiar to each country. Variation along one dimension reinforces, or undermines, variation along another dimension. The articulations of police behavior, or any other feature, conform to as well as support the configuration of other parts. Criminal justice systems are not made of interchangeable parts.

8

The Nation and the Police

A police force is more than an organization; it is an institution. It exists within a larger human community whose customary views about what is appropriate shape what the organization does. These views constitute a police force's normative environment, and they vary from society to society. So do the mechanisms whereby a community imposes its vision on the police. In some places the community regulates certain aspects of police behavior directly; in others only diffuse social controls operate. This too is a matter of institutional tradition. Police officers themselves are children of the community. They share inherited views about what is proper for police to do, though their views are sometimes modified as a result of experience within the organization. In order to understand why a police force behaves in distinctive ways, it is essential to examine what the community by tradition expects the police to be. In short, what are the traditions of a community with respect to the relations of the police with the community?

The institutional traditions of the police in Japan and the United States differ substantially with respect to three key features of any social organization—namely, its role, structure, and mode of external regulation. I shall examine each of these in turn, searching for what is distinctive in the institutional constraints on the police in each country. Then I shall examine the features of the Japanese police practice that the United States might reasonably adopt.

The role that the Japanese police are expected to play in society is much more ramified and less well defined than the American. While fundamental to the role of both is maintenance of order and the curbing of deviance, they have contrasting relations to processes of explicit social change. The Japanese police are expected to assist actively in inculcating values entailed by the community's vision of what it wants to be. They have a teaching function as well as a legal brief. Japanese police have a positive orientation toward the polity. American police, on the other hand, have a negative orientation. They are not viewed as an active agency shaping social development. At best their function is prophylactic, to maintain conditions suitable to the performance of formative acts by others. A diffuse role in politics is anathema; the only civic lesson they can reinforce is the importance of remaining passively within the injunctions of law, in effect, of being apolitical.

There have been two formative periods in the development of the modern Japanese police—the Meiji Restoration, especially the years 1872–1889, and the Allied Occupation, 1945–1952. In both periods, police development was informed by a clear vision of political objectives. Meiji statesmen saw the police as an instrument for creating a new nation. Along with schools, courts, and the military, the police were to be used to mold feudal Japan into a strong nation respected in the world. In addition to maintaining law and order, the police were to embody national ideals and instruct the people in the new political vision.[1] Speeches of police officials at the time are filled with words like "spirit," "dedication," and "virtue." American police forces, assuming modern form also in the nineteenth century, were created to deal with quite specific law-enforcement problems—urban riots, drunkenness, especially among immigrant groups, hooliganism, prostitution, and gambling. State police forces too, which began to be developed in the early twentieth century, were created not as part of a new political dispensation, but to enforce state laws that local communities were neglecting.[2] Instruction in civic lessons has historically been left to schoolteachers and to politicians. All that Americans expected of their police was vigorous and honest enforcement of the law.

The Allied Occupation after World War II also reformed the Japanese police in accordance with an explicit political vision. Like the Meiji

1. Shuichi Sugai, "The Japanese Police System," in *Five Studies in Japanese Politics*, ed. Robert E. Ward (Ann Arbor: University of Michigan Press, 1957), p. 2.

2. Bruce Smith, *Police Systems in the United States*, 2d ed. (New York: Harper and Row, 1960), pp. 147–54.

statesmen before them, Occupation officials were determined to change the political orientation of the Japanese people and they saw the police as an instrument for this purpose. The police were to be one of several demonstration projects in democracy. They had to be nonauthoritarian in manner, responsive to public opinion, restrained by constitutional rights, and accountable to local communities.[3] In contrast, efforts to reform the police in the United States have always been prompted by particular shortcomings of the police, either inefficient enforcement, especially of vice laws, or impropriety, such as corruption and brutality. It is one of history's delightful ironies that American officials during the Occupation, some of them experienced police officers, undertook to reshape Japanese police institutions with a sensitivity to general political objectives that had never been reflected in police reform in the United States. They became aware that police officers are more than enforcement technicians, that the actions of police officers can affect the moral basis of political community.

In Japan, determination of the character of the police has preceded specification of tasks; in the United States, specification of tasks has preceded concern with character. American police officers fulfill their responsibilities when they bring people into compliance with law; Japanese police officers seek more than compliance; they seek acceptance of the community's moral values. They are not merely the law's enforcers; they are teachers in the virtue of the law. The Japanese police have been given a moral mandate, based on recognition of their importance in shaping the polity; American police have been given legal instructions, and have been enjoined from straying beyond the law.

The structures of contemporary police organization in Japan and the United States also reflect distinctive historical traditions. Japan has a national police system, coordinated by the central government and standardized in operations. The United States has a radically decentralized system with little standardization and a marked lack of coordination. The Japanese police were created by an act of central initiative designed to consolidate national government.[4] They were formed from the top down—more accurately, the center out. By 1874 police affairs in every

3. In the words of Supreme Command Allied Powers (SCAP), "Police and Public Safety," p. 5, "These were not purely police problems, however, being but phases of the major occupation objective of a government responsible to the will of the people."

4. Eleanor D. Westney, *Imitation and Innovation: The Transfer of Western Organizational Patterns to Meiji Japan* (Cambridge: Harvard University Press, 1987); E. H. Norman, *Japan's Emergence as a Modern State* (New York: Institute of Pacific Relations, 1940),

prefecture except Tokyo were directed by governors appointed by the central government. A Police Bureau in the Ministry of Home Affairs coordinated police affairs nationally.[5] The Tokyo police became subordinate to the Home Ministry in 1886, superseding control by a semiautonomous local board.[6] The central government paid the salaries of all police officers above the rank of inspector and subsidized part of general expenditure.[7] Where the Japanese system is national by design, the American system is national by default. American police forces were created by action of autonomous local communities. Policing was considered an indispensable part of local government. Later state and national forces—such as state patrols and the Federal Bureau of Investigation—were established to supplement the law enforcement capabilities of local communities. In all cases police organizations sprang from existing units of government. They represented the elaboration of any government's function—namely, enforcement—not a decision to reorganize government in new structures.

Today in Japan command of police operations is vested in prefectural organizations. This makes forty-six police forces in Japan proper, plus Okinawa. The central government has no operational forces of its own; it can direct prefectural police operations only where there has been a declared state of national emergency.[8] The National Police Agency, which is located in Tokyo and is part of the national government, is entirely a staff organization devoted to planning, coordination, and supervision. It maintains a variety of facilities for the use of prefectural forces, such as criminal files, forensic laboratories, communications networks, and advanced training schools.

Though the National Police Agency cannot direct field operations, except with respect to clandestine intelligence-gathering, it has considerable power to shape police conduct and procedures. The National Police Agency's influence is exerted in several ways. First, it sets the cur-

p. 118; Roger F. Hackett, *Yamagata Arimoto in the Rise of Modern Japan, 1838–1922* (Cambridge: Harvard University Press), chaps. 2 and 3; Ruth Benedict, *The Chrysanthemum and the Sword* (Boston: Houghton Mifflin, 1946), chap. 4.

5. The Bureau was originally lodged in the Ministry of Justice, 1872, but was transferred to the Home Ministry in 1874.

6. Baron Kanetake Oura, "The Police in Japan," in *Fifty Years of New Japan*, ed. Count Shigenobu Okuma (London: Smith, Elder, 1905), pp. 282–83, Hidenori Nakahara, "The Japanese Police," *Journal of Criminal Law, Criminology, and Police Science* (November-December 1955), pp. 583–84.

7. Nakahara, pp. 583–84, and Sugai, *Five Studies*, pp. 1–4.

8. The Police Law, Articles 71–75.

ricula for all police schools, including recruit training schools run by each prefecture. The NPA maintains its own schools for training supervisory officers—sergeants and above. These are located in Tokyo and seven regional centers.

Second, though the size of prefectural police forces is determined by local ordinance, they must meet minimum standards established by the central government. This ensures that coverage is roughly the same from place to place.

Third, wage rates for police officers in each prefecture must conform to standards established by the National Police Agency. The NPA sets levels around which prefectural salaries may fluctuate. They vary within a range of about 15 percent.

Fourth, the national government makes financial contributions to prefectures to cover several categories of expenses connected with police operations. The national government is required by law to pay for all police schools, communications equipment, facilities for criminal identification and data collection, and the purchase and maintenance of all vehicles, boats, and arms. It must also pay for operations related to national public safety. By decision of the central governmnt, national funds are used to defray half of all construction costs and part of the cost of local police salaries.

Fifth, all officers with the rank of senior superintendent and above, wherever they may be stationed, are designated as national government employees and are paid out of central funds. They constitute a national corps of police administrators that may be rotated among the prefectures as the National Police Agency directs. There are two routes into this administrative elite. One is by promotion from the rank of patrol officer within a prefectural force. Most of these men continue to serve in the force to which they were recruited. The second is by direct appointment to the National Police Agency on the basis of having passed the national advanced public service examination.[9] These officers are paid by the central government throughout their careers except when they are on deputation to a prefectural force. They belong to what is called the "elite course." The top posts in most prefectures are reserved for them, with the result that the senior personnel are, by and large, not local men.[10]

9. They are recruited at the rank of assistant inspector but are very quickly promoted.

10. The practice of central appointment of senior personnel in the prefectures did not begin with the Police Law, 1954. The old Home Ministry appointed chiefs of police in every prefecture. The National Police Agency is merely following the tradition, with the

Japan has succeeded in standardizing performance while decentralizing command. In the United States, on the other hand, there are a greater number of autonomous commands relative to population and geographical extent, and the quality of policing varies enormously. Americans are so strongly attached to vigorous local government that attempts at standardization, even on a state basis, have met strong resistance. Most states have some law setting forth standards of police operations. Most deal only with standards for recruitment and training; they provide no mechanism for supervision. Standardization on a national basis, as in Japan, would be impractical given significant differences in scale. Japan is about the size of California; prefectures are the equivalent of American counties. The Japanese model is more appropriate to the states rather than the nation as a whole.[11]

The size of police jurisdictions in Japan and therefore the scale of force organization is much more rational than in the United States. Japan did not patch together a system of police coverage out of intensely jealous local government units. Impelled by a vision of a strong centralized government, Meiji statesmen were guided by administrative convenience. The average Japanese police force—one in each prefecture—contains on the average five thousand officers and covers about 2.5 million people. In the United States, there are about fifteen thousand police forces, each containing on the average about forty officers and covering sixteen thousand persons.[12] There are no overlapping jurisdictions in Japan, unlike the United States where city, county, and state police forces may have concurrent jurisdiction.

In American terms, the Japanese system is the equivalent of policing the United States exclusively by fifty state forces whose personnel are trained, paid, and organized identically and each of which is managed by the top graduates of Harvard or Stanford.

The costs of policing are affected by the scale of organization. It would be reasonable to expect that the Japanese have achieved lower

---

important modification that local public safety commissions may now veto appointments. The Police Law, Article 50.

11. Standardization is also being furthered in the United States through the mechanism of accreditation. Funded initially by a grant from the national government in 1979, the Commission on Accreditation of Law Enforcement Agencies, Inc., has developed standards for evaluating whether police departments have achieved appropriate standards of performance. By 1990 it had accredited 135 departments in the United States and Canada.

12. *Sourcebook of Criminal Justice Statistics, 1988,* pp. 78–79.

unit costs in providing coverage because of economies of scale of police forces and the absence of overlapping jurisdictions. This seems to be the case. Recognizing that fluctuating exchange rates make comparisons somewhat arbitrary, per capita costs of police coverage were lower in Japan than in the United States in 1989. At that time there was about one police officer for every 552 persons in Japan and one for every 429 in the United States.[13] Thus there were 22 percent more police per capita in the United States than in Japan. The per capita costs of policing in Japan were $156 and in the United States $195.[14] Americans paid 40 percent more per capita for police than the Japanese but got only 22 percent more coverage.

The Japanese, however, devote a larger share of national resources to policing than Americans do. They spend 0.76 percent of their gross national product on police, compared with 0.5 percent in the United States.[15] In per capita terms, however, the burden is greater on Americans: they spent 1.1 percent of per capita gross national product on police services, compared with 0.8 percent in Japan.

So far the measure of police output has been quantitative—the number of police officers and their cost per unit of population. If the quality of performance is considered—proportion of arrests to offenses, incidence of police corruption, accessibility of the police, cordiality of police-public relations—then the Japanese are getting a much better return than Americans are. At lower unit costs and lower costs per capita, they are obtaining a far superior performance. The United States, which has more police per capita, achieves less at a higher cost per officer.

The third difference in institutional tradition has to do with the way control is exerted by the community over the police. In the United States, the police, like any government agency, are accountable to elected political bodies. Americans fear the creation of police organizations that are immune from inspection and direction by elected representatives of the people. Politicians supervise the police directly. The

13. In 1988 there were approximately 221,000 police officers in Japan and 560,000 in the United States. *White Paper on Police, 1988*, p. 118, and *Sourcebook of Criminal Justice Statistics, 1988*, p. 78.

14. National Police Agency, 1989, and *Statistical Abstract of the United States, 1989*, p. 177, state and local government expenditures only. Based on an official exchange rate of 125 yen per dollar.

15. At an average rate of 125 yen per dollar, total police expenditures in Japan in 1988 were approximately $17.9 billion; in the United States in 1986 they were $22.7 billion. *White Paper on Police, 1988*, p. 120; *Sourcebook of Criminal Justice Statistics, 1988*, p. 14. Data on GNP come from the *Statistical Abstract of the United States, 1989*, p. 823.

disadvantages of this has been that politicians can be self-serving and irresponsible. American history is littered with cases of politicians using the police as a base of power or obtaining special favors from them in exchange for promotions and raises in pay. Reform efforts over the past one hundred years have tried to achieve political accountability while avoiding partisan intrusion. A variety of formal arrangements have been tried: direct election of senior police officers, supervision by elected bodies, appointment of nonpartisan regulating committees, state supervision of local forces, and appointment of senior officers by elected executive officials.[16] Today most police chiefs are appointed by an executive officer, usually an elected official, subject to confirmation by a representative assembly. Police forces are linked directly to politicians at the apex of the police hierarchy.

In Japan police officials are not accountable directly to politicians and never have been. From the Meiji Restoration until 1945 immediate supervision over the police was exercised by bureaucrats. Prefectural chiefs of police reported to governors appointed by the central government. National police affairs were coordinated through the Ministry of Home Affairs. The only politician involved was the home minister, quite removed from direct contact with uniformed officers. The Occupation abolished the powerful Home Ministry but kept a protective layer between police and elected officials—the public safety commissions.[17] Public safety commissions are composed of three to five members, depending on the size of the prefecture; members are appointed for fixed terms by the governor with the approval of the legislature.[18] Public safety commissions are hybrids, neither bureaucratic nor political, like regulatory agencies in the United States. Persons who have served in the police or the prosecutor's service within the preceding five years are ineligible for appointment.[19] A national public safety commission appointed by the prime minister and confirmed by the national

16. Smith, *Police Systems*, chap. 7; James F. Richardson, *The New York Police* (New York: Oxford University Press, 1970), chap. 9; Robert M. Fogelson, *Big-City Police* (Cambridge: Harvard University Press, 1977); Samuel Walker, *A Critical History of Police Reform* (Lexington, Mass.: D. C. Heath, 1977).

17. Contrary to what many Japanese think, the idea of public safety commissions does not appear to have originated with Americans. It came from the Katayama government in 1946, which suggested a three-member national public safety commission. SCAP, "Police and Public Safety," chaps. 2 and 3. There are appointed public safety commissions in some cities in the U.S., but they are not the rule.

18. The Police Law, Article 39. Commission members may be reappointed indefinitely.

19. There must be a balance among political party affiliations represented on a commission. The Police Law, Articles 9(3), 9(4), 41(3), 41(4), 41(5).

legislature is responsible through the National Police Agency for overall direction and coordination.[20] The public safety commissions have exclusive authority over the discipline and dismissal of all police officers. Prefectural chiefs are appointed and dismissed through coordinated action by local and national public safety commissions. Because Tokyo is the capital, it has a unique position in the system; the consent of the prime minister is required for a change in its chief of police.[21]

Although the public safety commissions have enormous residual power, they tend not to be very active. Their members are invariably elderly, male, and conservative politically. They are certainly friends of the police. The commissions meet once or twice a month, but their agenda is prepared by the police. Their influence is exerted by asking questions, thereby forcing the police to pay attention to new problems and to demonstrate that solutions are being implemented. Their supervision is relaxed, a matter of authority rather than power.[22]

Public safety commissions are not the only device for attenuating political pressure on the police. Mandated national standards for pay and size of local forces reduce dependence on local legislatures. Top administrative positions are filled with officers recruited nationally, paid by the central government, and nominated by the national public safety commissions. Local control can be exerted only through the prefectural public safety commission, which must be nonpartisan in composition. Prefectural forces are sufficiently large that personnel can be rotated through positions every two years. Officers cannot become too intimately involved with local communities. Because promotions are determined by the police organization itself, subject to approval by public safety commissions, there is nothing a local politician can do for a police officer. He controls neither money nor the prospects for advancement. Japanese police officers can afford to be confident and even condescending in their relations with politicians.

Japanese and Americans want their police to be responsive to community sentiment without becoming unprincipled. Reflecting different political traditions, they have chosen contrasting institutional arrangements for accomplishing this. Americans distrust bureaucratic govern-

---

20. The National Public Safety Commission is composed of five members plus a chairman who is a minister of state and therefore a cabinet official. This is the closest contact between police and politician that is allowed.

21. The Police Law, Article 55(4), and Articles 48, 49, 50.

22. For this reason the Japanese Community Party has long pressed for the election of members to public safety commissions.

ment and consider close supervision by politicians indispensable to liberty. Japanese readily accept bureaucratic government and consider intrusions by politicians dangerous to liberty because they are self-serving. Cultivation of the police by politicians is viewed as inappropriate and undesirable. On the other hand, the police sometimes play a significant role in politics by becoming candidates for office. Several prominent politicians, including former Prime Minister Nakasone, have used a career in the police as a stepping-stone to political office.[23]

Japanese police are insulated from politics because they, as well as the public more largely, are distinctly distrustful of it. In particular, they display a deep-seated suspicion of dissenting political opinion outside the mainstream. Ideology is the characteristic that police most often cite in explaining public cooperativeness, rudeness, or criticism. Ideological motivation is attributed to the few people who do not welcome the door-to-door household visits; to lawyers who investigate alleged abuses in "substitute prisons"; to scholars whose analysis suggests that the criminal justice system may not be working properly; and to journalists who write stories of police misbehavior. Although the constitution prohibits the denial of government employment on the basis of political belief or affiliation, the police screen applicants carefully for "antisocial" tendencies, which would be hard to distinguish from questionable political connections. Ideological orientation plays the same role in structuring the world for Japanese police that race does for American police. Ideology and race respectively are the features of human background that each group refers to in order to anticipate and explain interactions with the community.

The apprehensions of the police are not groundless. Undoubtedly the most dangerous work the police have faced since World War II are mass demonstrations organized by leftist political groups, as well as repeated incidents of terrorist bombings. President Eisenhower's visit to Japan was called off in 1960 because of paralyzing student demonstrations. During an upsurge of radical activity between 1968 and 1971, businesses were bombed, people were kidnapped, and the library of Tokyo University was occupied. In a second wave during 1974–75 there were 37 bombings of public facilities, injuring 432 and killing 14.[24] Narita International Airport was prevented from opening for several years and is still tightly secured against radical attack. Though vio-

23. In Japan former police officers run for political office, prosecutors rarely; in the United States prosecutors frequently do, police officers rarely.
24. *White Paper on Police, 1988,* chap. 1.

lent demonstrations have declined sharply since the mid-1970s, the police are concerned about ongoing links between "ultraleftist" groups in
Japan and international terrorism.[25] They were shocked into renewed
alertness in 1986 when terrorists fired rockets at the site of a summit
meeting of industrial democracies in central Tokyo.

To meet these recurrent outbreaks of violence and disorder, the police have developed highly skilled riot police—the *kidotai*—and maintain routine clandestine surveillance over political groups of both the
right and the left that might engage in violence. The National Police
Agency established a new counter-terrorism unit in April 1989 to monitor the activities of Japanese terrorists abroad. As a result of their surveillance, police estimate the number of "ultraleftists" at about thirty-
five thousand.[26] They also attribute approximately three hundred crimes
each year to right-wing political groups, involving four or five hundred
people.[27]

Justified or not, Japanese police are affected with a siege-mentality
with respect to radical political activity. American police have reacted
similarly in the past, as during the "Red Scare" after World War I or
during the Vietnam War and civil rights protests of the 1960s. But such
episodes are abnormal. American police are characteristically cynical
about politics but not frightened. Whereas Japanese police are insulated
from politics but preemptively alert to it, American police are regularly
affected by it but only reactively alert to it.

To summarize the discussion so far, we find the following differences
between the institutional traditions of the Japanese and the American
police. Police in Japan, though required not to act contrary to law, as-
sume diffuse social responsibilities and regulate themselves in accordance with standards of propriety shared with the community. They
have a tutelary position with respect to the public, which extends to
supervision of public morals and political activity. American police are
created to perform carefully specified tasks; the only legitimate im-

25. "Ultraleftist" refers to groups that split from the Communist Party in 1957 when
it adopted a policy of "peaceful revolution" as opposed to "armed struggle." The main
groups today are the Red Army Faction (Sekigun-ha) and the Revolutionary Communist
League-Core Faction (Chukaku-ha). Although the violence of demonstrations has certainly declined during the past fifteen years, it is worth noting that over an estimated five
million people joined various rallies in demonstrations in unexceptional 1987 to protest
against nuclear power, U.S. military operations, Narita Airport, and environmental hazards. *White Paper on Police, 1988*, p. 110.

26. *White Paper on Police, 1988*.

27. Ibid., p. 190.

pingement of the police on the community is what is detailed in law. They are instruments of law, not of diffuse community morality.[28] The best guarantee that this mandate is not exceeded is direct and vigorous supervision by elected officials, whose own conduct is their own responsibility, without monitoring by the police except in the most exceptional circumstances.

The American tradition is distinctive, certainly compared with the Japanese, and it has affected contemporary police practices in several ways. First, because only mandated actions are legitimate, the police are relatively insensitive to social effects flowing from authorized actions. Their denial of wider and more subtle impingement is self-protecting: police cannot be accused of failing to meet responsibilities they do not have. Second, operational requirements for performing particular tasks are the primary determinants of police behavior and organization. Tactical decisions shape strategy. Performance goals are defined primarily in terms of completing specific jobs, such as making arrests, regulating traffic, clearing drunks from the street, and solving sensational crimes. Preoccupied with concrete tasks, the police neglect development of an ethic supportive of underlying political and moral principles not specifically enjoined by law. Third, relying so extensively on external checks to ensure right behavior, police are not encouraged to develop a binding self-enforced disciplinary code. Discipline is accepted grudgingly, as an external demand, rather than pridefully as a condition of membership in a unique institution.

The fundamental argument of this book is that police institutions are shaped by social context. Police do not stand in isolation; they reflect society. The variety of circumstances that help to mold the police is very great. In searching for the roots of contrasting Japanese and American police practices, we have seen the importance of factors such as the following: social homogeneity, occupational mobility, the role of groups in developing personal identity, child-raising practices, sexual morality, deference to authority, and political philosophy. One implication of the

---

28. When James Q. Wilson and George L. Kelling proposed that police officers should enforce standards of public order and civility consonant with prevailing standards in different neighborhoods, Karl Klockars vigorously argued that this would lead to the police making up rules as they went and to egregiously unequal standards of law enforcement. The United States, Klockars feared, would return to "ass kicking" policing, which had been thoroughly discredited before the "professional era." James Q. Wilson, "Broken Windows," *Atlantic Monthly* (March 1982), and Karl B. Klockars, "Order Maintenance, the Quality of Urban Life, and Police: A Different Line of Argument," in *Police Leadership in America*, ed. William A. Geller (New York: Praeger, 1986), chap. 27.

conclusion that police behavior and social context are inextricably linked is that police practices may be difficult to import successfully from one country to another. Yet this would be tempting for Americans to do because Japan has such an enviable record of police efficiency and propriety. Can this be done? Specifically, what are the features of Japanese police practice that might be amenable to importation? Which, conversely, should not be attempted?

The short answer to how much might be imported from Japan to the United States is: a great deal more than might have been thought twenty years ago. The distinguishing feature of Japanese police practice, for which it is known worldwide, is the koban system—the delivery of police services to local communities from dispersed, fixed police posts, for the purpose of enhancing accessibility to the public for whatever problems they might have and to encourage the cooperative exchange of information. This is very much against the grain of American police practice, which deploys its uniformed personnel almost exclusively in patrol vehicles in order to maximize patrol coverage and rapid response in times of emergency. Yet there is no compelling reason of culture that koban cannot be used in the United States. Indeed, several cities, notably Detroit, Houston, and Santa Ana, have created neighborhood police stations in the past fifteen years with success and considerable public acclaim. Because of lesser population densities, it might be uneconomical to deploy police personnel everywhere in the United States in the koban fashion. But koban would be as appropriate as in Japan for the policing needs of American public-housing projects, or for high-density mixed commercial strips where there are many pedestrians, or in major shopping malls, or around transportation and commuting centers. Rather than being oriented almost entirely to the handling of radio-dispatched calls from the public, American police could experiment with deploying for involvement with communities according to local needs, but back this up with an overlay of rapid-response cars, as the Japanese do. This was in fact tried in Wilmington, Delaware, in the late 1970s.[29]

Foot patrols would certainly be welcomed by the public in the United States, who would recognize them as a return to an older, mythologized practice of neighborhood policing. So, too, would door-to-door visits. Although one might have thought Americans would re-

29. J. M. Tien, J. W. Simon, and R. C. Larson, *An Alternative Approach to Police Patrol: The Wilmington Split-Force Experiment* (Washington, D.C.: U.S. Department of Justice, Law Enforcement Assistance Administration, 1977).

sent unannounced visits, experiments with it in Houston, Detroit, Newark, and New York City have shown that the reaction of most people is not hostility but surprised delight. They are pleased to know that the police care enough to come around.[30] They are as keen as the police are to prevent crime before it happens by enhancing physical security or learning to take precautions in the routines of daily life. And inner cities, where relations between the public and the police are often strained, are exactly where response is best because those are also the areas that experience high crime and governmental neglect.

In short, the major impediment to importing the essence of the Japanese policing model is not the reaction of the American public, but rather the bureaucratic tradition of the police themselves. They could do these things if they wanted, which is not to say that making such a decision would be easy. But they need not hesitate because the American public will not stand for the changes. They will.

More difficult to import will be the managerial practices of Japanese policing, especially the development of a keen vocational sense that views policing as a high calling requiring tight internal discipline. Not only are Americans more reluctant than Japanese to trust self-regulating bureaucracies, but American police officers were raised like everyone else to distrust authority, to guard the perimeters of personal autonomy, and to be skeptical about moral crusades. Reform in this area is not a technical matter of efficiency or effectiveness, but touches on questions of personal identity and the salience of groups in human life. At the same time, some Japanese devices are being tried in American police forces, such as the development of explicit value statements and intensified training in the ethical dimensions of police work.

The United States may emulate the Japanese in providing professionally trained managers for senior executive positions, but it will not do so in the same way. Though more slowly than the Japanese, American police are learning the value of higher educational qualifications. They are also beginning to develop career tracks for people with managerial talent, although tradition is sharply against the Japanese custom of recruiting such people for immediate appointment at middle-rank levels. At the same time, the United States is moving much more quickly than the Japanese to utilize the training resources of universities and professional schools for its senior managers. The relative lack of clan-

30. See Anthony M. Pate et al., *Reducing Fear of Crime in Houston and Newark: A Summary Report* (Washington, D.C.: The Police Foundation, 1986), and Jerome H. Skolnick and David H. Bayley, *The New Blue Line* (Free Press, 1986).

nishness of American police, as well as their greater openness to outside observation, provides mechanisms for enhancing managerial capacity that would not be available to the Japanese. For the same reason, the United States may find it easier to appoint nonpolice to senior executive positions.

It is doubtful if American police have the capacity for regular study of police practices in other countries in order to provide guidance for themselves. The Japanese explore the world systematically, a tradition that goes back over one hundred years to the origin of the modern Japanese police.[31] American forces not only do not regard foreign experience as relevant to their continental country, but until recently have given little attention to the explicit design and reconsideration of police strategies. Scores of Japanese police are sent abroad by the government each year to study police practices; some are assigned to the embassies of major countries on a permanent basis. Although the FBI has liaison posts in many countries, American police abroad for the most part are on holiday or are conducting business on matters of narrow relevance at home. The radical decentralization of policing in the United States undoubtedly contributes to its failure to exploit foreign precedents. Few forces are large enough to be able to support such study, and the country as a whole lacks mechanisms for sharing, let alone implementing, what is learned on a national basis. That this might be an important role for the national government to play is just beginning to be appreciated.[32]

This suggests what will not be emulated at all in American policing: the development of a national police force composed of large operational commands. Population in the United States is still highly dispersed, with 51 percent living in communities smaller than ten thousand persons.[33] The police forces of the sixty largest cities cover only 18

31. Eleanor Westney, *Imitation and Innovation*. The concluding section of this informative book contains an interesting insight into the process of borrowing from abroad. Examining Japan's scouring of the world for lessons about modern policing in the 1870s and 1880s, she concludes that imitation was driven by national needs and not by a strong appreciation of cultural congruence between Japan and foreign countries. Japan borrowed what it thought it needed and then used tradition selectively to legitimate the borrowing. Tradition, then, was not allowed to become an easy excuse for failing to change. Rather, it was cunningly manipulated to provide legitimacy. The Japanese did not fit foreign practice to Japanese culture, they fitted Japanese culture to foreign practice.

32. The National Institute of Justice of the U.S. Department of Justice, successor to the Law Enforcement Assistance Administration created in 1968, is the appropriate vehicle, but it has deliberately avoided foreign study out of fear of congressional criticism. Only in the last few years has it taken the first cautious steps in this direction.

33. *Statistical Abstract of the United States*, 1989.

precent of the population. So command is fragmented across the country, each force is jealously autonomous, and performance is uneven. Change in American policing will therefore be more laborious than in Japan, which is exactly what Americans want. It has to occur force by force. Single state forces, let alone a national one, are anathema. Policing is power, and Americans want that power dispersed widely and held accountable locally, which is both more natural and perhaps more sensible in a country that is twenty-five times larger than Japan.[34]

As the United States begins to look to Japan for lessons about policing, the greatest impediment to successful borrowing is probably not culture but perspective. Japanese police strategies do not require a Japanese populace. What is required, and what the United States lacks, is a broader vision of the police. Americans are not accustomed to seeing the police as important social actors; they see them as enforcement technicians. Because Americans are anxious about the creation of governmental authority, the great injunction laid on the police is to fight crime within the letter of the law. Americans do not demand that they fight crime within the law in particular ways that reinforce the values undergirding democratic life. They do not see that legality and efficiency do not exhaust the contributions police make to society.

Can American perspectives on the police be extended? Yes, but slowly. Political tradition as well as contemporary misdeeds have combined to make the police protectively self-denying and the public loath to trust them further. The dilemma for the police in the United States can be posed in a single question: How can esteem be kindled for a role most people accept only as an unpleasant necessity?

34. The total land area of Japan is 378,000 square kilometers; of the United States, 9,373,000. Keizai Koho Center, Tokyo, *Japan 1989,* p. 7.

9

Lessons in Order

The gangster office was located in a modern two-story detached structure in an open space at the end of a passageway between two tall brick buildings. On the first floor was a large office containing desks and filing cabinets, along with an alcove furnished with leatherette couches and easy chairs providing a view through glass panels of a well-tended Japanese-style garden. The name of the gangster organization was etched onto a large, lacquered cross section of tree trunk displayed prominently just inside the door. The boss was a tough-looking man of forty-five, dressed in dark slacks and a maroon turtleneck under a buttoned cardigan. As the two patrol officers and I sat drinking green tea prepared by one of the casually dressed male underlings, the boss explained that this was a headquarters supervising forty or fifty branch offices. The two patrol officers took their hats off and enjoyed a relaxed smoke while prompting the boss with questions that they thought would interest me. After fifteen minutes, we were bowed out the door, past conical piles of salt arranged for good luck on the doorstep.

Police estimate that there are at least 80,000 *yakuza* in Japan—that is, full-fledged members of 1,500 organized criminal groups, loosely federated into several larger competing syndicates.[1] They commit 6 per-

---

1. *Yakuza* is a slang word for gangster. More politely, gangsters are known as *boryokudan*.

cent of all Penal Code crimes—3 percent of murders, 16 percent of rob-
eries, 15 percent of rapes—and are instrumental in drug and gun smug-
gling.[2] Frequently fighting among themselves for turf and position,
they commit most of the crimes involving firearms, as well as most of
the offenses against the gun laws. Their illegal activities include gambling, prostitution, selling protection, strikebreaking, blackmail, and
loan-sharking, although increasingly they are investing their illegal pro-
ceeds in legitimate businesses, especially in the entertainment industry.
Uniformed patrol officers routinely visit their offices to show the flag,
and also to note the names of gang members displayed on wall-mounted
rosters and the schedule of monthly events written on large chalkboards,
as in any Japanese office.

The visibility of organized criminal gangs and their close surveillance
by the police does not mean that Japan's reputation for being the safest
country among the developed democracies is false. Japan's rate of serious crime is indeed less than one-third of the American, and there is
no reason to doubt the figures.[3] But it certainly raises questions about
how this orderliness has been achieved and what the role of the police is
in it. To understand what is going on in Japan, I shall compare factors
that are commonly expected to affect crime and its control in order to
see if they can account for the remarkable difference in orderliness between Japan and the United States. I shall begin by examining crimi-
nalogenic conditions, then examine the contribution of the police.

Reasons for Public Order

In searching for an explanation of Japan's dramatically
lower crime rates, several factors can immediately be set aside. Japan is
fully as modern as the United States, transformed equally during the
last century by processes of urbanization, industrialization, and tech-
nological development. Japan is not a Third World backwater. Especially confounding is the fact that its population congestion, sometimes

2. M. Tamura, "Yakuza and Stimulants: Drug Problems in Japan" (Paper for the
International Conference on Crime, Drugs, and Social Control, Hong Kong, December
14–16, 1988), p. 3; S. Miyazawa, "Learning Lessons from Japanese Experience: Challenge for Japanese Criminologists" (Paper prepared for the U.S./Japan Bilateral Session,
Tokyo, 1988), Appendix 25. See also the *White Paper on Police, 1987*.
3. See chapter 1.

suspected of being associated with social disorganization and high crime, is much greater than that of the United States. To appreciate what it would be like if the United States were as densely populated as Japan, imagine California if half the U.S. population moved there. If they did, can one believe that our crime rate would fall?

Japan is also not politically repressive; its people are not subjected to the iron hand of government regimentation. It is as democratic as the United States, with the rights of speech, expression, association, and electoral competition protected by law and an independent judiciary. This has not always been the case. Democracy is less than fifty years old in Japan, dating from the Allied Occupation in 1945. For centuries government had exercised very tight control. While it seems doubtful that many Japanese are inhibited by fear of governmental abuses of power, one might argue that the habits of subservience to authority learned in earlier times remain a part of Japan's political culture and might inhibit expressive behavior. The sole serious contemporary exception to its fine human rights record is the practice of extended pre-charge detention.[4] Because it is used so seldomly and the cultural promptings of confession are so powerful, I doubt that this practice has any important effect on either crime- or clearance-rates.

Turning to economic conditions, informative differences between Japan and the United States begin to emerge. Although per capita wealth is about the same, the distribution of income is significantly more egalitarian in Japan than in the United States. That is, rich people earn a larger proportion of the country's income in the United States than they do in Japan.[5] Furthermore, unemployment is generally much lower in Japan than in the United States by a factor of two or three.[6] And a much smaller proportion of the working population is involved in strikes in Japan.[7] Although there is poverty in Japan and homeless-

4. See chapter 7, the issue of "substitute prisons."
5. Income inequality as measured by the gini-coefficient was 0.278 in Japan, 0.366 in the United States. *Japan Times,* 24 February 1989, p. 24, from data provided by the European Economic Community and the Japanese Economic Planning Agency. Values for the gini-coefficient run from 0 to 1, with higher values indicating greater inequality. Elliot Currie, *Confronting Crime: An American Challenge* (New York: Pantheon, 1985) 1, p. 161, says that Japan's equality of income was exceeded among OECD countries only by Holland, Sweden, and Norway.
6. In 1987, for example, unemployment rates were 2.8 percent in Japan and 6.2 percent in the United States; in 1989, 2.5 percent in Japan, 5.5 percent in the United States. *Japan Times,* 24 February 1989.
7. In 1987, 256,000 person-days were lost to strikes in Japan, 4,481,000 in the U.S. Ibid.

ness, there are few slums—that is, areas of chronic poverty, unemployment, family pathology, and high crime.[8] There are probably only two
in all of Japan that qualify—the Airin area of Osaka, home to 20,000
day laborers, and the Sanya section of Tokyo, which has 7,000.[9] These
areas are notorious throughout Japan.

More important, Japan does not have ghettoes, meaning areas inhabited by chronically impoverished people who are members of groups
that are subjected to discrimination by the general population. Only
about one-half of 1 percent of the population is ethnically not Japanese,
mostly Koreans and Chinese.[10] By contrast, about 13 percent of the
American population is African-American and 8 percent is Hispanic.[11]
Nor does Japan have the large, well-defined, and competitive religious
denominations of the United States. As Japanese often point out, Japan
probably has the largest homogeneous population of any country in the
world. This is not to suggest that crime is mostly interracial or inter-
ethnic. It is not. Rather, Japan lacks the kind of racial and cultural di-
versity that so frequently reinforces economic inequality to produce
successive generations of the misery, hopelessness, rage, and family dis-
integration that are so strongly associated with crime.

Americans expect the operations of the criminal justice system to inhibit crime. Comparing its operation in Japan and in the United States,
however, the few differences would seem to work to give Japan higher
rather than lower crime rates. The two systems are very similar in form,
which is hardly surprising, since the Japanese system is the product of
American reform after World War II, overlaying earlier borrowings
from Germany and France. The Japanese actually invest less of their
gross national product in police, courts, and corrections (0.88 percent)
than does the United States (1.26 percent).[12] Japan spends a smaller
proportion of government revenues on criminal justice (2.5 percent)
than does the United States (3.2 percent).[13] Japan does spend propor-

8. H. Wagatsuma, "Social Control of Juvenile Delinquency in Arakawa Ward of
Tokyo" (Paper prepared for the Social Science Research Council Workshop on the Japanese City, April 1976), pp. 34–39.

9. Figures supplied by the respective police forces.

10. See chapter 5.

11. *Statistical Abstract of the United States, 1989*, pp. 14, 16.

12. Japan spent Y2,900 billion in 1988 on police, prosecution, courts, and corrections; the United States, $53.5 billion in 1986. Information from the Ministry of Justice
and National Police Agency, 1989, and the *Sourcebook of Criminal Justice Statistics, 1988*,
p. 2. The GNP of Japan was Y330,116 billion in 1987; of the United States, $4,235 bil-
lion in 1986. *Japan, 1989*, p. 14.

13. Same sources as n. 12.

tionately more of its gross national product on police—0.76 percent versus 0.50 percent—but per capita expenditures on police are higher in the United States.[14] Altogether, criminal justice investments would hardly seem to account for Japan's lower crime rates.

Contrary to what Americans would expect in a country with low crime rates, sentences for similar crimes are invariably more lenient in Japan than in the United States, which is reflected in the fact that five times as many Americans as Japanese, proportionate to population, are in prison.[15] Japan did keep the death penalty while the United States experimented briefly from 1972 to 1976 with its abolition, but that single difference in deterrent severity was short-lived. Since World War II about 550 people have been executed in Japan, about 5 a year during the last fifteen years. In the United States from 1945 to 1987 1,640 were executed, about 20 a year in the mid-1980s.[16] If the Japanese criminal justice system is having an impact on crime, it is not, therefore, through the greater rigor of its punishments. It may, however, be doing so through its sureness. A suspect is charged and officially dealt with in some manner in more than one-third of all crimes reported to the Japanese police. In the United States, the comparable figure is a meager 5 percent. Crime is much more risky in Japan than in the United States. The sureness of punishment in Japan, even if it is mild, may have a more deterrent effect than the more severe but uncertain punishments in the United States.

There is only one difference in legal context that might help to account for the disparity in crime rates. Japan has the toughest laws on the ownership of firearms, especially handguns, of any democratic country in the world. Registration is required for all firearms, knives, and swords.[17] No handguns are permitted in private hands, even registered, with the exception of people who participate in international shooting competitions.[18] There were forty-five such persons in 1989.[19] Even they cannot take their guns home, but must deposit them at a police station or with registered administrators of shooting ranges. Shot-

14. See chapter 8.
15. See chapter 7.
16. Ministry of Justice, 1989, and *Sourcebook of Criminal Justice Statistics, 1988,* p. 671.
17. This includes rivet guns, rope-discharging guns, and signal guns for athletic games. "Law Controlling Possession, Etc., of Fire-arms and Swords," Article 3(1), clause 8 (Law No. 6, March 1958). Swords and knives over six inches long or with blades that automatically extend by mechanical action are prohibited except under permit.
18. Article 4.
19. National Police Agency, 1989.

guns and small-caliber rifles are permitted for hunting. There were 29,000 registered rifles and about 450,000 registered shotguns in 1989. Permits for owning weapons are issued by prefectural public safety commissions.[20] No one knows how many handguns are privately held in the United States, although estimates run into the hundreds of millions. Surveys have shown that 23 percent of American homes have handguns.[21]

As a result, the use of firearms in Japanese crime is negligible. Out of approximately 51,000 felonious or violent offenses committed in Japan in 1988, less than 250 involved handguns.[22] Ninety-four percent of these were committed by yakuza. In the United States, about 59 percent of all murders (17,859 instances) in 1987 were committed with firearms, 21 percent of all aggravated assaults (792,457 instances), and 33 percent of all robberies (498,632 instances).[23] The uncertainty, wariness, and honest fear that American police officers feel in making street contacts and responding to summonses for assistance are totally unfamiliar to the Japanese police. Less than twenty officers are killed feloniously each year, hardly ever by firearms. In the United States eighty-four officers on average were killed each year during the last decade, three-quarters of them by handguns.[24]

The National Rifle Association, the major source of opposition to efforts to restrict gun ownership in the United States, developed a slogan that many believe makes the case convincingly against legislation restricting gun ownership. "When guns are outlawed, only outlaws will have guns." This is exactly what has occurred in Japan. And the Japanese think this is a very good thing.[25]

A final factor that is often considered influential in explaining crime, especially violent crime, is popular culture. Japan's is hardly less violent than that of the United States. Its history is certainly as blood-soaked. For centuries justice was meted out on the basis of class; until a little

20. Article 4.

21. *Sourcebook of Criminal Justice Statistics, 1988*, pp. 231–32.

22. *White Paper on Police, 1988*, p. 78.

23. *Sourcebook of Criminal Justice Statistics, 1988*, pp. 446, 454, 453.

24. Federal Bureau of Investigation, *Uniform Crime Reports: Law Enforcement Officers Killed and Assaulted 1988* (Washington, D.C.: U.S. Department of Justice, 1989).

25. The place of firearms in Japan is even more interesting because they were once fairly widely used and manufactured in Japan. Japan is disarmed today as a result of deliberate government policy. This experience, and the reasons for the government's decision, is described in a short illustrated book by Noel Perrin, *Giving Up the Gun: Japan's Reversion to the Sword* (Boston: Godine, 1979).

over a hundred years ago a samurai had the right to cut down with a sword any peasant who insulted him. Executions for crime were quick and brutal. There was and still is a cult of the sword in Japan similar to the cult of the gun in the United States. Martial values and regimen, which Americans tend to deprecate, have been extolled in Japan for generations. Political assassination has been far more common in Japanese history than in American. Since 1945 eight political leaders have been killed or injured in attacks.[26] Several assassination plans are discovered in their early stages each year. Both countries fought civil wars at approximately the same time. Although the bloodletting was less extensive in Japan, the parochial loyalties overcome were probably as intense. Furthermore, two generations ago Japan launched a fanatical imperial war whose excesses are still remembered throughout Asia as well as in the United States.

Contemporary popular culture, too, is replete with violence. Theater, films, television, and the ubiquitous "manga"—adult comic books—are saturated with violence, much of it with strong erotic overtones that feature women as victims.[27] Violence on television, on which many American ills are blamed, appears to be as prevalent in Japan as in the United States.[28] Samurai dramas are a staple of television, as Westerns used to be and police detective shows now are in the United States. The sword-wielding warrior, especially if he has turned outlaw, fascinates the Japanese. However, there may be some important differences in the portrayal of violence in both countries. Violence in Japan is more ritualized, more easily recognized as theater, distanced more from the settings of contemporary life. Furthermore, violence is usually portrayed tragically; people who use it die, often with their problems unresolved.[29]

Looking generally then at the circumstances within which Japanese and Americans live, there are some differences that would explain the lower crime rates in Japan. On the one hand, income distribution is more equitable in Japan, unemployment is less, and poverty is less concentrated in particular localities, especially neighborhoods defined by race or ethnicity. Japan also regulates gun ownership much more stringently than does the United States. On the other hand, its popular cul-

26. National Police Agency, 1989.

27. Ian Baruma, *Behind the Mask* (New York: Pantheon, 1984), chap. 10.

28. Albert Axelbank, *Black Star over Japan* (London: Allen and Unwin, 1972), and George Comstock, Syracuse University, speech, 12 May 1982.

29. Baruma and Comstock.

ture is as violent as that of the United States, and its criminal justice system, while more efficient, is less rigorous in its punishments. Criminal prosecution is hampered by civil rights, very much as in the United States, except for the extended precharge detention period.

It is impossible to determine scientifically, given limitations on data in both countries, whether these differences in social circumstances can account entirely for Japan's enviable crime record. At the same time, it is clear that there are other processes at work in Japan that help to produce its remarkable orderliness. These are processes of social interaction, part of general culture, that bear directly on the behavior of the Japanese. Crime, more generally the impulse to deviance, is inhibited by mechanisms that are peculiar to Japan in their strength and extensiveness. Although these mechanisms can be found in American society too, they are much weaker and more attenuated. Control of deviant behavior in Japan, I shall argue, is obtained through a unique combination of propriety, presumption, and pride.

First: propriety. Japanese are bound by an infinite number of rules about what is proper. To an American, Japan is supremely uptight. There is nothing casual or relaxed about it. In order to avoid giving offense, modes of speech shift as one addresses a man or a woman, a child or an adult, an older or a younger sibling, an elderly person, one's peer, a first-time acquaintance or a long-time friend, a workmate or an outsider, and so forth. Informal dress codes are strict, and people dress exactingly so as to conform to what is expected on particular occasions as well as in particular roles. All schoolchildren wear the uniform distinctive of the school they attend, identical down to purses, backpacks, width of trousers, and length of skirts. Businessmen and government bureaucrats invariably wear dark suits, dark ties, white shirts, and black shoes. Construction workers can be recognized by knickers, soft two-toed boots, and woolen belly-warmers. Female street sweepers wear long scarves; truck and taxi drivers often wear white gloves. Revealingly, a customer in a Western-style dress shop will be asked, "What size are you?" in a kimono store, "How old are you?"[30] People in Japan are what they look like, which means they must conform in order to be what they want to be.

30. W. Caudill and H. Weinstein, "Maternal Care and Infant Behavior in Japan and America," in *Japanese Culture and Behavior,* ed. T. S. and W. Lebra (Honolulu: University of Hawaii Press, 1974), pp. 225–76.

Decorum is all-encompassing: not sitting on desks and surfaces people use for work; not putting shod feet on chairs, so that mothers carefully take off the tiny tennis shoes of their children when they pull them onto subway seats; encasing wet umbrellas in disposable plastic sacks when entering department stores; tying a *ukata* (bathrobe) one way for a man, another for a woman; and not looking directly into the eyes of another person in public. Japanese calculate the depth as well as the number of bows so that proper deference is shown. Department stores have mechanical calibrators that help personnel learn the appropriate bowing angle for different sorts of people.[31] Late one morning in a popular Tokyo restaurant I heard chanting from the kitchen. Peering surreptitiously through an open door, I saw the manager rehearsing the staff in saying, "What can I do for you?" "How can I help you?" and "Thank you, come back," in the proper bright and cheery way.

Japanese are surrounded by rules in all they do, from the serious to the trivial. In relation to Americans, they are compulsively watchful about decorum. Etiquette, civility, morality, and law blend together. Japanese learn early that someone is paying attention to everything they do, and that departures from propriety will be met with visible expressions of disapproval. A sense of constraining order is always present in Japanese life. A person is never offstage.

The pervading sense of propriety produces startling demonstrations of orderliness. An English businessman was so astonished at the absence of litter that he personally inspected 1,200 yards of subway corridors in the Yurakicho-Ginza subway station during an evening rush hour to count discarded trash. Although this complex is ten times larger than London's Picadilly Circus Underground station, he found only nineteen cigarette ends, twenty-eight matchsticks, eleven candy wrappers, and four pieces of paper.[32] Japanese pedestrians rarely jaywalk, dutifully waiting for the crossing-lights to turn green even if there is no car in sight and it is late at night.

The instinctive obedience to shared rules of order is wonderfully captured in a story about a burglar who was caught fleeing an apartment in the daytime. It is important to understand that Japanese remove their shoes on entering a private home, especially if its floor is the traditional raised floor made of thick woven-straw (tatami). The burglar had crossed

31. Peter Hazelhurst, formerly Tokyo correspondent for the *Sunday Times* and the *Straits Times*.
32. Peter Hazelhurst.

such a room to ransack a bureau, but was apprehended by the police because, when he heard them, he had stopped to put his shoes back on.[33]

Japanese orderliness in large matters, such as crime, seems to be related to orderliness in small things. If this is true, then the lack of regimentation that Americans value in personal life may affect the amount of criminal disorder in public life. Would Americans, one wonders, be willing to obtain a greater measure of safety if they were required to tie their bathrobes in a prescribed way?[34]

Second: presumption. Japanese are enmeshed in closely knit groups that inhibit behavior through informal social controls. Japanese are not raised to stand alone, develop their individual potential, or "do their own thing." They are taught to fit into groups and to subordinate themselves to the purposes of those groups. The most important and enduring groups are family, school, and workplace. Becoming an organic part of them—belonging—is the source of the deepest emotional satisfaction Japanese feel. Thus, fitting in becomes the ultimate discipline in Japan. Japanese are encapsulated in small groups of well-known people who have the presumptive right to tell them how to behave.

Accepting the obligations of belonging is not like being directed to conform, though that is the result. Japanese tolerate the presumptions of membership because in exchange they are nurtured, supported, and cared for. This may take the form of lifetime employment, or the covering up of errors, or assistance in carrying out tasks, or simply an understanding of personal problems. Americans are more calculating about the costs and benefits of membership. Groups are instruments of individual purpose, rather than being ends in themselves. Americans are therefore less bound by the obligations of membership in any particular group, whether it be family, marriage, job, sports team, or social club. Because Japanese depend so entirely on a much smaller number of affiliations, they lose the ability to discriminate between the claims of the individual and those of the group, the obligations of the personal as opposed to those of the public.

33. Robert Trumbull, formerly Tokyo correspondent for the *New York Times*. I once saw a squad of plainclothes detectives break into a yakuza apartment on a drug-bust and stop inside the front door to remove their shoes before undertaking their search.

34. James Q. Wilson and George L. Kelling have argued that police should concentrate on maintaining decorum on the streets in order to discourage more serious criminal behavior. "Broken Windows," *Atlantic Monthly* (March 1982), pp. 29–38. Experimental evidence for a connection between visible signs of disorder and criminal actions was found by Professor Philip Zimbardo, Stanford University, in 1969.

The difference between Japanese and Americans is not in valuing the favorable regard of others or in the need to conform; it lies in the range of significant external references. Americans are "outer directed," to use David Reisman's famous phrase, in a generalized way; Japanese are "outer directed" in a focused way.[35] Studies have in fact shown that among strangers Americans conform more quickly than Japanese.[36] Japanese do not accept the presumptions of any group, but only of a small number of groups. The universal desire for fellowship and community provides enormous leverage in Japan because it is not counterbalanced by the obligations of other affiliations.

The presumptive control that immediate social groups can exercise can be seen in the importance placed on unspoken communication in Japan. People who properly belong do not have to be told; they understand instinctively what the wishes of the group are. For example, a husband in a properly attuned marriage does not need to apologize to his wife if he spills hot tea-water on her hand, because she understands without being told that he did not intend to hurt her and also that he is sorry. The most cutting remark a man can make about his wife is that she has to be told what he needs.[37] Businessmen complain that they do not like to be sent abroad for long periods because they lose instinctive knowledge of their group. When they return they feel like strangers, having to be told what everyone else understands. As the Japanese say, the expectation in most of life is that when you talk "others can finish the sentence." It is not an acceptable excuse in Japan to say "I wasn't told."[38]

Japanese learn the value of belonging early in life. In schools children advance automatically, as a group, helping one another as they go. Individual achievements are deemphasized in favor of group accomplishments. Children learn not to embarrass schoolmates by showing them

35. David Riesman, *The Lonely Crowd* (Garden City, N.Y.: Doubleday, 1953).

36. H. Wagatsuma and Arthur Rosett, "Cultural Attitudes toward Contract Law: Japan and the U.S. Compared" (Draft article, 1982), p. 22.

37. Robert J. Smith, *Japanese Society: Tradition, Self, and the Social Order* (Cambridge: Cambridge University Press, 1983), pp. 57–58.

38. In *Hidden Differences: Doing Business with the Japanese* (New York: Anchor Press/Doubleday, 1987), Part I, Edward T. and Mildred R. Hall describe Japan as a "high context" society, meaning that people need a great deal of information about the people they work with in order to work together successfully. Americans, on the other hand, need much less, preferring to limit the dimensions of interaction with the people they work with. The same distinction is made by Howard Gardner, *Frames of Mind* (New York: Basic Books, 1985), in distinguishing "particle" societies, where autonomous individuals interact, from "field" societies, where individuals are subordinated to groups.

to be wrong. Instead, they correct others by saying "I want to help Yakuda-kun" or "I agree with Kato-san but I also think this way."[39] Individual test scores are not known among classmates. Separation according to ability occurs impersonally, usually as the result of formal examinations allowing students to move from one level of schooling to another. Young children compete athletically by classes, not as individuals. Students also perform together many of the custodial chores at schools, like sweeping floors, washing dishes after lunch, picking up trash, putting away equipment, and rearranging chairs. Teachers and students explain constantly to laggards what is expected, reiterating that unless something or other is done the class will be disappointed, the student will be letting down the side, or everyone will be ashamed if the student does not try. Emotional blackmail, Americans would call this, and would resent it.

Even before schooling, Japanese children learn that fitting in brings warmth and love. Observers of early child-raising practices have noted that Japanese mothers carry their children with them everywhere, both inside and outside the house. Children sleep with their parents until the age of four or five. American mothers put down happy children, encouraging them to play by themselves. American children are left with baby-sitters, a practice still uncommon in Japan. They learn early to attract attention by crying and demanding; Japanese mothers anticipate the needs of their children so they do not have to cry or demand.[40]

When Japanese preschool children misbehave, parents threaten them with being locked out of the home. They tearfully bang on the front doors, pleading to be allowed back in. In the United States parents threaten badly behaving children with exactly the reverse—being kept in. The children are "grounded." The effect is that American children are taught that it is punishment to be locked up with one's family; Japanese children are taught that punishment is being excluded from one's family.[41] Small wonder, then, that Japanese schools and work groups have leverage over individual behavior later in life—and that adult affiliations in the United States have less.

The power of informal social control is what the Japanese criminal

39. Takie S. Lebra, *Japanese Women: Constraint and Fulfillment* (Honolulu: University of Hawaii Press, 1984), chap. 5.

40. See Caudill and Weinstein (n. 30 above).

41. *Mura hachibu* is the term for being excluded. It was a very serious punishment in villages. This is similar to the practice in the British labor movement of sending colleagues "to Coventry," not talking to them, when they defied group norms.

justice system relies on when it accepts apologies for minor infractions, does not insist on arresting suspects, allows people to be free without bail pending trial, and suspends prosecution or the execution of sentences. The vitality of group supervision is what allows police, prosecutors, and judges to act on the philosophy that they "hate the crime but not the criminal." The Japanese criminal justice system is founded not on deterrence but rather on "reintegrative shaming."[42] The purpose of the system is to shame individuals into accepting the obligations of their social setting and to shame groups into accepting responsibility for the errant member. Individuation makes sense in Japan, as it often does in the United States as well, when people are situated in specific, binding social networks.

Learning to accept the presumptions of groups does not mean that groups are without conflict and disagreement. Japanese often feel frustrated and inhibited. Unlike Americans, however, they are more willing to manage the conflict, deflecting or repressing it.[43] They make an explicit distinction linguistically between what is apparent and what is real in social situations. *Tatemae* refers to the appearance that must be maintained; *honne* is the inside story, what is truly felt. Americans too understand the tension between gut-feeling and propriety, but are more likely to be led by the former. Conversely, they value sincerity, being uncomfortable with hollow conformity. Japanese stifle nonconformity for the sake of maintaining the *tatemae* of group harmony, even though they know it is a pretense.

Social order in an individualistic society like the United States requires the discipline of conscience; social order in a communitarian society like Japan requires the discipline of presumption. Both societies learn to accommodate some of the other perspective. Japanese society does not wholly trample individual identity; American society does not forfeit entirely the capacity for cooperative endeavor. But the balance is different. As two observers of both countries have said, "One may even venture to suggest that while Americans learn to live with an illusion of complete self-reliance, self-sufficiency and autonomy, many Japanese tend to live with an illusion of total harmony, mutual understanding and consensus among them."[44]

---

42. John Braithwaite, *Crime, Shame, and Reintegration* (Cambridge: Cambridge University Press, 1989).

43. Takie S. Lebra, "Nonconfrontational Strategies for Management of Interpersonal Conflicts," in Ellis S. Krauss et al., *Conflict in Japan* (Honolulu: University of Hawaii Press, 1984), chap. 3.

44. Wagatsuma and Rosett, "Cultural Attitudes."

Third: pride. Discipline is maintained in Japan because people take enormous pride in performing well the roles demanded of them. Distinctive occupational dress is one indication of the prideful identification people have with their work. Japanese society is hierarchical in terms of authority, but it is egalitarian in its evaluation of the worth of work. What is important is the dedication brought to the job, not its status. Interestingly, anyone who teaches in Japan, from university professors to instructors in cutting up raw fish, are called *sensei*. One reason Japanese women have accepted differentiated sex roles more readily than American women may be that the emotional rewards are greater. Being a wife and mother is regarded as a demanding and responsible job in Japan. It is not denigrated as being "just housework."[45]

The essential ingredient in achieving success at anything is *seishin*, literally "spirit." But the word has strong overtones of effort, discipline, self-control, and even suffering. Inner fulfillment comes from developing the *seishin* necessary to accept demanding obligations willingly, whether artistic and craft skills, work routines, athletic feats, or social responsibilities. Japanese respect the *seishin* shown by the daughter-in-law who uncomplainingly performs her duties in the house of an overbearing mother-in-law for the sake of the family, or the student who practices tea-ceremony for years in order to achieve a higher ranking, or the baseball player who trains despite personal injury without asking for time off.[46] In arts, crafts, and social relations, Japanese learn by rote, by endlessly copying approved behavior. High achievement is obtained by fanatical application, not by gifted innovation. Great effort earns great respect. Indeed, Japanese tend to excuse marginal performance as long as exemplary *seishin* was shown. By being perfectionist in effort, Japanese protect themselves against censure. Americans, on the other hand, are more ends-oriented, excusing slipshod preparation if the results are good.

Pride given to work helps Japanese accept conformity. As Edwin O. Reischauer, former ambassador to Japan, has said, "social conformity to the Japanese is no sign of weakness but rather the proud, tempered product of inner strength."[47] A symbol of this is the bonzai tree, a unique expression of aesthetic taste with which Japanese identify. Bonzai is a dwarf tree that has been restricted by binding and pruning so that it grows into strange, artificial shapes. A bonzai tree achieves beauty by

45. Suzanne H. Vogel, "Professional Housewife: The Career of Urban Middle Class Japanese Women," *Japan Interpreter* 12, no. 1 (Winter 1978): 16–43.
46. Robert Whiting, *You Gotta Have Wa* (New York: Macmillan, 1989), p. 317.
47. *The Japanese Today* (Cambridge: Harvard University Press, 1988), p. 166.

being constricted, some might say deformed. Japanese orderliness is achieved in the same way.

In conclusion, propriety, presumption, and pride can be analytically and anecdotally separated, but they are part of a single dynamic. The enwrapping web of propriety is held in place by the myriad presumptive corrections of primary social groups. Careful attention to the forms of human interaction allows tightly knit groups to hold together despite the vagaries of circumstance and personality. Pride allows for the internalization of the discipline necessary for subordination to small groups. Presumption becomes bearable when society rewards those who accept it.

Americans can understand, perhaps even empathize with, this dynamic. But they reverse the values. Propriety in the United States is limited, individuals being free to live their lives bound only by the commodious limits of the law. Behavior is bound more exclusively by law, or a very general morality, because the texture of American society is too loosely knit to rely on the presumptive enforcement of small groups. Norms of decorum and civility are not shared across the spectrum of American life. American pride is rooted in individual accomplishment, not in the acceptance of the disciplines of primary social groups. Americans kick against the restrictions of propriety, having been taught to question conventions of dress, language, taste, and morality.

If crime is caused to an important extent by customary patterns of social interaction, then Japan and the United States may both be getting what they have contrived.

The Role of the Police

The Japanese frequently assert that an important reason for their success in limiting the amount of crime is the effectiveness of their police. It certainly looks that way. The Japanese police are undoubtedly well equipped, superbly trained, tightly disciplined, technologically sophisticated, and well managed. For years the crime clearance rate has been between 57 and 60 percent, compared with 20–22 percent in the United States. The Japanese police are a substantial deterrent presence. But is their effectiveness, especially their deterrent impact, due to the skill and sophistication with which they fight crime? Should the police be given as much credit as they are willing to take?

From an American perspective the Japanese police could hardly fail to succeed. The New York City Police Department, for example, handles almost twice the number of emergency calls for service in a year as all the police in Japan, with a force that is one-eighth as large.[48] American police confront 3 times the amount of serious crime per officer as their Japanese counterparts.[49] The homicide rate per officer is 5 times higher in the United States; 20 times for rape; 110 times for robbery; 34.2 times for assault; and 2.2 times for larceny. Yet despite this avalanche of work, individual American police officers solve the same number of serious crimes as Japanese officers—3.8 cases in Japan, 3.6 in the United States.[50] For serious crimes excluding larceny, the American police on a per officer basis are much more efficient, solving 3.3 times more homicides, 10.9 times more rapes, 34.4 times more robberies, and 19.7 times more assaults. American police would think they were on vacation if their volume of work was similar to the Japanese. Furthermore, considering that the Japanese people are more compliant and less adversarial than Americans, one begins to wonder if the Japanese police are not significantly overstaffed?

They would be overstaffed if their primary role were crime fighting—but it is not. The primary function of the Japanese police is not deterrence; it is crime prevention through enhancing the capacity of the society to discipline itself. They do this in three ways—prodding, guiding, and alerting.

Despite the fact that Japan is the safest developed society in the world, the police continually prod the populace to report suspicious activity, buy security hardware, learn avoidance techniques, and join crime-prevention groups. At the urging of the police, Japanese houses are barred and double-locked even though burglary is a remote contingency. Crime-prevention material circulates constantly through neighborhoods that are safer than American suburbs. During the twice-yearly home visits, koban officers distribute crime-prevention material, discuss recent crimes in the general area, offer security inspections, and raise the level of consciousness about the dangers of victimization. Spe-

48. New York City handles more than six million calls per year, compared with two and one-half million in Japan.
49. Comparing homicide, rape, robbery, assault, and larceny in 1987, the rate per officer was 2.6 times higher in the United States. Computed from the *White Paper on Police, 1988,* p. 18, and *Sourcebook of Criminal Justice Statistics, 1988,* p. 427. Japan had 221,000 police officers, the United States 555,364, including state, local, and sheriff department sworn personnel. National Police Agency, 1989, and *Sourcebook,* p. 78.
50. Computed using 1987 figures for homicide, rape, robbery, assault, and larceny.

cial crime-prevention teams regularly visit schools, community centers, and facilities for the elderly to demonstrate how criminals may attack them and what defensive actions to take.

Police in the United States, where crime is much more threatening than in Japan, go to lengths to reassure the public that their fears are exaggerated, while the police of Japan, where crime is insignificant, continually tell people the situation is worse than they imagine. American police still worry that distribution of neighborhood newsletters about crime will cause undue alarm, in particular curtail mobility so that people become virtual prisoners in their own homes. Japanese police publicize tiny increases in crime precisely so as to change behavior, in particular to encourage cooperative crime prevention. It has been suggested that there is a sinister motive behind this, namely, that by raising the fear of crime the police legitimate their community-penetrating and community-mobilizing strategies.[51] This is certainly one result, but historical tradition, rather than conspiratorial foresight, is the more likely motivator.

The Japanese police also prod people suspected of criminal activity. Street interrogations by koban officers are designed for this, as well as the polite harassment of people peddling goods on the street without permits or the warnings giving to salespersons about overly aggressive tactics. Yakuza are a continual target of surveillance and interrogation. Gangster offices are routinely visited, cars with yakuza license plates stopped and searched, and gangster gatherings photographed. Occasionally, police launch large-scale crackdowns in which hundreds of yakuza are rounded up. These are usually a response to an upsurge in gang warfare.[52] Communities are encouraged to mobilize against yakuza. For instance, one prefectural police force distributed a pamphlet entitled "Let's Drive Out Boryokudan" and showing a fist squeezing a man. Recently the police have encouraged neighborhoods to hold demonstrations against yakuza activity. In 1987, for example, 187 yakuza offices were closed as a result of community pressure.[53] This is similar to efforts by American communities to close "crack-houses" in inner cities.

Although Japanese police are certainly interested in arresting, prosecuting, and sending to prison yakuza members, their enforcement

51. Karel van Wolferin, *The Enigma of Japanese Power* (New York: Alfred P. Knopf, 1989), chap. 7.

52. David E. Kaplan and Alec Dubro, *Yakuza* (Reading, Mass.: Addison-Wesley, 1986), p. 128.

53. *White Paper on Police, 1988,* pp. 29–31.

strategy seems weak by American standards. Most notably, they do not do undercover work against the criminal gangs, apart from surveillance. They do not try to penetrate yakuza, except through informers, nor do they set up "stings" to trap yakuza in illegal activities. The reasons for this reluctance to attack yakuza through undercover operations are complex, involving strict interpretation by courts of the laws against entrapment, difficulties in remaining undetected in the tight yakuza world, and fears about corruption and subordination of police officers. "Unthinkable" or "It just isn't done" is what police, prosecutors, and legal scholars all say about the possibility that the Japanese police will undertake American-style undercover operations.[54] Another explanation may be that there is a tacit agreement, sometimes renegotiated in face-to-face meetings, between police and yakuza to the effect that the police will turn a blind eye to certain forms of yakuza criminality as long as they will protect the public from the violence of their members, hangers-on, and street punks in general and do not import and sell drugs.[55]

The Japanese police continually guide communities in the exercise of presumptive discipline. Viewing themselves as "nurses of the people," in the famous words of Toshiyoshi Kawaji, founder of the Tokyo Metropolitan Police Department in the 1870s, they enlist thousands of volunteers to monitor and supervise behavior in every neighborhood. The crime-prevention associations, described in chapter 5, are a prime vehicle. But they are only the tip of the iceberg. Perhaps the best example of cooperative presumption are the activities directed at juveniles. The National Police Agency regularly advises prefectures about books, magazines, pictures, movies, toys, and advertisements that are appropriate for adults but not for children.[56] Regulation is carried out by members of the crime-prevention associations, which were designated by law in 1985 as Committees on a Clean Moral Environment. They have been instrumental, for example, in the past several years in pressuring small shops throughout Japan to remove pornography-vending machines. These are in addition to materials judged obscene, which would be seized straight-

54. Japan also does not have a RICO statute—Racketeering Influenced Corrupt Organizations act—which allows the government to seize assets obtained through organized crime. It is being studied, however, by the Japanese government.

55. Karel van Wolferin, *Enigma*, pp. 101–3, and Walter Ames, *Police and Community in Japan* (Berkeley and Los Angeles: University of California Press, 1981), p. 107.

56. In 1987, for example, various prefectural governments, under authority of the Juvenile Protection Ordinance, designated the following materials harmful to children and placed restrictions on their availability for sale: 23,306 books and magazines, 7,104 theaters and movies, 282 advertisements, and 94 toys. *White Paper on Police, 1988,* p. 63.

away by the police and prosecution instituted. Crime-prevention specialists in the police also provide guidance to a mind-boggling array of juvenile counselors. There are over 2,000 police-school liaison councils, covering 90 percent of all primary and secondary schools.[57] Prefectural Public Safety Commissions have appointed nearly 5,000 juvenile guidance counselors, who work with 57,000 volunteers offering advice and support to juveniles who are already in trouble with the law or whose behavior could be considered predelinquent. These people, largely teachers, parents, and juvenile probation officers, patrol the streets, usually accompanied by crime-prevention officers in plainclothes, "protecting" juveniles. The patrols concentrate on places where adolescents gather, such as parks, shopping arcades, pachinko parlors, video-games stores, bus and subway terminals, and McDonald's and Kentucky Fried Chicken restaurants. During the day they look for truants, but after school and during early evening hours they quietly accost juveniles who are behaving in unseemly and improper ways, which may mean "hanging out" in school uniform in public places, riding bicycles on prohibited walkways, playing video-games outside of allowed hours, wearing running shoes with the heels pushed down so that they can be put on without lacing, wearing abnormally long skirts, or having "permed" hair.

The most serious transgression of all is smoking in public. Under Japanese law minors under twenty may not smoke, although exception is made for people who are working or have graduated. Smoking is considered a very serious indicator of delinquent tendencies. On a cold, drizzly night, for example, seven volunteers with flashlights and green armbands over winter jackets noticed two teenage boys and three girls sitting on playground equipment in a small park, all still in school uniforms, although it was early evening. Separating the boys and girls, the volunteers asked their names and for an explanation of what they were doing. The boys were asked to turn out their pockets, and their cigarettes were confiscated. Confiscating is not authorized by law, but few juveniles are going to refuse an authoritative request. Admonished by two female volunteers about behaving improperly, the now tearful girls were told to go straight home. The boys tried to argue that they had a right not to be hassled, but were slowly cowed, and they finally left with perfunctory bows and downcast heads.

Throughout Japan, day in and day out, over weekends and vacations, thousands of respectable "busybodies" like these work hand in glove

57. *White Paper on Police, 1988,* p. 59.

with the police to extend the boundaries of family and school discipline into public places. Americans would undoubtedly see this as Big Brother on the streets. The Japanese do too, but without the capital letters. The police and community believe that they are providing protective guidance with the loving concern of an elder brother in order to ensure that children do not fall into life-destroying habits.

Primary and secondary schools are central to this presumptive concern, and their power is astonishing. This was dramatically demonstrated when the police pulled over two teenage boys riding double on a motorcycle without helmets. After being given a stern lecture, prelude, I thought, to being issued a ticket, one police officer concluded the interview by shaking his finger at them and saying that if they were caught doing this again, he would *notify their teachers*. When I was unable to believe my ears, the officers said that this was a very powerful threat because it meant the boys would become known as troublemakers, even delinquents, in the school and possibly before their peers. They would be labeled for ongoing supervision. What a colossal difference in social control there is in a country where the police call the schools for support and a country where the schools must call the police for security.

Patrol officers, too, constantly offer "guidance" to juveniles. In 1987, for instance, they gave advice concerning "immoral conduct" to 1,295,196 juveniles throughout Japan.[58] Forty percent was for smoking, 30 percent for violating the midnight curfew, 8 percent for hotrodding, 5 percent for associating with unsavory—meaning gangster-affiliated—people, 3 percent for drinking, and 3 percent for truancy. This means that as much as 4 percent of the school-age population may have received police advice about proper behavior during the year.

The enforcement of the ban on teenage smoking is a dramatic indicator of the power of community presumption in Japan, encouraged by the police. Japan is a nation of heavy smoking, with over 60 percent of adult males being regular smokers. Nonetheless, the country is preoccupied with enforcing the ban against smoking by juveniles. The Tokyo police in 1987, for example, advised 48,000 minors about smoking in public. Imagine the reaction in New York City if the police tried that. But imagine what it would say about law-and-order if they could get away with it. The Japanese can enforce this blatant double standard in behavior because the older generation is united in the standards of be-

58. National Police Agency, 1989.

havior it wants juveniles to follow. As one Japanese put it, the community has the "confidence" to enforce moral prescriptions. Children are not adults. Moral discipline, and by extension crime control, are created by consensus and will. The role of the police is to maintain both.

Finally, the Japanese police play an important part in anticipating emerging problems of order and then working with other agencies to take preventive action. Even though crime is relatively infrequent, the police are hypersensitive to small changes. For example, even though foreign residents in Japan committed less than one-tenth of one percent of crime in 1986, the National Police Agency and the Tokyo Metropolitan Police Department set up special units to deal with the problem because the trend was upward over the preceding decade. When violence in schools against teachers and property increased in the late 1970s, the government immediately sent study teams abroad and charged various departments, including the police, with devising corrective plans. The "epidemic" in stimulant drugs is another objectively small problem that government has organized to squash in its early stages.

During the 1980s police in the United States developed a new strategy known as "problem-oriented policing."[59] It called for patrol officers to analyze recurring patterns of calls for service and devise long-range solutions for them if possible, rather than going from one call to the other without addressing underlying conditions. Police officers were to formulate plans and monitor implementation, working with other public and private agencies. The Japanese are doing the same thing but at a different command level. They do it at the top rather than the bottom. Diagnosis and problem-solving are responsibilities of headquarters personnel. And they do not wait until crises emerge. They anticipate problems and coordinate planning with other government departments, including the drafting of new legislation. To the Japanese police, problem-solving American style is like closing the barn door after the horse has escaped. Part of their perfectionist mentality involves stopping problems before they become too large to handle. This explains why Japanese police seem to exaggerate crime. They, as well as government generally, are like white corpuscles in the human body—they swarm around the first signs of infection, trying to save society from

59. Herman Goldstein, "Improving Policing: A Problem-Oriented Approach," *Journal of Crime and Delinquency* (April 1979), pp. 236–58; Goldstein, "Toward Community-Oriented Policing: Potential, Basic Requirements, and Threshold Questions," *Crime and Delinquency* 33, no. 1 (January 1987): 6–30; John E. Eck and William Spelman, *Problem-Solving* (Washington, D.C.: Police Executive Research Forum, 1987).

getting more than a mild fever. The Japanese police are always alert to departures from social order and are ready to take the lead in developing encompassing strategies of response.

Conclusion

Several lessons about orderliness may be learned from Japan. First, paraphrasing a former prime minister, Japan is a free country but not a free society.[60] Mechanisms of order do not arise solely out of government. The most important ones stem from private social relationships, because such contacts are more numerous, more intrusive, more varied, and more consequential than those of government. A corollary to this lesson is that order depends on regimes of behavior that cannot be left exclusively to governmental initiative.

Second, orderliness is affected by more than structural conditions. Customary patterns of social interaction, passed on from generation to generation, are also important. They are also independent of social circumstance. Japanese orderliness depends both on an equitable prosperity and on a distinctive set of behavioral predispositions.

Americans tend to be structuralist in their thinking about crime, circumstances being seen as the primary determinants of order. Japan, which is so similar to the United States on many structural dimensions, should prompt Americans to reconsider whether behavioral patterns that are a part of general culture do not also exert a powerful influence on crime. American criminological theory recognizes that structures produce mind-sets, sometimes referred to as "subcultures," that do affect deviance. But it gives little attention to the idea that mind-sets, in the sense of expected behavior agreed upon by communities, have a life of their own. But only very unobservant people could argue that Japanese order is not strongly affected by regimes of order enforced by community as well as governmental sanctions.

Third, orderliness is a seamless web, encompassing etiquette, decorum, civility, politeness, morality, and law. Propriety and crime are related. Violations of law are related to habits of defiance learned in other normative realms.

60. M. Ohira, quoted in Lawrence W. Beer, "Postwar Law on Civil Liberties in Japan," *UCLA Pacific Basin Law Journal* 2, nos. 1–2 (Spring and Fall 1983): 98.

Fourth, the success of the police in exerting a deterrent effect on crime depends less on their own endeavors than on the character of society within which they work. If Japanese and American police changed places, Americans would perform as efficiently as Japanese and Japanese police might come unhinged.

Fifth, police can prevent crime by deterring criminal activity through assuredly catching and helping to punish criminals. But they also contribute to the prevention of crime by enhancing society's private capacity to regulate behavior. The anticipatory crime-prevention role may be the more efficacious in the long run.

Sixth, effective crime prevention by the police, and probably meaningful problem-solving as well, must be undertaken before crime problems reach crisis proportions. This is ironic. Working within a context of low crime, Japanese police have the time and resources to devote to crime prevention. American police, overwhelmed by crime, are too busy to do much more than respond to emergencies. It would be tragic indeed if low crime rates were a precondition to effective crime prevention. Certainly, high crime rates are a significant inhibitor of effective prevention, both deterrent and anticipatory. The challenge for the United States, therefore, is to develop the political and governmental capacity to devise and implement strategies that prevent disorder before disorder becomes so great it cannot be controlled.

Index

Compositor:	G&S Typesetters, Inc.
Text:	10/13 Galliard
Display:	Galliard
Printer:	Edwards Brothers, Inc.
Binder:	Edwards Brothers, Inc.